Thoughts Out of Season
Part One and Part Two

Thoughts Out of Season
Part One and Part Two

by Friedrich Nietzsche
Translated by Anthony M. Ludovici and Adrian Collins

Table of Contents

Part I

Part II

Part I

Translator's Preface.

To the reader who knows Nietzsche, who has studied his Zarathustra and understood it, and who, in addition, has digested the works entitled Beyond Good and Evil, The Genealogy of Morals, The Twilight of the Idols, and The Antichrist,— to such a reader everything in this volume will be perfectly clear and comprehensible. In the attack on Strauss he will immediately detect the germ of the whole of Nietzsche's subsequent attitude towards too hasty contentment and the foolish beatitude of the "easily pleased"; in the paper on Wagner he will recognise Nietzsche the indefatigable borer, miner and underminer, seeking to define his ideals, striving after self-knowledge above all, and availing himself of any contemporary approximation to his ideal man, in order to press it forward as the incarnation of his thoughts. Wagner the reformer of mankind! Wagner the dithyrambic dramatist!—The reader who knows Nietzsche will not be misled by these expressions.

To the uninitiated reader, however, some words of explanation are due, not only in regard to the two papers before us, but in regard to Nietzsche himself. So much in our time is learnt from hearsay concerning prominent figures in science, art, religion, or philosophy, that it is hardly possible for anybody to-day, however badly informed he may be, to begin the study of any great writer or scientist with a perfectly open mind. It were well, therefore, to begin the study of Nietzsche with some definite idea as to his unaltered purpose, if he ever possessed such a thing; as to his lifelong ideal, if he ever kept one so long; and as to the one direction in which he always travelled, despite apparent deviations and windings. Had he such a purpose, such an ideal, such a direction? We have no wish to open a controversy here, neither do we think that in replying to this question in the affirmative we shall give rise to one; for every careful student of Nietzsche, we know, will uphold us in our view. Nietzsche had one very definite and unaltered purpose, ideal and direction, and this was "the elevation of the type man." He tells us in The Will to Power: "All is truth to me that tends to elevate man!" To this principle he was already pledged as a student at Leipzig; we owe every line that he ever wrote to his devotion to it, and it is the key to all his complexities, blasphemies, prolixities, and terrible earnestness. All was good to Nietzsche that tended to elevate man; all was bad that kept man stationary or sent him backwards. Hence he wrote David Strauss, the Confessor and Writer (1873).

The Franco-German War had only just come to an end, and the keynote of this polemical pamphlet is, "Beware of the intoxication of success." When the whole of Germany was delirious with joy over her victory, at a time when the unquestioned triumph of her arms tended rather to reflect unearned glory upon every department of her social organisation, it required both courage and discernment to raise the warning voice and to apply the wet blanket. But Nietzsche did both, and with spirit, because his worst fears were aroused. Smug content (erbärmliches Behagen) was threatening to thwart his one purpose—the elevation of man; smug content personified in the German scholar was giving itself airs of omniscience, omnipotence, and ubiquity, and all the while it was a mere cover for hidden rottenness and jejune pedantry.

Nietzsche's attack on Hegelian optimism alone (pp. 46, 53-54), in the first paper, fully reveals the fundamental idea underlying this essay; and if the personal attack on Strauss seems sometimes to throw the main theme into the background, we must remember the author's own attitude towards this aspect of the case. Nietzsche, as a matter of fact, had neither the spite nor the meanness requisite for the purely personal attack. In his Ecce Homo, he tells us most emphatically: "I have no desire to attack particular persons—I do but use a personality as a magnifying glass; I place it over the subject to which I wish to call attention, merely that the appeal may be stronger." David Strauss, in a letter to a friend, soon after the publication of the first Thought out of Season, expresses his utter astonishment that a total stranger should have made such a dead set at him. The same problem may possibly face the reader on every page of this fssay: if, however, we realise Nietzsche's purpose, if we understand his struggle to be one against "Culture-Philistinism" in general, as a stemming, stultifying and therefore degenerate factor, and regard David Strauss—as the author himself did, that is to say, simply as a glass, focusing the whole light of our understanding upon the main theme— then the Strauss paper is seen to be one of such enormous power, and its aim appears to us so lofty, that, whatever our views may be concerning the nature of the person assailed, we are forced to conclude that, to Nietzsche at least, he was but the incarnation and concrete example of the evil and danger then threatening to overtake his country, which it was the object of this essay to expose.

When we read that at the time of Strauss's death (February 7th, 1874) Nietzsche was greatly tormented by the fear that the old scholar might have been hastened to his end by the use that had been made of his personality in the first Unzeitgemässe Betrachtung; when we remember that in the midst of this torment he ejaculated, "I was indeed not made to hate and have enemies!"—we are then in a better position to judge of the motives which, throughout his life, led him to engage such formidable opponents and to undertake such relentless attacks. It was merely his ruling principle that, all is true and good that tends to elevate man; everything is bad and false that keeps man stationary or sends him backwards.

Those who may think that his attacks were often unwarrantable and ill-judged will do well, therefore, to bear this in mind, that whatever his value or merits may have been as an iconoclast, at least the aim he had was sufficiently lofty and honourable, and that he never shirked the duties which he rightly or wrongly imagined would help him to

Wagner paper (1875-1876) we are faced by a somewhat different problem. Most readers who will have heard of Nietzsche's subsequent denunciation of Wagner's music will probably stand aghast before this panegyric of him; those who, like Professor Saintsbury, will fail to discover the internal evidence in this essay which points so infallibly to Nietzsche's real but still subconscious opinion of his hero, may even be content to regard his later attitude as the result of a complete volte-face, and at any rate a flat contradiction of the one revealed in this paper. Let us, however, examine the internal evidence we speak of, and let us also discuss the purpose and spirit of the essay.

We have said that Nietzsche was a man with a very fixed and powerful ideal, and we have heard what this ideal was. Can we picture him, then,—a young and enthusiastic scholar with a cultured love of music, and particularly of Wagner's music, eagerly scanning all his circle, the whole city and country in which he lived—yea, even the whole continent on which he lived—for something or some one that would set his doubts at rest concerning the feasibility of his ideal? Can we now picture this young man coming face to face with probably one of the greatest geniuses of his age—with a man whose very presence must have been electric, whose every word or movement must have imparted some power to his surroundings—with Richard Wagner?

If we can conceive of what the mere attention, even, of a man like Wagner must have meant to Nietzsche in his twenties, if we can form any idea of the intoxicating effect produced upon him when this attention developed into friendship, we almost refuse to believe that Nietzsche could have been critical at all at first. In Wagner, as was but natural, he soon began to see the ideal, or at least the means to the ideal, which was his one obsession. All his hope for the future of Germany and Europe cleaved, as it were, to this highest manifestation of their people's life, and gradually he began to invest his already great friend with all the extra greatness which he himself drew from the depths of his own soul.

The friendship which grew between them was of that rare order in which neither can tell who influences the other more. Wagner would often declare that the beautiful music in the third act of Siegfried was to be ascribed to Nietzsche's influence over him; he also adopted the young man's terminology in art matters, and the concepts implied by the words "Dionysian" and "Apollonian" were borrowed by him from his friend's discourses. How much Nietzsche owed to Wagner may perhaps never be definitely known; to those who are sufficiently interested to undertake the investigation of this matter, we would recommend Hans Belart's book, Nietzsche's Ethik; in it references will be found which give some clue as to the probable sources from which the necessary information may be derived. In any case, however, the reciprocal effects of their conversations will never be exactly known; and although it would be ridiculous to assume that Nietzsche was essentially the same when he left as when he met him, what the real nature of the change was it is now difficult to say.

For some years their friendship continued firm, and grew ever more and more intimate. The Birth Of Tragedy was one of the first public declarations of it, and after its publication many were led to consider that Wagner's art was a sort of resurrection of the Dionysian Grecian art. Enemies of Nietzsche began to whisper that he was merely Wagner's "literary lackey"; many friends frowned upon the promising young philologist, and questioned the exaggerated importance he was beginning to ascribe to the art of music and to art in general, in their influence upon the world; and all the while Nietzsche's one thought and one aim was to help the cause and further the prospects of the man who he earnestly believed was destined to be the salvation of European culture.

Every great ideal coined in his own brain he imagined to be the ideal of his hero; all his sublimest hopes for society were presented gratis, in his writings, to Wagner, as though products of the latter's own mind; and just as the prophet of old never possessed the requisite assurance to suppose that his noblest ideas were his own, but attributed them to some higher and supernatural power, whom he thereby learnt to worship for its fancied nobility of sentiment, so Nietzsche, still doubting his own powers, created a fetich out of nis most distinguished friend, and was ultimately wounded and well-nigh wrecked with disappointment when he found that the Wagner of the Gotterdammerung and Parsifal was not the Wagner of his own mind.

While writing Ecce Homo, he was so well aware of the extent to which he had gone in idealising his friend, that he even felt able to say: "Wagner in Bayreuth is a vision of my own future.... Now that I can look back upon this work, I would not like to deny that, at bottom, it speaks only of myself" (p. 74). And on another page of the same book we read: "... What I heard, as a young man, in Wagnerian music, had absolutely nothing to do with Wagner: when I described Dionysian music, I only described what I had heard, and I thus translated and transfigured all that I bore in my own soul into the spirit of the new art. The strongest proof of this is my essay, Wagner in Bayreuth: in all decidedly psychological passages of this book the reader may simply read my name, or the name 'Zarathustra,' wherever the text contains the name 'Wagner'" (p. 68).

As we have already hinted, there are evidences of his having subconsciously discerned the REAL Wagner, even in the heyday of their friendship, behind the ideal he had formed of him; for his eyes were too intelligent to be deceived, even though his understanding refused at first to heed the messages they sent it: both the Birth of Tragedy and Wagner in Bayreuth are with us to prove this, and not merely when we read these works between the lines, but when we take such passages as those found on pp. 115, 149, 150, 151, 156, 158, 159 of this book quite literally.

Nietzsche's infatuation we have explained; the consequent idealisation of the object of his infatuation he himself has confessed; we have also pointed certain passages which we believe show beyond a doubt that almost everything to be found in The Case of Wagner and Nietzsche contra Wagner was already subconscious in our author, long before he had begun to feel even a coolness towards his hero: let those who think our interpretation of the said passages is either strained or unjustified turn to the literature to which we have referred and judge for themselves. It seems to us that those distinguished critics who complain of Nietzsche's complete volte-face and his uncontrollable recantations and revulsions of feeling have completely overlooked this aspect of the question.

It were well for us to bear in mind that we are not altogether free to dispose of Nietzsche's attitude to Wagner, at any given period in their relationship, with a single sentence of praise or of blame. After all, we are faced by a problem which no objectivity or dispassionate detachment on our parts can solve. Nietzsche endowed both Schopenhauer and Wagner with qualities and aspirations so utterly foreign to them both, that neither of them would have recognised himself in the images he painted of them. His love for them was unusual; perhaps it can only be fully understood emotionally by us: like all men who are capable of very great love, Nietzsche lent the objects of his affection anything they might happen to lack in the way of greatness, and when at last his eyes were opened, genuine pain, not malice, was the motive of even the most bitter of his diatribes.

Finally, we should just like to give one more passage from Ecce Homo bearing upon the subject under discussion. It is particularly interesting from an autobiographical standpoint, and will perhaps afford the best possible conclusion to this preface.

Nietzsche is writing about Wagner's music, and he says: "The world must indeed be empty for him who has never been unhealthy enough for this 'infernal voluptuousness'; it is allowable and yet almost forbidden to use a mystical expression in this behalf. I suppose I know better than any one the prodigies Wagner was capable of, the fifty worlds of strange raptures to which no one save him could soar; and as I stand to-day—strong enough to convert even the most suspicious and dangerous phenomenon to my own use and be the stronger for it—I declare Wagner to be the great benefactor of my life. Something will always keep our names associated in the minds of men, and that is, that we are two who have suffered more excruciatingly—even at each other's hands—than most men are able to suffer nowadays. And just as Wagner is merely a misunderstanding among Germans, so am I and ever will be. You lack two centuries of psychological and artistic discipline, my dear countrymen!... But it will be impossible for you ever to recover the time now lost" (p. 43).

ANTHONY M. LUDOVICI.

David Strauss: The Confessor and the Writer.

I.

Public opinion in Germany seems strictly to forbid any allusion to the evil and dangeious consequences of a war, more particularly when the war in question has been a victorious one. Those writers, therefore, command a more ready attention who, regarding this public opinion as final, proceed to vie with each other in their jubilant praise of the war, and of the powerful influences it has brought to bear upon morality, culture, and art. Yet it must be confessed that a gieat victory is a great danger. Human nature bears a triumph less easily than a defeat; indeed, it might even be urged that it is simpler to gain a victory of this sort than to turn it to such account that it may not ultimately proxe a seiious rout.

But of all evil results due to the last contest with France, the most deplorable, peihaps, is that widespread and even universal error of public opinion and of all who think publicly, that German culture was also victorious in the struggle, and that it should now, therefore, be decked with garlands, as a fit recognition of such extraordinary events and successes. This error is in the highest degree pernicious: not because it is an error,—for there are illusions which are both salutary and blessed,—but because it threatens to convert our victory into a signal defeat. A defeat? —I should say rather, into the uprooting of the "German Mind" for the benefit of the "German Empire."

Even supposing that the fight had been between the two cultures, the standard for the value of the victor would still be a very relative one, and, in any case, would certainly not justify such exaggerated triumph or self-glorification. For, in the first place, it would be necessary to ascertain the worth of the conquered culture. This might be very little; in which case, even if the victory had involved the most glorious display of arms, it would still offer no warrant for inordinate rapture.

Even so, however, there can be no question, in our case, of the victory of German culture; and for the simple reason, that French culture remains as heretofore, and that we depend upon it as heretofore. It did not even help towards the success of our arms. Severe military discipline, natural bravery and sustaining power, the superior generalship, unity and obedience in the rank and file—in short, factors which have nothing to do with culture, were instrumental in making us conquer an opponent in whom the most essential of these factors were absent. The only wonder is, that precisely what is now called "culture" in Germany did not prove an obstacle to the military operations which seemed vitally necessary to a great victory. Perhaps, though, this was only owing to the fact that this "thing" which dubs itself "culture" saw its advantage, for once, in keeping in the background.

If however, it be permitted to grow and to spread, if it be spoilt by the flattering and nonsensical assurance that it has been victorious,—then, as I have said, it will have the power to extirpate German mind, and, when that is done, who knows whether there will still be anything to be made out of the surviving German body!

Provided it were possible to direct that calm and tenacious bravery which the German opposed to the pathetic and spontaneous fury of the Frenchman, against the inward enemy, against the highly suspicious and, at all events, unnative "cultivation" which, owing to a dangerous misunderstanding, is called "culture" in Germany, then all hope of a really genuine German "culture"—the reverse of that "cultivation"—would not be entirely lost. For the Germans have never known any lack of clear-sighted and heroic leaders, though these, often enough, probably, have lacked Germans. But whether it be possible to turn German bravery into a new direction seems to me to become ever more and more doubtful; for I realise how fully convinced every one is that such a struggle and such bravery are no longer requisite; on the contrary, that most things are regulated as satisactorily as they possibly can be—or, at all events, that everything of moment has long ago been discovered and accomplished: in a word, that the seed of culture is already sown everywhere, and is now either shooting up its fresh green blades, or, here and there, even bursting forth into luxuriant blossom. In this sphere, not only happiness but ecstasy reigns supreme. I am conscious of this ecstasy and happiness, in the ineffable, truculent assurance of German journalists and manufacturers of novels, tragedies, poems, and histories (for it must be clear that these people belong to one category), who seem to have conspired to improve the leisure and ruminative hours—that is to say, "the intellectual lapses"—of the modern man, by bewildering him with their printed paper. Since the war, all is gladness, dignity, and self-consciousness in this merry throng. After the startling successes of German culture, it regards itself, not only as approved and sanctioned, but almost as sanctified. It therefore speaks with gravity, affects to apostrophise the German People, and issues complete works, after the manner of the classics; nor does it shrink from proclaiming in those journals which are open to it some few of its adherents as new German classical writers and model authors. It might be supposed that the dangers of such an abuse of success would be recognised by the more thoughtful and enlightened among cultivated Germans; or, at least, that these would feel how painful is the comedy that is being enacted around them: for what in truth could more readily inspire pity than the sight of a cripple strutting like a cock before a mirror, and exchanging complacent glances with his reflection! But the "scholar" caste willingly allow things to remain as they are, and re too much concerned with their own affairs to busy themselves with the care of the German mind. Moreover, the units of this caste are too thoroughly convinced that their own scholarship is the ripest and most perfect fruit of the age—in fact, of all ages—to see any necessity for a care of German culture in general; since, in so far as they and the legion of their brethren are concerned, preoccupations of this order have everywhere been, so to speak, surpassed. The more conscientious observer, more particularly if he be a foreigner, cannot help noticing withal that no great disparity exists between that which the German scholar regards as his culture and that other triumphant culture of the new German classics, save in respect of the quantum of knowledge. Everywhere, where knowledge and not ability, where information and not art, hold the first rank,—everywhere, therefore, where life bears testimony to the kind of culture extant, there is now only one specific German culture—and this is the culture that is supposed to have conquered France?

The contention appears to be altogether too preposterous. It was solely to the more extensive knowledge of German officers, to the superior training of their soldiers, and to their more scientific military strategy, that all impartial Judges, and even the French nation, in the end, ascribed the victory. Hence, if it be intended to regard German erudition as a thing apart, in what sense can German culture be said to have conquered? In none whatsoever; for the moral qualities of severe discipline, of more placid obedience, have nothing in common with culture: these were characteristic of the Macedonian army, for instance, despite the fact that the Greek soldiers were infinitely more cultivated. To speak of German scholarship and culture as having conquered, therefore, can only be the outcome of a misapprehension, probably resulting from the circumstance that every precise notion of culture has now vanished from Germany.

Culture is, before all things, the unity of artistic style, in every expression of the life of a people. Abundant knowledge and learning, however, are not essential to it, nor are they a sign of its existence; and, at a pinch, they might coexist much more harmoniously with the very opposite of culture—with barbarity: that is to say, with a complete lack of style, or with a riotous jumble of all styles. But it is precisely amid this riotous jumble that the German of to-day subsists; and the serious problem to be solved is: how, with all his learning, he can possibly avoid noticing it; how, into the bargain, he can rejoice with all his heart in his present "culture"? For everything conduces to open his eyes for him—every glance he casts at his clothes, his room, his house; every walk he takes through the streets of his town; every visit he pays to his art-dealers and to his trader in the articles of fashion. In his social intercourse he ought to realise the origin of his manners and movements; in the heart of our art-institutions, the pleasures of our concerts, theatres, and museums, he ought to become apprised of the super- and juxta-position of all imaginable styles. The German heaps up around him the forms, colours, products, and curiosities of all ages and zones, and thereby succeeds in producing that garish newness, as of a country fair, which his scholars then proceed to contemplate and to define as "Modernism per se"; and there he remains, squatting peacefully, in the midst of this conflict of styles. But with this kind of culture, which is, at bottom, nothing more nor less than a phlegmatic insensibility to real culture, men cannot vanquish an enemy, least of all an enemy like the French, who, whatever their worth may be, do actually possess a genuine and productive culture, and whom, up to the present, we have systematically copied, though in the majority of cases without skill.

Even supposing we had really ceased copying them, it would still not mean that we had overcome them, but merely that we had lifted their yoke from our necks. Not before we have succeeded in forcing an original German culture upon them can there be any question of the triumph of German culture. Meanwhile, let us not forget that in all matters of form we are, and must be, just as dependent upon Paris now as we were before the war; for up to the present there has been no such thing as a original German culture.

We all ought to have become aware of this, of our own accord. Besides, one of the few who had he right to speak to Germans in terms of reproach Publicly drew attention to the fact. "We Germans are of yesterday," Goethe once said to Eckermann. "True, for the last hundred years we have diligently cultivated ourselves, but a few centuries may yet have to run their course before our fellow-countrymen become permeated with sufficient intellectuality and higher culture to have it said of them, it is a long time since they were barbarians."

II.

If, however, our public and private life is so manifestly devoid of all signs of a productive and characteristic culture; if, moreover, our great artists, with that earnest vehemence and honesty which is peculiar to greatness admit, and have admitted, this monstrous fact—so very humiliating to a gifted nation; how can it still be possible for contentment to reign to such an astonishing extent among German scholars? And since the last war this complacent spirit has seemed ever more and morerready to break forth into exultant cries and demonstrations of triumph. At all events, the belief seems to be rife that we are in possession of a genuine culture, and the enormous incongruity of this triumphant satisfaction in the face of the inferiority which should be patent to all, seems only to be noticed by the few and the select. For all those who think with the public mind have blindfolded their eyes and closed their ears. The incongruity is not even acknowledged to exist. How is this possible? What power is sufficiently influential to deny this existence? What species of men must have attained to supremacy in Germany that feelings which are so strong and simple should he denied or prevented from obtaining expression? This power, this species of men, I will name—they are the Philistines of Culture.

As every one knows, the word "Philistine" is borrowed from the vernacular of student-life, and, in its widest and most popular sense, it signifies the reverse of a son of the Muses, of an artist, and of the genuine man of culture. The Philistine of culture, however, the study of whose type and the hearing of whose confessions (when he makes them) have now become tiresome duties, distinguishes himself from the general notion of the order "Philistine" by means of a superstition: he fancies that he is himself a son of the Muses and a man of culture. This incomprehensible error clearly shows that he does not even know the difference between a Philistine and his opposite. We must not be surprised, therefore, if we find him, for the most part, solemnly protesting that he is no Philistine. Owing to this lack of self-knowledge, he is convinced that his "culture" is the consummate manifestation of real German culture; and, since he everywhere meets with scholars of his own type, since all public institutions, whether schools, universities, or academies, are so organised as to be in complete harmony with his education and needs, wherever he goes he bears with him the triumphant feeling that he is the worthy champion of prevailing German culture, and he frames his pretensions and claims accordingly.

If, however, real culture takes unity of style for granted (and even an inferior and degenerate culture cannot be imagined in which a certain coalescence of the profusion of forms has not taken place), it is just possible that the confusion underlying the Culture-Philistine's error may arise from the fact that, since he comes into contact everywhere with creatures cast in the same mould as himself, he concludes that this uniformity among all "scholars" must point to a certain uniformity in German education—hence to culture. All round him, he sees only needs and views similar to his own; wherever he goes, he finds himself embraced by a ring of tacit conventions concerning almost everything, but more especially matters of religion and art. This imposing sameness, this *tutti unisono* which, though it responds to no word of command, is yet ever ready to burst forth, cozens him into the belief that here a culture must be established and flourishing. But Philistinism, despite its systematic organisation and power, does not constitute a culture by virtue of its system alone; it does not even constitute an inferior culture, but invariably the reverse—namely, firmly established barbarity. For the uniformity of character which is so apparent in the German scholars of to-day is only the result of a conscious or unconscious exclusion and negation of all the artistically productive forms and requirements of a genuine style. The mind of the cultured Philistine must have become sadly unhinged; for precisely what culture repudiates he regards as culture itself; and, since he proceeds logically, he succeeds in creating a connected group of these repudiations—a system of non-culture, to which one might at a pinch grant a certain "unity of style," provided of course it were Ot nonsense to attribute style to barbarity. If he have to choose between a stylish act and its opposite, he will invariably adopt the latter, and, since this rule holds good throughout, every one of his acts bears the same negative stamp. Now, it is by means of this stamp that he is able to identify the character of the "German culture," which is his own patent; and all things that do not bear it are so many enemies and obstacles drawn up against him. In the presence of these arrayed forces the Culture-Philistine either does no more than ward off the blows, or else he denies, holds his tongue, stops his ears, and refuses to face facts. He is a negative creature—even in his hatred and animosity. Nobody, however, is more disliked by him than the man who regards him as a Philistine, and tells him what he is—namely, the barrier in the way of all powerful men and creators, the labyrinth for all who doubt and go astray, the swamp for all the weak and the weary, the fetters of those who would run towards lofty goals, the poisonous mist that chokes all germinating hopes, the scorching sand to all those German thinkers who seek for, and thirst after, a new life. For the mind of Germany is seeking; and ye hate it because it is seeking, and because it will not accept your word, when ye declare that ye have found what it is seeking. How could it have been possible for a type like that of the Culture-Philistine to develop? and even granting its development, how was it able to rise to the powerful Position of supreme judge concerning all questions of German culture? How could this have been possible, seeing that a whole procession of grand and heroic figures has already filed past us, whose every movement, the expression of whose every feature, whose questioning voice and burning eye betrayed the one fact, that they were seekers, and that they sought that which the Culture-Philistine had long fancied he had found—to wit, a genuine original German culture? Is there a soil—thus they seemed to ask—a soil that is pure enough, unhandselled enough, of sufficient virgin sanctity, to allow the mind of Germany to build its house upon it? Questioning thus, they wandered through the wilderness, and the woods of wretched ages and narrow conditions, and as seekers they disappeared from our vision; one of them, at an advanced age, was even able to say, in the name of all: "For half a century my life has been hard and bitter enough; I have allowed myself no rest, but have ever striven, sought and done, to the best and to the utmost of my ability."

What does our Culture-Philistinism say of these seekers? It regards them simply as discoverers, and seems to forget that they themselves only claimed to be seekers. We have our culture, say her sons; for have we not our "classics"? Not only is the foundation there, but the building already stands upon it—we ourselves constitute that building. And, so saying, the Philistine raises his hand to his brow.

But, in order to be able thus to misjudge, and thus to grant left-handed veneration to our classics, people must have ceased to know them. This, generally speaking, is precisely what has happened. For, otherwise, one ought to know that there is only one way of honouring them, and that is to continue seeking with the same spirit and with the same courage, and not to weary of the search. But to foist the doubtful title of "classics" upon them, and to "edify" oneself from time to time by reading their works, means to yield to those feeble and selfish emotions which all the paying public may purchase at concert-halls and theatres. Even the raising of monuments to their memory, and the christening of feasts and societies with their names—all these things are but so many ringing cash payments by means of which the Culture-Philistine discharges his indebtedness to them, so that in all other respects he may be rid of them, and, above all, not bound to follow in their wake and prosecute his search further. For henceforth inquiry is to cease: that is the Philistine watchword.

This watchword once had some meaning. In Germany, during the first decade of the nineteenth century, for instance, when the heyday and confusion of seeking, experimenting, destroying, promising, surmising, and hoping was sweeping in currents and cross-currents over the land, the thinking middle-classes were right in their concern for their own security. It was then quite right of them to dismiss from their minds with a shrug of their shoulders the omnium gatherum of fantastic and language-maiming philosophies, and of rabid special-pleading historical studies, the carnival of all gods and myths, and the poetical affectations and fooleries which a drunken spirit may be responsible for. In this respect they were quite right; for the Philistine has not even the privilege of licence. With the cunning proper to base natures, however, he availed himself of the opportunity, in order to throw suspicion even upon the seeking spirit, and to invite people to join in the more comfortable pastime of finding. His eye opened to the joy of Philistinism; he saved himself from wild experimenting by clinging to the idyllic, and opposed the restless creative spirit that animates the artist, by means of a certain smug ease—the ease of self-conscious narrowness, tranquillity, and self-sufficiency. His tapering finger pointed, without any affectation of modesty, to all the hidden and intimate incidents of his life, to the many touching and ingenuous joys which sprang into existence in the wretched depths of his uncultivated existence, and which modestly blossomed forth on the bog-land of Philistinism.

There were, naturally, a few gifted narrators who, with a nice touch, drew vivid pictures of the happiness, the prosaic simplicity, the bucolic robustness, and all the well-being which floods the quarters of children, scholars, and peasants. With picture-books of this class in their hands, these smug ones now once and for all sought to escape from the yoke of these dubious classics and the command which they contained—to seek further and to find. They only started the notion of an epigone-age in order to secure peace for themselves, and to be able to reject all the efforts of disturbing innovators summarily as the work of epigones. With the view of ensuring their own tranquillity, these smug ones even appropriated history, and sought to transform all sciences that threatened to disturb their wretched ease into branches of history—more particularly philosophy and classical philology. Through historical consciousness, they saved themselves from enthusiasm; for, in opposition to Goethe, it was maintained that history would no longer kindle enthusiasm. No, in their desire to acquire an historical grasp of everything, stultification became the sole aim of these philosophical admirers of "nil admirari." While professing to hate every form of fanaticism and intolerance, what they really hated, at bottom, was the dominating genius and the tyranny of the real claims of culture. They therefore concentrated and utilised all their forces in those quarters where a fresh and vigorous movement was to be expected, and then paralysed, stupefied, and tore it to shreds. In this way, a philosophy which veiled the Philistine confessions of its founder beneath neat twists and flourishes of language proceeded further to discover a formula for the canonisation of the commonplace. It expatiated upon the rationalism of all reality, and thus ingratiated itself with the Culture-Philistine, who also loves neat twists and flourishes, and who, above all, considers himself real, and regards his reality as the standard of reason for the world. From this time forward he began to allow every one, and even himself, to reflect, to investigate, to astheticise, and, more particularly, to make poetry, rnusic, and even pictures—not to mention systems philosophy; provided, of course, that everything were done according to the old pattern, and that no assault were made upon the "reasonable" and the "real"—that is to say, upon the Philistine. The latter really does not at all mind giving himself up, from time to time, to the delightful and daring transgressions of art or of sceptical historical studies, and he does not underestimate the charm of such recreations and entertainments; but he strictly separates "the earnestness of life" (under which term he understands his calling, his business, and his wife and child) from such trivialities, and among the latter he includes all things which have any relation to culture. Therefore, woe to the art that takes itself seriously, that has a notion of what it may exact, and that dares to endanger his income, his business, and his habits! Upon such an art he turns his back, as though it were something dissolute; and, affecting the attitude of a. guardian of chastity, he cautions every unprotected virtue on no account to look.

Being such an adept at cautioning people, he is always grateful to any artist who heeds him and listens to caution. He then assures his protege that things are to be made more easy for him; that, as a kindred spirit, he will no longer be expected to make sublime masterpieces, but that his work must be one of two kinds—either the imitation of reality to the point of simian mimicry, in idylls or gentle and humorous satires, or the free copying of the best-known and most famous classical works, albeit with shamefast concessions to the taste of the age. For, although he may only be able to appreciate slavish copying or accurate portraiture of the present, still he knows that the latter will but glorify him, and increase the well-being of "reality"; while the former, far from doing him any harm, rather helps to establish his reputation as a classical judge of taste, and is not otherwise troublesome; for he has, once and for all, come to terms with the classics. Finally, he discovers the general and effective formula "Health" for his habits, methods of observation, judgments, and the objects of his patronage; while he dismisses the importunate disturber of the peace with the epithets "hysterical" and "morbid." It is thus that David Strauss—a genuine example of the satisfait in regard to our scholastic institutions, and a typical Philistine—it is thus that he speaks of "the philosophy of Schopenhauer" as being "thoroughly intellectual, yet often unhealthy and unprofitable." It is indeed a deplorable fact that intellect should show such a decided preference for the "unhealthy" and the "unprofitable"; and even the Philistine, if he be true to himself, will admit that, in regard to the philosophies which men of his stamp produce, he is conscious of a frequent lack of intellectuality, although of course they are always thoroughly healthy and profitable.

Now and again, the Philistines, provided they are by themselves, indulge in a bottle of wine, and then they grow reminiscent, and speak of the great deeds of the war, honestly and ingenuously. On such occasions it often happens that a great deal comes to light which would otherwise have been most stead-fastly concealed, and one of them may even be heard to blurt out the most precious secrets of the whole brotherhood. Indeed, a lapse of this sort occurred but a short while ago, to a well-known aesthete of the Hegelian school of reasoning. It must, however, be admitted that the provocation thereto was of an unusual character. A company of Philistines were feasting together, in celebration of the memory of a genuine anti-Philistine—one who, moreover, had been, in the strictest sense of the words, wrecked by Philistinism. This man was Holderlin, and the afore-mentioned aesthete was therefore justified, under the circumstances, in speaking of the tragic souls who had foundered on "reality"—reality being understood, here, to mean Philistine reason. But the "reality" is now different, and it might well be asked whether Holderlin would be able to find his way at all in the present great age. "I doubt," says Dr. Vischer, "whether his delicate soul could have borne all the roughness which is inseparable from war, and whether it had survived the amount of perversity which, since the war, we now see flourishing in every quarter. Perhaps he would have succumbed to despair. His was one of the unarmed souls; he was the Werther of Greece, a hopeless lover; his life was full of softness and yearning, but there was strength and substance in his will, and in his style, greatness, riches and life; here and there it is even reminiscent of AEschylus. His spirit, however, lacked hardness. He lacked the weapon humour; he could not grant that one may be a Philistine and still be no barbarian." Not the sugary condolence of the post-prandial speaker, but this last sentence concerns us. Yes, it is admitted that one is a Philistine; but, a barbarian?—No, not at any price! Unfortunately, poor Holderlin could not make such flne distinctions. If one reads the reverse of civilisation, or perhaps sea-pirating, or cannibalism, into the word "barbarian," then the distinction is justifiable enough. But what the aesthete obviously wishes to prove to us is, that we may be Philistines and at the same time men of culture. Therein lies the humour which poor Holderlin lacked and the need of which ultimately wrecked him.*

[Footnote * : Nietzsche's allusion to Holderlin here is full of tragic significance; for, like Holderlin, he too was ultimately wrecked and driven insane by the Philistinism of his age. —Translator's note.]

On this occasion a second admission was made by the speaker: "It is not always strength of will, but weakness, which makes us superior to those tragic souls which are so passionately responsive to the attractions of beauty," or words to this effect. And this was said in the name of the assembled "We"; that is to say, the "superiors," the "superiors through weakness." Let us content ourselves with these admissions. We are now in possession of information concerning two matters from one of the initiated: first, that these "We" stand beyond the passion for beauty; secondly, that their position was reached by means of weakness. In less confidential moments, however, it was just this weakness which masqueraded in the guise of a much more beautiful name: it was the famous "healthiness" of the Culture-Philistine. In view of this very recent restatement of the case, however, it would be as well not to speak of them any longer as the "healthy ones," but as the "weakly," or, still better, as the "feeble." Oh, if only these feeble ones were not in power! How is it that they concern themselves at all about what we call them! They are the rulers, and he is a poor ruler who cannot endure to be called by a nickname. Yes, if one only have power, one soon learns to poke fun—even at oneself. It cannot matter so very much, therefore, even if one do give oneself away; for what could not the purple mantle of triumph conceal? The strength of the Culture-Philistine steps into the broad light of day when he acknowledges his weakness; and the more he acknowledges it— the more cynically he acknowledges it—the more completely he betrays his consciousness of his own importance and superiority. We are living in a period of cynical Philistine confessions. Just as Friedrich Vischer gave us his in a word, so has David Strauss handed us his in a book; and both that word and that book are cynical.

III.

Concerning Culture-Philistinism, David Strauss makes a double confession, by word and by deed; that is to say, by the word of the confessor, and the act of the writer. His book entitled The Old Faith and the New is, first in regard to its contents, and secondly in regard to its being a book and a literary production, an uninterrupted confession; while, in the very fact that he allows himself to write confessions at all about his faith, there already lies a confession. Presumably, every one seems to have the right to compile an autobiography after his fortieth year; for the humblest amongst us may have experienced things, and may have seen them at such close quarters, that the recording of them may prove of use and value to the thinker. But to write a confession of one's faith cannot but be regarded as a thousand times more pretentious, since it takes for granted that the writer attaches worth, not only to the experiences and investigations of his life, but also to his beliefs. Now, what the nice thinker will require to know, above all else, is the kind of faith which happens to be compatible with natures of the Straussian order, and what it is they have "half dreamily conjured up" (p. 10) concerning matters of which those alone have the right to speak who are acquainted with them at first hand. Whoever would have desired to possess the confessions, say, of a Ranke or a Mommsen? And these men were scholars and historians of a very different stamp from David Strauss. If, however, they had ever ventured to interest us in their faith instead of in their scientific investigations, we should have felt that they were overstepping their limits in a most irritating fashion. Yet Strauss does this when he discusses his faith. Nobody wants to know anything about it, save, perhaps, a few bigoted opponents of the Straussian doctrines, who, suspecting, as they do, a substratum of satanic principles beneath these doctrines, hope that he may compromise his learned utterances by revealing the nature of those principles. These clumsy creatures may, perhaps, have found what they sought in the last book; but we, who had no occasion to suspect a satanic substratum, discovered nothing of the sort, and would have felt rather pleased than not had we been able to discern even a dash of the diabolical in any part of the volume. But surely no evil spirit could speak as Strauss speaks of his new faith. In fact, spirit in general seems to be altogether foreign to the book— more particularly the spirit of genius. Only those whom Strauss designates as his "We," speak as he does, and then, when they expatiate upon their faith to us, they bore us even more than when they relate their dreams; be they "scholars, artists, military men, civil employes, merchants, or landed proprietors; come they in their thousands, and not the worst people in the land either!" If they do not wish to remain the peaceful ones in town or county, but threaten to wax noisy, then let not the din of their unisono deceive us concerning the poverty and vulgarity of the melody they sing. How can it dispose us more favourably towards a profession of faith to hear that it is approved by a crowd, when it is of such an order that if any individual of that crowd attempted to make it known to us, we should not only fail to hear him out, but should interrupt him with a yawn? If thou sharest such a belief, we should say unto him, in Heaven's name, keep it to thyself! Maybe, in the past, some few harmless types looked for the thinker in David Strauss; now they have discovered the "believer" in him, and are disappointed. Had he kept silent, he would have remained, for these, at least, the philosopher; whereas, now, no one regards him as such. He no longer craved the honours of the thinker, however; all he wanted to be was a new believer, and he is proud of his new belief. In making a written declaration of it, he fancied he was writing the catechism of "modern thought," and building the "broad highway of the world's future." Indeed, our Philistines have ceased to be faint-hearted and bashful, and have acquired almost cynical assurance. There was a time, long, long ago, when the Philistine was only tolerated as something that did not speak, and about which no one spoke; then a period ensued during which his roughness was smoothed, during which he was found amusing, and people talked about him. Under this treatment he gradually became a prig, rejoiced with all his heart over his rough places and his wrongheaded and candid singularities, and began to talk, on his own account, after the style of Riehl's music for the home.

"But what do I see? Is it a shadow? Is it reality? How long and broad my poodle grows!"

For now he is already rolling like a hippopotamus along "the broad highway of the world's future," and his growling and barking have become transformed into the proud incantations of a religious founder. And is it your own sweet wish, Great Master, to found the religion of the future? "The times seem to us not yet ripe (p. 7). It does not occur to us to wish to destroy a church." But why not, Great Master? One but needs the ability. Besides, to speak quite openly in the latter, you yourself are convinced that you Possess this ability. Look at the last page of your book. There you actually state, forsooth, that your new way "alone is the future highway of the world, which now only requires partial completion, and especially general use, in order also to become easy and pleasant."

Make no further denials, then. The religious founder is unmasked, the convenient and agreeable highway leading to the Straussian Paradise is built. It is only the coach in which you wish to convey us that does not altogether satisfy you, unpretentious man that you are! You tell us in your concluding remarks: "Nor will I pretend that the coach to which my esteemed readers have been obliged to trust themselves with me fulfils every requirement,... all through one is much jolted" (p. 438). Ah! you are casting about for a compliment, you gallant old religious founder! But let us be straightforward with you. If your reader so regulates the perusal of the 368 pages of your religious catechism as to read only one page a day—that is to say, if he take it in the smallest possible doses–then, perhaps, we should be able to believe that he might suffer some evil effect from the book—if only as the outcome of his vexation when the results he expected fail to make themselves felt. Gulped down more heartily, however, and as much as possible being taken at each draught, according to the prescription to be recommended in the case of all modern books, the drink can work no mischief; and, after taking it, the reader will not necessarily be either out of sorts or out of temper, but rather merry and well-disposed, as though nothing had happened; as though no religion had been assailed, no world's highway been built, and no profession of faith been made. And I do indeed call this a result! The doctor, the drug, and the disease—everything forgotten! And the joyous laughter! The continual provocation to hilarity! You are to be envied, Sir; for you have founded the most attractive of all religions —one whose followers do honour to its founder by laughing at him.

IV.

The Philistine as founder of the religion of the future—that is the new belief in its most emphatic form of expression. The Philistine becomes a dreamer—that is the unheard-of occurrence which distinguishes the German nation of to-day. But for the present, in any case, let us maintain an attitude of caution towards this fantastic exaltation. For does not David Strauss himself advise us to exercise such caution, in the following profound passage, the general tone of which leads us to think of the Founder of Christianity rather than of our particular author? (p. 92): "We know there have been noble enthusiasts—enthusiasts of genius; the influence of an enthusiast can rouse, exalt, and produce prolonged historic effects; but we do not wish to choose him as the guide of our life. He will be sure to mislead us, if we do not subject his influence to the control of reason." But we know something more: we know that there are enthusiasts who are not intellectual, who do not rouse or exalt, and who, nevertheless, not only expect to be the guides of our lives, but, as such, to exercise a very lasting historical influence into the bargain, and to rule the future;—all the more reason why we should place their influence under the control of reason. Lichtenberg even said: "There are enthusiasts quite devoid of ability, and these are really dangerous people." In the first place, as regards the above-mentioned control of reason, we should like to have candid answers to the three following questions: First, how does the new believer picture his heaven? Secondly, how far does the courage lent him by the new faith extend? And, thirdly, how does he write his books? Strauss the Confessor must answer the first and second questions; Strauss the Writer must answer the third.

The heaven of the new believer must, perforce, be a heaven upon earth; for the Christian "prospect of an immortal life in heaven," together with the other consolations, "must irretrievably vanish" for him who has but "one foot" on the Straussian platform. The way in which a religion represents its heaven is significant, and if it be true that Christianity knows no other heavenly occupations than singing and making music, the prospect of the Philistine, à la Strauss, is truly not a very comforting one. In the book of confessions, however, there is a page which treats of Paradise (p. 342). Happiest of Philistines, unroll this parchment scroll before anything else, and the whole of heaven will seem to clamber down to thee! "We would but indicate how we act, how we have acted these many years. Besides our profession—for we are members of the most various professions, and by no means exclusively consist of scholars or artists, but of military men and civil employes, of merchants and landed proprietors;... and again, as I have said already, there are not a few of us, but many thousands, and not the worst people in the country;—besides our profession, then, I say, we are eagerly accessible to all the higher interests of humanity; we have taken a vivid interest, during late years, and each after his manner has participated in the great national war, and the reconstruction of the German State; and we have been profoundly exalted by the turn events have taken, as unexpected as glorious, for our much tried nation. To the end of forming just conclusions in these things, we study history, which has now been made easy, even to the unlearned, by a series of attractively and popularly written works; at the same time, we endeavour to enlarge our knowledge of the natural sciences, where also there is no lack of sources of information; and lastly, in the writings of our great poets, in the performances of our great musicians, we find a stimulus for the intellect and heart, for wit and imagination, which leaves nothing to be desired. Thus we live, and hold on our way in joy."

"Here is our man!" cries the Philistine exultingly, who reads this: "for this is exactly how we live; it is indeed our daily life."* And how perfectly he understands the euphemism! When, for example, he refers to the historical studies by means of which we help ourselves in forming just conclusions regarding the political situation, what can he be thinking of, if it be not our newspaper-reading? When he speaks of the active part we take in the reconstruction of the German State, he surely has only our daily visits to the beer-garden in his mind; and is not a walk in the Zoological Gardens implied by 'the sources of information through which we endeavour to enlarge our knowledge of the natural sciences'? Finally, the theatres and concert-halls are referred to as places from which we take home 'a stimulus for wit and imagination which leaves nothing to be desired.'—With what dignity and wit he describes even the most suspicious of our doings! Here indeed is our man; for his heaven is our heaven!"

[Footnote * : This alludes to a German student-song.]

Thus cries the Philistine; and if we are not quite so satisfied as he, it is merely owing to the fact that we wanted to know more. Scaliger used to say: "What does it matter to us whether Montaigne drank red or white wine?" But, in this more important case, how greatly ought we to value definite particulars of this sort! If we could but learn how many pipes the Philistine smokes daily, according to the prescriptions of the new faith, and whether it is the Spener or the National Gazette that appeals to him over his coffee! But our curiosity is not satisfied. With regard to one point only do we receive more exhaustive information, and fortunately this point relates to the heaven in heaven—the private little art-rooms which will be consecrated to the use of great poets and musicians, and to which the Philistine will go to edify himself; in which, moreover, according to his own showing, he will even get "all his stains removed and wiped away" (p. 433); so that we are led to regard these private little art-rooms as a kind of bath-rooms. "But this is only effected for some fleeting moments; it happens and counts only in the realms of phantasy; as soon as we return to rude reality, and the cramping confines of actual life, we are again on all sides assailed by the old cares,"—thus our Master sighs. Let us, however, avail ourselves of the fleeting moments during which we remain in those little rooms; there is just sufficient time to get a glimpse of the apotheosis of the Philistine— that is to say, the Philistine whose stains have been removed and wiped away, and who is now an absolutely pure sample of his type. In truth, the opportunity we have here may prove instructive: let no one who happens to have fallen a victim to the confession-book lay it aside before having read the two appendices, "Of our Great Poets" and "Of our Great Musicians." Here the rainbow of the new brotherhood is set, and he who can find no pleasure in it "for such an one there is no help," as Strauss says on another occasion; and, as he might well say here, "he is not yet ripe for our point of view." For are we not in the heaven of heavens? The enthusiastic explorer undertakes to lead us about, and begs us to excuse him if, in the excess of his joy at all the beauties to be seen, he should by any chance be tempted to talk too much. "If I should, perhaps, become more garrulous than may seem warranted in this place, let the reader be indulgent to me; for out of the abundance of the heart the mouth speaketh. Let him only be assured that what he is now about to read does not consist of older materials, which I take the opportunity of inserting here, but that these remarks have been written for their present place and purpose" (pp. 345-46). This confession surprises us somewhat for the moment. What can it matter to us whether or not the little chapters were freshly written? As if it were a matter of writing! Between ourselves, I should have been glad if they had been written a quarter of a century earlier; then, at least, I should have understood why the thoughts seem to be so bleached, and why they are so redolent of resuscitated antiquities. But that a thing should have been written in 1872 and already smell of decay in 1872 strikes me as suspicious. Let us imagine some one's falling asleep while reading these chapters—what would he most probably dream about? A friend answered this question for me, because he happened to have had the experience himself. He dreamt of a wax-work show. The classical writers stood there, elegantly represented in wax and beads. Their arms and eyes moved, and a screw inside them creaked an accompaniment to their movements. He saw something gruesome among them—a misshapen figure, decked with tapes and jaundiced paper, out of whose mouth a ticket hung, on which "Lessing" was written. My friend went close up to it and learned the worst: it was the Homeric Chimera; in front it was Strauss, behind it was Gervinus, and in the middle Chimera. The tout-ensemble was Lessing. This discovery caused him to shriek with terror: he waked, and read no more. In sooth, Great Master, why have you written such fusty little chapters?

We do, indeed, learn something new from them; for instance, that Gervinus made it known to the world how and why Goethe was no dramatic genius; that, in the second part of Faust, he had only produced a world of phantoms and of symbols; that Wallenstein is a Macbeth as well as a Hamlet; that the Straussian reader extracts the short stories out of the Wanderjahre "much as naughty children pick the raisins and almonds out of a tough plum-cake"; that no complete effect can be produced on the stage without the forcible element, and that Schiller emerged from Kant as from a cold-water cure. All this is certainly new and striking; but, even so, it does not strike us with wonder, and so sure as it is new, it will never grow old, for it never was young; it was senile at birth. What extraordinary ideas seem to occur to these Blessed Ones, after the New Style, in their aesthetic heaven! And why can they not manage to forget a few of them, more particularly when they are of that unaesthetic, earthly, and ephemeral order to which the scholarly thoughts of Gervinus belong, and when they so obviously bear the stamp of puerility? But it almost seems as though the modest greatness of a Strauss and the vain insignificance of a Gervinus were only too well able to harmonise: then long live all those Blessed Ones! may we, the rejected, also live long, if this unchallenged judge of art continues any longer to teach his borrowed enthusiasm, and the gallop of that hired steed of which the honest Grillparzer speaks with such delightful clearness, until the whole of heaven rings beneath the hoof of that galumphing enthusiasm. Then, at least, things will be livelier and noisier than they are at the present moment, in which the carpet-slippered rapture of our heavenly leader and the lukewarm eloquence of his lips only succeed in the end in making us sick and tired. I should like to know how a Hallelujah sung by Strauss would sound: I believe one would have to listen very carefully, lest it should seem no more than a courteous apology or a lisped compliment. Apropos of this, I might adduce an instructive and somewhat forbidding example. Strauss strongly resented the action of one of his opponents who happened to refer to his reverence for Lessing. The unfortunate man had misunderstood;—true, Strauss did declare that one must be of a very obtuse mind not to recognise that the simple words of paragraph 86 come from the writer's heart. Now, I do not question this warmth in the very least; on the contrary, the fact that Strauss fosters these feelings towards Lessing has always excited my suspicion; I find the same warmth for Lessing raised almost to heat in Gervinus—yea, on the whole, no great German writer is so popular among little German writers as Lessing is; but for all that, they deserve no thanks for their predilection; for what is it, in sooth, that they praise in Lessing? At one moment it is his catholicity— the fact that he was critic and poet, archaeologist and philosopher, dramatist and theologian. Anon, "it is the unity in him of the writer and the man, of the head and the heart." The last quality, as a rule, is just as characteristic of the great writer as of the little one; as a rule, a narrow head agrees only too fatally with a narrow heart. And as to the catholicity; this is no distinction, more especially when, as in Lessing's case, it was a dire necessity. What astonishes one in regard to Lessing-enthusiasts is rather that they have no conception of the devouring necessity which drove him on through life and to this catholicity; no feeling for the fact that such a man is too prone to consume himself rapidly, like a flame; nor any indignation at the thought that the vulgar narrowness and pusillanimity of his whole environment, especially of his learned contemporaries, so saddened, tormented, and stifled the tender and ardent creature that he was, that the very universality for which he is praised should give rise to feelings of the deepest compassion. "Have pity on the exceptional man!" Goethe cries to us; "for it was his lot to live in such a wretched age that his life was one long polemical effort." How can ye, my worthy Philistines, think of Lessing without shame? He who was ruined precisely on account of your stupidity, while struggling with your ludicrous fetiches and idols, with the defects of your theatres, scholars, and theologists, without once daring to attempt that eternal flight for which he had been born. And what are your feelings when ye think of Winckelman, who, in order to turn his eyes from your grotesque puerilities, went begging to the Jesuits for help, and whose ignominious conversion dishonours not him, but you? Dare ye mention Schiller's name without blushing? Look at his portrait. See the flashing eyes that glance contemptuously over your heads, the deadly red cheek—do these things mean nothing to you? In him ye had such a magnificent and divine toy that ye shattered it. Suppose, for a moment, it had been possible to deprive this harassed and hunted life of Goethe's friendship, ye would then have been reponsible for its still earlier end. Ye have had no finger in any one of the life-works of your great geniuses, and yet ye would make a dogma to the effect that no one is to be helped in the future. But for every one of them, ye were "the resistance of the obtuse world," which Goethe calls by its name in his epilogue to the Bell; for all of them ye were the grumbling imbeciles, or the envious bigots, or the malicious egoists: in spite of you each of them created his works, against you each directed his attacks, and thanks to you each prematurely sank, while his work was still unfinished, broken and bewildered by the stress of the battle. And now ye presume that ye are going to be permitted, tamquam re bene gesta, to praise such men! and with words which leave no one in any doubt as to whom ye have in your minds when ye utter your encomiums, which therefore "spring forth with such hearty warmth" that one must be blind not to see to whom ye are really bowing. Even Goethe in his day had to cry: "Upon my honour, we are in need of a Lessing, and woe unto all vain masters and to the whole aesthetic kingdom of heaven, when the young tiger, whose restless strength will be visible in his every distended muscle and his every glance, shall sally forth to seek his prey!"

V.

How clever it was of my friend to read no further, once he had been enlightened (thanks to that chimerical vision) concerning the Straussian Lessing and Strauss himself. We, however, read on further, and even craved admission of the Doorkeeper of the New Faith to the sanctum of music. The Master threw the door open for us, accompanied us, and began quoting certain names, until, at last, overcome with mistrust, we stood still and looked at him. Was it possible that we were the victims of the same hallucination as that to which our friend had been subjected in his dream? The musicians to whom Strauss referred seemed to us to be wrongly designated as long as he spoke about them, and we began to think that the talk must certainly be about somebody else, even admitting that it did not relate to incongruous phantoms. When, for instance, he mentioned Haydn with that same warmth which made us so suspicious when he praised Lessing, and when he posed as the epopt and priest of a mysterious Haydn cult; when, in a discussion upon quartette-music, if you please, he even likened Haydn to a "good unpretending soup" and Beethoven to "sweetmeats" (p. 432); then, to our minds, one thing, and one thing alone, became certain—namely, that his Sweetmeat-Beethoven is not our Beethoven, and his Soup-Haydn is not our Haydn. The Master was moreover of the opinion that our orchestra is too good to perform Haydn, and that only the most unpretentious amateurs can do justice to that music—a further proof that he was referring to some other artist and some other work, possibly to Riehl's music for the home.

But whoever can this Sweetmeat-Beethoven of Strauss's be? He is said to have composed nine symphonies, of which the Pastoral is "the least remarkable"; we are told that "each time in composing the third, he seemed impelled to exceed his bounds, and depart on an adventurous quest," from which we might infer that we are here concerned with a sort of double monster, half horse and half cavalier. With regard to a certain Eroica, this Centaur is very hard pressed, because he did not succeed in making it clear "whether it is a question of a conflict on the open field or in the deep heart of man." In the Pastoral there is said to be "a furiously raging storm," for which it is "almost too insignificant" to interrupt a dance of country-folk, and which, owing to "its arbitrary connection with a trivial motive," as Strauss so adroitly and correctly puts it, renders this symphony "the least remarkable." A more drastic expression appears to have occurred to the Master; but he prefers to speak here, as he says, "with becoming modesty." But no, for once our Master is wrong; in this case he is really a little too modest. Who, indeed, will enlighten us concerning this Sweetmeat-Beethoven, if not Strauss himself—the only person who seems to know anything about him? But, immediately below, a strong judgment is uttered with becoming non-modesty, and precisely in regard to the Ninth Symphony. It is said, for instance, that this symphony "is naturally the favourite of a prevalent taste, which in art, and music especially, mistakes the grotesque for the genial, and the formless for the sublime" (p. 428). It is true that a critic as severe as Gervinus was gave this work a hearty welcome, because it happened to confirm one of his doctrines; but Strauss is "far from going to these problematic productions" in search of the merits of his Beethoven. "It is a pity," cries our Master, with a convulsive sigh, "that one is compelled, by such reservations, to mar one's enjoyment of Beethoven, as well as the admiration gladly accorded to him." For our Master is a favourite of the Graces, and these have informed him that they only accompanied Beethoven part of the way, and that he then lost sight of them. "This is a defect," he cries, "but can you believe that it may also appear as an advantage?" "He who is painfully and breathlessly rolling the musical idea along will seem to be moving the weightier one, and thus appear to be the stronger" (pp. 423-24). This is a confession, and not necessarily one concerning Beethoven alone, but concerning "the classical prose-writer" himself. He, the celebrated author, is not abandoned by the Graces. From the play of airy jests—that is to say, Straussian jests—to the heights of solemn earnestness—that is to say, Straussian earnestness—they remain stolidly at his elbow. He, the classical prose-writer, slides his burden along playfully and with a light heart, whereas Beethoven rolls his painfully and breathlessly. He seems merely to dandle his load; this is indeed an advantage. But would anybody believe that it might equally be a sign of something wanting? In any case, only those could believe this who mistake the grotesque for the genial, and the formless for the sublime—is not that so, you dandling favourite of the Graces? We envy no one the edifying moments he may have, either in the stillness of his little private room or in a new heaven specially fitted out for him; but of all possible pleasures of this order, that of Strauss's is surely one of the most wonderful, for he is even edified by a little holocaust. He calmly throws the sublimest works of the German nation into the flames, in order to cense his idols with their smoke. Suppose, for a moment, that by some accident, the Eroica, the Pastoral, and the Ninth Symphony had fallen into the hands of our priest of the Graces, and that it had been in his power to suppress such problematic productions, in order to keep the image of the Master pure, who doubts but what he would have burned them? And it is precisely in this way that the Strausses of our time demean themselves: they only wish to know so much of an artist as is compatible with the service of their rooms; they know only the extremes— censing or burning. To all this they are heartily welcome; the one surprising feature of the whole case is that public opinion, in matters artistic, should be so feeble, vacillating, and corruptible as contentedly to allow these exhibitions of indigent Philistinism to go by without raising an objection; yea, that it does not even possess sufficient sense of humour to feel tickled at the sight of an unaesthetic little master's sitting in judgment upon Beethoven. As to Mozart, what Aristotle says of Plato ought really to be applied here: "Insignificant people ought not to be permitted even to praise him." In this respect, however, all shame has vanished—from the public as well as from the Master's mind: he is allowed, not merely to cross himself before the greatest and purest creations of German genius, as though he had perceived something godless and immoral in them, but people actually rejoice over his candid confessions and admission of sins—more particularly as he makes no mention of his own, but only of those which great men are said to have committed. Oh, if only our Master be in the right! his readers sometimes think, when attacked by a paroxysm of doubt; he himself, however, stands there, smiling and convinced, perorating, condemning, blessing, raising his hat to himself, and is at any minute capable of saying what the Duchesse Delaforte said to Madame de Staël, to wit: "My dear, I must confess that I find no one but myself invariably right."

VI.

A corpse is a pleasant thought for a worm, and a worm is a dreadful thought for every living creature. Worms fancy their kingdom of heaven in a fat body; professors of philosophy seek theirs in rummaging among Schopenhauer's entrails, and as long as rodents exist, there will exist a heaven for rodents. In this, we have the answer to our first question: How does the believer in the new faith picture his heaven? The Straussian Philistine harbours in the works of our great poets and musicians like a parasitic worm whose life is destruction, whose admiration is devouring, and whose worship is digesting.

Now, however, our second question must be answered: How far does the courage lent to its adherents by this new faith extend? Even this question would already have been answered, if courage and pretentiousness had been one; for then Strauss would not be lacking even in the just and veritable courage of a Mameluke. At all events, the "becoming modesty" of which Strauss speaks in the above-mentioned passage, where he is referring to Beethoven, can only be a stylistic and not a moral manner of speech. Strauss has his full share of the temerity to which every successful hero assumes the right: all flowers grow only for him—the conqueror; and he praises the sun because it shines in at his window just at the right time. He does not even spare the venerable old universe in his eulogies—as though it were only now and henceforward sufficiently sanctified by praise to revolve around the central monad David Strauss. The universe, he is happy to inform us, is, it is true, a machine with jagged iron wheels, stamping and hammering ponderously, but: "We do not only find the revolution of pitiless wheels in our world-machine, but also the shedding of soothing oil" (p. 435). The universe, provided it submit to Strauss's encomiums, is not likely to overflow with gratitude towards this master of weird metaphors, who was unable to discover better similes in its praise. But what is the oil called which trickles down upon the hammers and stampers? And how would it console a workman who chanced to get one of his limbs caught in the mechanism to know that this oil was trickling over him? Passing over this simile as bad, let us turn our attention to another of Strauss's artifices, whereby he tries to ascertain how he feels disposed towards the universe; this question of Marguerite's, "He loves me—loves me not—loves me?" hanging on his lips the while. Now, although Strauss is not telling flower-petals or the buttons on his waistcoat, still what he does is not less harmless, despite the fact that it needs perhaps a little more courage. Strauss wishes to make certain whether his feeling for the "All" is either paralysed or withered, and he pricks himself; for he knows that one can prick a limb that is either paralysed or withered without causing any pain. As a matter of fact, he does not really prick himself, but selects another more violent method, which he describes thus: "We open Schopenhauer, who takes every occasion of slapping our idea in the face" (p. 167). Now, as an idea—even that of Strauss's concerning the universe—has no face, if there be any face in the question at all it must be that of the idealist, and the procedure may be subdivided into the following separate actions:—Strauss, in any case, throws Schopenhauer open, whereupon the latter slaps Strauss in the face. Strauss then reacts religiously; that is to say, he again begins to belabour Schopenhauer, to abuse him, to speak of absurdities, blasphemies, dissipations, and even to allege that Schopenhauer could not have been in his right senses. Result of the dispute: "We demand the same piety for our Cosmos that the devout of old demanded for his God"; or, briefly, "He loves me." Our favourite of the Graces makes his life a hard one, but he is as brave as a Mameluke, and fears neither the Devil nor Schopenhauer. How much "soothing oil" must he use if such incidents are of frequent occurrence!

On the other hand, we readily understand Strauss's gratitude to this tickling, pricking, and slapping Schopenhauer; hence we are not so very much surprised when we find him expressing himself in the following kind way about him: "We need only turn over the leaves of Arthur Schopenhauer's works (although we shall on many other accounts do well not only to glance over but to study them), etc." (p. 166). Now, to whom does this captain of Philistines address these words? To him who has clearly never even studied Schopenhauer, the latter might well have retorted, "This is an author who does not even deserve to be scanned, much less to be studied." Obviously, he gulped Schopenhauer down "the wrong way," and this hoarse coughing is merely his attempt to clear his throat. But, in order to fill the measure of his ingenuous encomiums, Strauss even arrogates to himself the right of commending old Kant: he speaks of the latter's General History of the Heavens of the Year 1755 as of "a work which has always appeared to me not less important than his later Critique of Pure Reason. If in the latter we admire the depth of insight, the breadth of observation strikes us in the former. If in the latter we can trace the old man's anxiety to secure even a limited possession of knowledge—so it be but on a firm basis—in the former we encounter the mature man, full of the daring of the discoverer and conqueror in the realm of thought." This judgment of Strauss's concerning Kant did not strike me as being more modest than the one concerning Schopenhauer. In the one case, we have the little captain, who is above all anxious to express even the most insignificant opinion with certainty, and in the other we have the famous prose-writer, who, with all the courage of ignorance, exudes his eulogistic secretions over Kant. It is almost incredible that Strauss availed himself of nothing in Kant's Critique of Pure Reason while compiling his Testament of modern ideas, and that he knew only how to appeal to the coarsest realistic taste must also be numbered among the more striking characteristics of this new gospel, the which professes to be but the result of the laborious and continuous study of history and science, and therefore tacitly repudiates all connection with philosophy. For the Philistine captain and his "We," Kantian philosophy does not exist. He does not dream of the fundamental antinomy of idealism and of the highly relative sense of all science and reason. And it is precisely reason that ought to tell him how little it is possible to know of things in themselves. It is true, however, that people of a certain age cannot possibly understand Kant, especially when, in their youth, they understood or fancied they understood that "gigantic mind," Hegel, as

Strauss did; and had moreover concerned themselves with Schleiermacher, who, according to Strauss, "was gifted with perhaps too much acumen." It will sound odd to our author when I tell him that, even now, he stands absolutely dependent upon Hegel and Schleiermacher, and that his teaching of the Cosmos, his way of regarding things sub specie biennii, his salaams to the state of affairs now existing in Germany, and, above all, his shameless Philistine optimism, can only be explained by an appeal to certain impressions of youth, early habits, and disorders; for he who has once sickened on Hegel and Schleiermacher never completely recovers.

There is one passage in the confession-book where the incurable optimism referred to above bursts forth with the full joyousness of holiday spirits (pp. 166-67). "If the universe is a thing which had better not have existed," says Strauss, "then surely the speculation of the philosopher, as forming part of this universe, is a speculation which had better not have speculated. The pessimist philosopher fails to perceive that he, above all, declares his own thought, which declares the world to be bad, as bad also; but if the thought which declares the world to be bad is a bad thought, then it follows naturally that the world is good. As a rule, optimism may take things too easily. Schopenhauer's references to the colossal part which sorrow and evil play in the world are quite in their right place as a counterpoise; but every true philosophy is necessarily optimistic, as otherwise she hews down the branch on which she herself is sitting." If this refutation of Schopenhauer is not the same as that to which Strauss refers somewhere else as "the refutation loudly and jubilantly acclaimed in higher spheres," then I quite fail to understand the dramatic phraseology used by him elsewhere to strike an opponent. Here optimism has for once intentionally simplified her task. But the master-stroke lay in thus pretending that the refutation of Schopenhauer was not such a very difficult task after all, and in playfully wielding the burden in such a manner that the three Graces attendant on the dandling optimist might constantly be delighted by his methods. The whole purpose of the deed was to demonstrate this one truth, that it is quite unnecessary to take a pessimist seriously; the most vapid sophisms become justified, provided they show that, in regard to a philosophy as "unhealthy and unprofitable" as Schopenhauer's, not proofs but quips and sallies alone are suitable. While perusing such passages, the reader will grasp the full meaning of Schopenhauer's solemn utterance to the effect that, where optimism is not merely the idle prattle of those beneath whose flat brows words and only words are stored, it seemed to him not merely an absurd but a vicious attitude of mind, and one full of scornful irony towards the indescribable sufferings of humanity. When a philosopher like Strauss is able to frame it into a system, it becomes more than a vicious attitude of mind—it is then an imbecile gospel of comfort for the "I" or for the "We," and can only provoke indignation.

Who could read the following psychological avowal, for instance, without indignation, seeing that it is obviously but an offshoot from this vicious gospel of comfort?—"Beethoven remarked that he could never have composed a text like Figaro or Don Juan. Life had not been so profuse of its snubs to him that he could treat it so gaily, or deal so lightly with the foibles of men" (p. 430). In order, however, to adduce the most striking instance of this dissolute vulgarity of sentiment, let it suffice, here, to observe that Strauss knows no other means of accounting for the terribly serious negative instinct and the movement of ascetic sanctification which characterised the first century of the Christian era, than by supposing the existence of a previous period of surfeit in the matter of all kinds of sexual indulgence, which of itself brought about a state of revulsion and disgust.

"The Persians call it bidamag buden, The Germans say 'Katzenjammer.'"[Footnote: Remorse for the previous night's excesses.]

Strauss quotes this himself, and is not ashamed. As for us, we turn aside for a moment, that we may overcome our loathing.

VII.

As a matter of fact, our Philistine captain is brave, even audacious, in words; particularly when he hopes by such bravery to delight his noble colleagues—the "We," as he calls them. So the asceticism and self-denial of the ancient anchorite and saint was merely a form of Katzenjammer? Jesus may be described as an enthusiast who nowadays would scarcely have escaped the madhouse, and the story of the

Resurrection may be termed a "world-wide deception." For once we will allow these views to pass without raising any objection, seeing that they may help us to gauge the amount of courage which our "classical Philistine" Strauss is capable of. Let us first hear his confession: "It is certainly an unpleasant and a thankless task to tell the world those truths which it is least desirous of hearing. It prefers, in fact, to manage its affairs on a profuse scale, receiving and spending after the magnificent fashion of the great, as long as there is anything left; should any person, however, add up the various items of its liabilities, and anxiously call its attention to the sum-total, he is certain to be regarded as an importunate meddler. And yet this has always been the bent of my moral and intellectual nature." A moral and intellectual nature of this sort might possibly be regarded as courageous; but what still remains to be proved is, whether this courage is natural and inborn, or whether it is not rather acquired and artificial. Perhaps Strauss only accustomed himself by degrees to the rôle of an importunate meddler, until he gradually acquired the courage of his calling. Innate cowardice, which is the Philistine's birthright, would not be incompatible with this mode of development, and it is precisely this cowardice which is perceptible in the want of logic of those sentences of Strauss's which it needed courage to pronounce. They sound like thunder, but they do not clear the air. No aggressive action is performed: aggressive words alone are used, and these he selects from among the most insulting he can find. He moreover exhausts all his accumulated strength and energy in coarse and noisy expression, and when once his utterances have died away he is more of a coward even than he who has always held his tongue. The very shadow of his deeds—his morality—shows us that he is a word-hero, and that he avoids everything which might induce him to transfer his energies from mere verbosity to really serious things. With admirable frankness, he announces that he is no longer a Christian, but disclaims all idea of wishing to disturb the contentment of any one: he seems to recognise a contradiction in the notion of abolishing one society by instituting another—whereas there is nothing contradictory in it at all. With a certain rude self-satisfaction, he swathes himself in the hirsute garment of our Simian genealogists, and extols Darwin as one of mankind's greatest benefactors; but our perplexity is great when we find him constructing his ethics quite independently of the question, "What is our conception of the universe?" In this department he had an opportunity of exhibiting native pluck; for he ought to have turned his back on his "We," and have established a moral code for life out of bellum omnium contra omnes and the privileges of the strong. But it is to be feared that such a code could only have emanated from a bold spirit like that of Hobbes', and must have taken its root in a love of truth quite different from that which was only able to vent itself in explosive outbursts against parsons, miracles, and the "world-wide humbug" of the Resurrection. For, whereas the Philistine remained on Strauss's side in regard to these explosive outbursts, he would have been against him had he been confronted with a genuine and seriously constructed ethical system, based upon Darwin's teaching.

Says Strauss: "I should say that all moral action arises from the individual's acting in consonance with the idea of kind" (p. 274). Put quite clearly and comprehensively, this means: "Live as a man, and not as an ape or a seal." Unfortunately, this imperative is both useless and feeble; for in the class Man what a multitude of different types are included—to mention only the Patagonian and the Master, Strauss; and no one would ever dare to say with any right, "Live like a Patagonian," and "Live like the Master Strauss"! Should any one, however, make it his rule to live like a genius—that is to say, like the ideal type of the genus Man—and should he perchance at the same time be either a Patagonian or Strauss himself, what should we then not have to suffer from the importunities of genius-mad eccentrics (concerning whose mushroom growth in Germany even Lichtenberg had already spoken), who with savage cries would compel us to listen to the confession of their most recent belief! Strauss has not yet learned that no "idea" can ever make man better or more moral, and that the preaching of a morality is as easy as the establishment of it is difficult. His business ought rather to have been, to take the phenomena of human goodness, such—for instance—as pity, love, and self-abnegation, which are already to hand, and seriously to explain them and show their relation to his Darwinian first principle. But no; he preferred to soar into the imperative, and thus escape the task of explaining. But even in his flight he was irresponsible enough to soar beyond the very first principles of which we speak.

"Ever remember," says Strauss, "that thou art human, not merely a natural production; ever remember that all others are human also, and, with all individual differences, the same as thou, having the same needs and claims as thyself: this is the sum and the substance of morality" (p. 277). But where does this imperative hail from? How can it be intuitive in man, seeing that, according to Darwin, man is indeed a creature of nature, and that his ascent to his present stage of development has been conditioned by quite different laws—by the very fact that be was continually forgetting that others were constituted like him and shared the same rights with him; by the very fact that he regarded himself as the stronger, and thus brought about the gradual suppression of weaker types. Though Strauss is bound to admit that no two creatures have ever been quite alike, and that the ascent of man from the lowest species of animals to the exalted height of the Culture—Philistine depended upon the law of individual distinctness, he still sees no difficulty in declaring exactly the reverse in his law: "Behave thyself as though there were no such things as individual distinctions." Where is the Strauss-Darwin morality here? Whither, above all, has the courage gone?

In the very next paragraph we find further evidence tending to show us the point at which this courage veers round to its opposite; for Strauss continues: "Ever remember that thou, and all that thou beholdest within and around thee, all that befalls thee and others, is no disjointed fragment, no wild chaos of atoms or casualties, but that, following eternal law, it springs from the one primal source of all life, all reason, and all good: this is the essence of religion" (pp. 277-78). Out of that "one primal source," however, all ruin and irrationality, all evil flows as well, and its name, according to Strauss, is Cosmos.

Now, how can this Cosmos, with all the contradictions and the self-annihilating characteristics which Strauss gives it, be worthy of religious veneration and be addressed by the name "God," as Strauss addresses it?—"Our God does not, indeed, take us into His arms from the outside (here one expects, as an antithesis, a somewhat miraculous process of being "taken into His arms from the inside"), but He

unseals the well-springs of consolation within our own bosoms. He
shows us that although Chance would be an unreasonable ruler, yet
necessity, or the enchainment of causes in the world, is Reason itself."
(A misapprehension of which only the "We" can fail to perceive the
folly; because they were brought up in the Hegelian worship of Reality
as the Reasonable—that is to say, in the canonisation of success.) "He
teaches us to perceive that to demand an exception in the
accomplishment of a single natural law would be to demand the
destruction of the universe" (pp. 435-36). On the contrary, Great
Master: an honest natural scientist believes in the unconditional rule
of natural laws in the world, without, however, taking up any position
in regard to the ethical or intellectual value of these laws. Wherever
neutrality is abandoned in this respect, it is owing to an
anthropomorphic attitude of mind which allows reason to exceed its
proper bounds. But it is just at the point where the natural scientist
resigns that Strauss, to put it in his own words, "reacts religiously," and
leaves the scientific and scholarly standpoint in order to proceed along
less honest lines of his own. Without any further warrant, he assumes
that all that has happened possesses the highest intellectual value; that
it was therefore absolutely reasonably and intentionally so arranged,
and that it even contained a revelation of eternal goodness. He
therefore has to appeal to a complete cosmodicy, and finds himself at
a disadvantage in regard to him who is contented with a theodicy, and
who, for instance, regards the whole of man's existence as a
punishment for sin or a process of purification. At this stage, and in
this embarrassing position, Strauss even suggests a metaphysical
hypothesis—the driest and most palsied ever conceived—and, in reality,
but an unconscious parody of one of Lessing's sayings. We read on
page 255: "And that other saying of Lessing's— 'If God, holding truth
in His right hand, and in His left only the ever-living desire for it,
although on condition of perpetual error, left him the choice of the
two, he would, considering that truth belongs to God alone, humbly
seize His left hand, and beg its contents for Himself'— this saying of
Lessing's has always been accounted one of the most magnificent
which he has left us. It has been found to contain the general
expression of his restless love of inquiry and activity. The saying has

always made a special impression upon me; because, behind its subjective meaning, I still seemed to hear the faint ring of an objective one of infinite import. For does it not contain the best possible answer to the rude speech of Schopenhauer, respecting the ill-advised God who had nothing better to do than to transform Himself into this miserable world? if, for example, the Creator Himself had shared Lessing's conviction of the superiority of struggle to tranquil possession?" What!—a God who would choose perpetual error, together with a striving after truth, and who would, perhaps, fall humbly at Strauss's feet and cry to him,"Take thou all Truth, it is thine!"? If ever a God and a man were ill-advised, they are this Straussian God, whose hobby is to err and to fail, and this Straussian man, who must atone for this erring and failing. Here, indeed, one hears "a faint ring of infinite import"; here flows Strauss's cosmic soothing oil; here one has a notion of the rationale of all becoming and all natural laws. Really? Is not our universe rather the work of an inferior being, as Lichtenberg suggests?—of an inferior being who did not quite understand his business; therefore an experiment, an attempt, upon which work is still proceeding? Strauss himself, then, would be compelled to admit that our universe is by no means the theatre of reason, but of error, and that no conformity to law can contain anything consoling, since all laws have been promulgated by an erratic God who even finds pleasure in blundering. It really is a most amusing spectacle to watch Strauss as a metaphysical architect, building castles in the air. But for whose benefit is this entertainment given? For the smug and noble "We," that they may not lose conceit with themselves: they may possibly have taken sudden fright, in the midst of the inflexible and pitiless wheel-works of the world-machine, and are tremulously imploring their leader to come to their aid. That is why Strauss pours forth the "soothing oil," that is why he leads forth on a leash a God whose passion it is to err; it is for the same reason, too, that he assumes for once the utterly unsuitable rôle of a metaphysical architect. He does all this, because the noble souls already referred to are frightened, and because he is too. And it is here that we reach the limit of his courage, even in the presence of his "We." He does not dare to be honest, and to tell them, for instance: "I have liberated you from a helping and pitiful God: the Cosmos is no more than an inflexible machine; beware of its wheels, that they do not crush you." He dare not do this. Consequently, he must enlist the help of a witch, and he turns to metaphysics. To the Philistine, however, even Strauss's metaphysics is preferable to Christianity's, and the notion of an erratic God more congenial than that of one who works miracles. For the Philistine himself errs, but has never yet performed a miracle. Hence his hatred of the genius; for the latter is justly famous for the working of miracles. It is therefore highly instructive to ascertain why Strauss, in one passage alone, suddenly takes up the cudgels for genius and the aristocracy of intellect in general. Whatever does he do it for? He does it out of fear—fear of the social democrat. He refers to Bismarck and Moltke, "whose greatness is the less open to controversy as it manifests itself in the domain of tangible external facts. No help for it, therefore; even the most stiff-necked and obdurate of these fellows must condescend to look up a little, if only to get a sight, be it no farther than the knees, of those august figures" (p.327). Do you, Master Metaphysician, perhaps intend to instruct the social democrats in the art of getting kicks? The willingness to bestow them may be met with everywhere, and you are perfectly justified in promising to those who happen to be kicked a sight of those sublime beings as far as the knee. "Also in the domain of art and science," Strauss continues, "there will never be a dearth of kings whose architectural undertakings will find employment for a multitude of carters." Granted; but what if the carters should begin building? It does happen at times, Great Master, as you know, and then the kings must grin and bear it.

As a matter of fact, this union of impudence and weakness, of daring words and cowardly concessions, this cautious deliberation as to which sentences will or will not impress the Philistine or smooth him down the right way, this lack of character and power masquerading as character and power, this meagre wisdom in the guise of omniscience,—these are the features in this book which I detest. If I could conceive of young men having patience to read it and to value it, I should sorrowfully renounce all hope for their future. And is this confession of wretched, hopeless, and really despicable Philistinism supposed to be the expression of the thousands constituting the "We" of whom Strauss speaks, and who are to be the fathers of the coming generation? Unto him who would fain help this coming generation to acquire what the present one does not yet possess, namely, a genuine German culture, the prospect is a horrible one. To such a man, the ground seems strewn with ashes, and all stars are obscured; while every withered tree and field laid waste seems to cry to him: Barren! Forsaken! Springtime is no longer possible here! He must feel as young Goethe felt when he first peered into the melancholy atheistic twilight of the Système de la Nature; to him this book seemed so grey, so Cimmerian and deadly, that he could only endure its presence with difficulty, and shuddered at it as one shudders at a spectre.

VIII.

We ought now to be sufficiently informed concerning the heaven and the courage of our new believer to be able to turn to the last question: How does he write his books? and of what order are his religious documents?

He who can answer this question uprightly and without prejudice will be confronted by yet another serious problem, and that is: How this Straussian pocket-oracle of the German Philistine was able to pass through six editions? And he will grow more than ever suspicious when he hears that it was actually welcomed as a pocket-oracle, not only in scholastic circles, but even in German universities as well. Students are said to have greeted it as a canon for strong intellects, and, from all accounts, the professors raised no objections to this view; while here and there people have declared it to be a religions book for scholars. Strauss himself gave out that he did not intend his profession of faith to be merely a reference-book for learned and cultured people; but here let us abide by the fact that it was first and foremost a work appealing to his colleagues, and was ostensibly a mirror in which they were to see their own way of living faithfully reflected. For therein lay the feat. The Master feigned to have presented us with a new ideal conception of the universe, and now adulation is being paid him out of every mouth; because each is in a position to suppose that he too regards the universe and life in the same way. Thus Strauss has seen fulfilled in each of his readers what he only demanded of the future.

In this way, the extraordinary success of his book is partly explained: "Thus we live and hold on our way in joy," the scholar cries in his book, and delights to see others rejoicing over the announcement. If the reader happen to think differently from the Master in regard to Darwin or to capital punishment, it is of very little consequence; for he is too conscious throughout of breathing an atmosphere that is familiar to him, and of hearing but the echoes of his own voice and wants. However painfully this unanimity may strike the true friend of German culture, it is his duty to be unrelenting in his explanation of it as a phenomenon, and not to shrink from making this explanation public.

We all know the peculiar methods adopted in our own time of cultivating the sciences: we all know them, because they form a part of our lives. And, for this very reason, scarcely anybody seems to ask himself what the result of such a cultivation of the sciences will mean to culture in general, even supposing that everywhere the highest abilities and the most earnest will be available for the promotion of culture. In the heart of the average scientific type (quite irrespective of the examples thereof with which we meet to-day) there lies a pure paradox: he behaves like the veriest idler of independent means, to whom life is not a dreadful and serious business, but a sound piece of property, settled upon him for all eternity; and it seems to him justifiable to spend his whole life in answering questions which, after all is said and done, can only be of interest to that person who believes in eternal life as an absolute certainty. The heir of but a few hours, he sees himself encompassed by yawning abysses, terrible to behold; and every step he takes should recall the questions, Wherefore? Whither? and Whence? to his mind. But his soul rather warms to his work, and, be this the counting of a floweret's petals or the breaking of stones by the roadside, he spends his whole fund of interest, pleasure, strength, and aspirations upon it. This paradox—the scientific man—has lately dashed ahead at such a frantic speed in Germany, that one would almost think the scientific world were a factory, in which every minute wasted meant a fine. To-day the man of science works as arduously as the fourth or slave caste: his study has ceased to be an occupation, it is a necessity; he looks neither to the right nor to the left, but rushes through all things—even through the serious matters which life bears in its train—with that semi-listlessness and repulsive need of rest so characteristic of the exhausted labourer. This is also his attitude towards culture. He behaves as if life to him were not only otium but sine dignitate: even in his sleep he does not throw off the yoke, but like an emancipated slave still dreams of his misery, his forced haste and his floggings. Our scholars can scarcely be distinguished—and, even then, not to their advantage—from agricultural labourers, who in order to increase a small patrimony, assiduously strive, day and night, to cultivate their fields, drive their ploughs, and urge on their oxen. Now, Pascal suggests that men only endeavour to work hard at their business and sciences with the view of escaping those questions of greatest import which every moment of loneliness or leisure presses upon them—the questions relating to the wherefore, the whence, and the whither of life. Curiously enough, our scholars never think of the most vital question of all—the wherefore of their work, their haste, and their painful ecstasies. Surely their object is not the earning of bread or the acquiring of posts of honour? No, certainly not. But ye take as much pains as the famishing and breadless; and, with that eagerness and lack of discernment which characterises the starving, ye even snatch the dishes from the sideboard of science. If, however, as scientific men, ye proceed with science as the labourers with the tasks which the exigencies of life impose upon them, what will become of a culture which must await the hour of its birth and its salvation in the very midst of all this agitated and breathless running to and fro—this sprawling scientifically?

For it no one has time—and yet for what shall science have time if not for culture? Answer us here, then, at least: whence, whither, wherefore all science, if it do not lead to culture? Belike to barbarity? And in this direction we already see the scholar caste ominously advanced, if we are to believe that such superficial books as this one of Strauss's meet the demand of their present degree of culture. For precisely in him do we find that repulsive need of rest and that incidental semi-listless attention to, and coming to terms with, philosophy, culture, and every serious thing on earth. It will be remembered that, at the meetings held by scholars, as soon as each individual has had his say in his own particular department of knowledge, signs of fatigue, of a desire for distraction at any price, of waning memory, and of incoherent experiences of life, begin to be noticeable. While listening to Strauss discussing any worldly question, be it marriage, the war, or capital punishment, we are startled by his complete lack of anything like first-hand experience, or of any original thought on human nature. All his judgments are so redolent of books, yea even of newspapers. Literary reminiscences do duty for genuine ideas and views, and the assumption of a moderate and grandfatherly tone take the place of wisdom and mature thought. How perfectly in keeping all this is with the fulsome spirit animating the holders of the highest places in German science in large cities! How thoroughly this spirit must appeal to that other! for it is precisely in those quarters that culture is in the saddest plight; it is precisely there that its fresh growth is made impossible—so boisterous are the preparations made by science, so sheepishly are favourite subjects of knowledge allowed to oust questions of much greater import. What kind of lantern would be needed here, in order to find men capable of a complete surrender to genius, and of an intimate knowledge of its depths—men possessed of sufficient courage and strength to exorcise the demons that have forsaken our age? Viewed from the outside, such quarters certainly do appear to possess the whole pomp of culture; with their imposing apparatus they resemble great arsenals fitted with huge guns and other machinery of war; we see preparations in progress and the most strenuous activity, as though the heavens themselves were to be stormed, and truth were to be drawn out of the deepest of all wells; and yet, in war, the largest machines are the most unwieldy. Genuine culture therefore leaves such places as these religiously alone, for its best instincts warn it that in their midst it has nothing to hope for, and very much to fear. For the only kind of culture with which the inflamed eye and obtuse brain of the scholar working-classes concern themselves is of that Philistine order of which Strauss has announced the gospel. If we consider for a moment the fundamental causes underlying the sympathy which binds the learned working-classes to Culture-Philistinism, we shall discover the road leading to Strauss the Writer, who has been acknowledged classical, and tihence to our last and principal theme.

To begin with, that culture has contentment written in its every feature, and will allow of no important changes being introduced into the present state of German education. It is above all convinced of the originality of all German educational institutions, more particularly the public schools and universities; it does not cease recommending these to foreigners, and never doubts that if the Germans have become the most cultivated and discriminating people on earth, it is owing to such institutions. Culture-Philistinism believes in itself, consequently it also believes in the methods and means at its disposal. Secondly, however, it leaves the highest judgment concerning all questions of taste and culture to the scholar, and even regards itself as the ever-increasing compendium of scholarly opinions regarding art, literature, and philosophy. Its first care is to urge the scholar to express his opinions; these it proceeds to mix, dilute, and systematise, and then it administers them to the German people in the form of a bottle of medicine. What conies to life outside this circle is either not heard or attended at all, or if heard, is heeded half-heartedly; until, at last, a voice (it does not matter whose, provided it belong to some one who is strictly typical of the scholar tribe) is heard to issue from the temple in which traditional infallibility of taste is said to reside; and from that time forward public opinion has one conviction more, which it echoes and re-echoes hundreds and hundreds of times. As a matter of fact, though, the aesthetic infallibility of any utterance emanating from the temple is the more doubtful, seeing that the lack of taste, thought, and artistic feeling in any scholar can be taken for granted, unless it has previously been proved that, in his particular case, the reverse is true. And only a few can prove this. For how many who have had a share in the breathless and unending scurry of modern science have preserved that quiet and courageous gaze of the struggling man of culture—if they ever possessed it—that gaze which condemns even the scurry we speak of as a barbarous state of affairs? That is why these few are forced to live in an almost perpetual contradiction. What could they do against the uniform belief of the thousands who have enlisted public opinion in their cause, and who mutually defend each other in this belief? What purpose can it serve when one individual openly declares war against Strauss, seeing that a crowd have decided in his favour, and that the masses led by this crowd have learned to ask six consecutive times for the Master's Philistine sleeping-mixture?

If, without further ado, we here assumed that the Straussian confession-book had triumphed over public opinion and had been acclaimed and welcomed as conqueror, its author might call our attention to the fact that the multitudinous criticisms of his work in the various public organs are not of an altogether unanimous or even favourable character, and that he therefore felt it incumbent upon him to defend himself against some of the more malicious, impudent, and provoking of these newspaper pugilists by means of a postscript. How can there be a public opinion concerning my book, he cries to us, if every journalist is to regard me as an outlaw, and to mishandle me as much as he likes? This contradiction is easily explained, as soon as one considers the two aspects of the Straussian book—the theological and the literary, and it is only the latter that has anything to do with German culture. Thanks to its theological colouring, it stands beyond the pale of our German culture, and provokes the animosity of the various theological groups—yea, even of every individual German, in so far as he is a theological sectarian from birth, and only invents his own peculiar private belief in order to be able to dissent from every other form of belief. But when the question arises of talking about Strauss THE WRITER, pray listen to what the theological sectarians have to say about him. As soon as his literary side comes under notice, all theological objections immediately subside, and the dictum comes plain and clear, as if from the lips of one congregation: In spite of it all, he is still a classical writer!

Everybody—even the most bigoted, orthodox Churchman—pays the writer the most gratifying compliments, while there is always a word or two thrown in as a tribute to his almost Lessingesque language, his delicacy of touch, or the beauty and accuracy of his aesthetic views. As a book, therefore, the Straussian performance appears to meet all the demands of an ideal example of its kind. The theological opponents, despite the fact that their voices were the loudest of all, nevertheless constitute but an infinitesimal portion of the great public; and even with regard to them, Strauss still maintains that he is right when he says: "Compared with my thousands of readers, a few dozen public cavillers form but an insignificant minority, and they can hardly prove that they are their faithful interpreters. It was obviously in the nature of things that opposition should be clamorous and assent tacit." Thus, apart from the angry bitterness which Strauss's profession of faith may have provoked here and there, even the most fanatical of his opponents, to whom his voice seems to rise out of an abyss, like the voice of a beast, are agreed as to his merits as a writer; and that is why the treatment which Strauss has received at the hands of the literary lackeys of the theological groups proves nothing against our contention that Culture-Philistinism celebrated its triumph in this book. It must be admitted that the average educated Philistine is a degree less honest than Strauss, or is at least more reserved in his public utterances. But this fact only tends to increase his admiration for honesty in another. At home, or in the company of his equals, he may applaud with wild enthusiasm, but takes care not to put on paper how entirely Strauss's words are in harmony with his own innermost feelings. For, as we have already maintained, our Culture-Philistine is somewhat of a coward, even in his strongest sympathies; hence Strauss, who can boast of a trifle more courage than he, becomes his leader, notwithstanding the fact that even Straussian pluck has its very definite limits. If he overstepped these limits, as Schopenhauer does in almost every sentence, he would then forfeit his position at the head of the Philistines, and everybody would flee from him as precipitately as they are now following in his wake. He who would regard this artful if not sagacious moderation and this mediocre valour as an Aristotelian virtue, would certainly be wrong; for the valour in question is not the golden mean between two faults, but between a virtue and a fault—and in this mean, between virtue and fault, all Philistine qualities are to be found.

IX.

"In spite of it all, he is still a classical writer." Well, let us see! Perhaps we may now be allowed to discuss Strauss the stylist and master of language; but in the first place let us inquire whether, as a literary man, he is equal to the task of building his house, and whether he really understands the architecture of a book. From this inquiry we shall be able to conclude whether he is a respectable, thoughtful, and experienced author; and even should we be forced to answer "No" to these questions, he may still, as a last shift, take refuge in his fame as a classical prose-writer. This last-mentioned talent alone, it is true, would not suffice to class him with the classical authors, but at most with the classical improvisers and virtuosos of style, who, however, in regard to power of expression and the whole planning and framing of the work, reveal the awkward hand and the embarrassed eye of the bungler. We therefore put the question, whether Strauss really possesses the artistic strength necessary for the purpose of presenting us with a thing that is a whole, *totum ponere?*

As a rule, it ought to be possible to tell from the first rough sketch of a work whether the author conceived the thing as a whole, and whether, in view of this original conception, he has discovered the correct way of proceeding with his task and of fixing its proportions. Should this most important Part of the problem be solved, and should the framework of the building have been given its most favourable proportions, even then there remains enough to be done: how many smaller faults have to be corrected, how many gaps require filling in! Here and there a temporary partition or floor was found to answer the requirements; everywhere dust and fragments litter the ground, and no matter where we look, we see the signs of work done and work still to be done. The house, as a whole, is still uninhabitable and gloomy, its walls are bare, and the wind blows in through the open windows. Now, whether this remaining, necessary, and very irksome work has been satisfactorily accomplished by Strauss does not concern us at present; our question is, whether the building itself has been conceived as a whole, and whether its proportions are good? The reverse of this, of course, would be a compilation of fragments—a method generally adopted by scholars. They rely upon it that these fragments are related among themselves, and thus confound the logical and the artistic relation between them. Now, the relation between the four questions which provide the chapter-headings of Strauss's book cannot be called a logical one. Are we still Christians? Have we still a religion? What is our conception of the universe? What is our rule of life? And it is by no means contended that the relation is illogical simply because the third question has nothing to do with the second, nor the fourth with the third, nor all three with the first. The natural scientist who puts the third question, for instance, shows his unsullied love of truth by the simple fact that he tacitly passes over the second. And with regard to the subject of the fourth chapter—marriage, republicanism, and capital punishment—Strauss himself seems to have been aware that they could only have been muddled and obscured by being associated with the Darwinian theory expounded in the third chapter; for he carefully avoids all reference to this theory when discussing them. But the question, "Are we still Christians?" destroys the freedom of the philosophical standpoint at one stroke, by lending it an unpleasant theological colouring. Moreover, in this matter, he quite forgot that the majority of men to-day are not Christians at all, but Buddhists. Why should one, without further ceremony, immediately think of Christianity at the sound of the words "old faith"? Is this a sign that Strauss has never ceased to be a Christian theologian, and that he has therefore never learned to be a philosopher? For we find still greater cause for surprise in the fact that he quite fails to distinguish between belief and knowledge, and continually mentions his "new belief" and the still newer science in one breath. Or is "new belief" merely an ironical concession to ordinary parlance? This almost seems to be the case; for here and there he actually allows "new belief" and "newer science" to be interchangeable terms, as for instance on page II, where he asks on which side, whether on that of the ancient orthodoxy or of modern science, "exist more of the obscurities and insufficiencies unavoidable in human speculation."

Moreover, according to the scheme laid down in the Introduction, his desire is to disclose those proofs upon which the modern view of life is based; but he derives all these proofs from science, and in this respect assumes far more the attitude of a scientist than of a believer.

At bottom, therefore, the religion is not a new belief, but, being of a piece with modern science, it has nothing to do with religion at all. If Strauss, however, persists in his claims to be religious, the grounds for these claims must be beyond the pale of recent science. Only the smallest portion of the Straussian book—that is to say, but a few isolated pages—refer to what Strauss in all justice might call a belief, namely, that feeling for the "All" for which he demands the piety that the old believer demanded for his God. On the pages in question, however, he cannot claim to be altogether scientific; but if only he could lay claim to being a little stronger, more natural, more outspoken, more pious, we should be content. Indeed, what perhaps strikes us most forcibly about him is the multitude of artificial procedures of which he avails himself before he ultimately gets the feeling that he still possesses a belief and a religion; he reaches it by means of stings and blows, as we have already seen. How indigently and feebly this emergency-belief presents itself to us! We shiver at the sight of it.

Although Strauss, in the plan laid down in his Introduction, promises to compare the two faiths, the old and the new, and to show that the latter will answer the same purpose as the former, even he begins to feel, in the end, that he has promised too much. For the question whether the new belief answers the same purpose as the old, or is better or worse, is disposed of incidentally, so to speak, and with uncomfortable haste, in two or three pages (p. 436 et seq.-), and is actually bolstered up by the following subterfuge: "He who cannot help himself in this matter is beyond help, is not yet ripe for our standpoint" (p. 436). How differently, and with what intensity of conviction, did the ancient Stoic believe in the All and the rationality of the All! And, viewed in this light, how does Strauss's claim to originality appear? But, as we have already observed, it would be a matter of indifference to us whether it were new, old, original, or imitated, so that it were only more powerful, more healthy, and more natural. Even Strauss himself leaves this double-distilled emergency-belief to take care of itself as often as he can do so, in order to protect himself and us from danger, and to present his recently acquired biological knowledge to his "We" with a clear conscience. The more embarrassed he may happen to be when he speaks of faith, the rounder and fuller his mouth becomes when he quotes the greatest benefactor to modern men-Darwin. Then he not only exacts belief for the new Messiah, but also for himself-the new apostle. For instance, while discussing one of the most intricate questions in natural history, he declares with true ancient pride: "I shall be told that I am here speaking of things about which I understand nothing. Very well; but others will come who will understand them, and who will also have understood me" (p. 241).

According to this, it would almost seem as though the famous "We" were not only in duty bound to believe in the "All," but also in the naturalist Strauss; in this case we can only hope that in order to acquire the feeling for this last belief, other processes are requisite than the painful and cruel ones demanded by the first belief. Or is it perhaps sufficient in this case that the subject of belief himself be tormented and stabbed with the view of bringing the believers to that "religious reaction" which is the distinguishing sign of the "new faith." What merit should we then discover in the piety of those whom Strauss calls "We"?

Otherwise, it is almost to be feared that modern men will pass on in pursuit of their business without troubling themselves overmuch concerning the new furniture of faith offered them by the apostle: just as they have done heretofore, without the doctrine of the rationality of the All. The whole of modern biological and historical research has nothing to do with the Straussian belief in the All, and the fact that the modern Philistine does not require the belief is proved by the description of his life given by Strauss in the chapter,"What is our Rule of Life?" He is therefore quite right in doubting whether the coach to which his esteemed readers have been obliged to trust themselves "with him, fulfils every requirement." It certainly does not; for the modern man makes more rapid progress when he does not take his place in the Straussian coach, or rather, he got ahead much more quickly long before the Straussian coach ever existed. Now, if it be true that the famous "minority" which is "not to be overlooked," and of which, and in whose name, Strauss speaks, "attaches great importance to consistency," it must be just as dissatisfied with Strauss the Coachbuilder as we are with Strauss the Logician.

Let us, however, drop the question of the logician. Perhaps, from the artistic point of view, the book really is an example of a. well-conceived plan, and does, after all, answer to the requirements of the laws of beauty, despite the fact that it fails to meet with the demands of a well-conducted argument. And now, having shown that he is neither

a scientist nor a strictly correct and systematic scholar, for the first time
we approach the question: Is Strauss a capable writer? Perhaps the task
he set himself was not so much to scare people away from the old faith
as to captivate them by a picturesque and graceful description of what
life would be with the new. If he regarded scholars and educated men
as his most probable audience, experience ought certainly to have told
him that whereas one can shoot such men down with the heavy guns
of scientific proof, but cannot make them surrender, they may be got
to capitulate all the more quickly before "lightly equipped" measures
of seduction. "Lightly equipped," and "intentionally so," thus Strauss
himself speaks of his own book. Nor do his public eulogisers refrain
from using the same expression in reference to the work, as the
following passage, quoted from one of the least remarkable among
them, and in which the same expression is merely paraphrased, will go
to prove:—

"The discourse flows on with delightful harmony: wherever it directs
its criticism against old ideas it wields the art of demonstration, almost
playfully; and it is with some spirit that it prepares the new ideas it
brings so enticingly, and presents them to the simple as well as to the
fastidious taste. The arrangement of such diverse and conflicting
material is well thought out for every portion of it required to be
touched upon, without being made too prominent; at times the
transitions leading from one subject to another are artistically
managed, and one hardly knows what to admire most—the skill with
which unpleasant questions are shelved, or the discretion with which
they are hushed up."

The spirit of such eulogies, as the above clearly shows, is not quite so
subtle in regard to judging of what an author is able to do as in regard
to what he wishes. What Strauss wishes, however, is best revealed by
his own emphatic and not quite harmless commendation of Voltaire's
charms, in whose service he might have learned precisely those "lightly
equipped" arts of which his admirer speaks—granting, of course, that
virtue may be acquired and a pedagogue can ever be a dancer.

Who could help having a suspicion or two, when reading the
following passage, for instance, in which Strauss says of Voltaire, "As
a philosopher [he] is certainly not original, but in the main a mere

exponent of English investigations: in this respect, however, he shows himself to be completely master of his subject, which he presents with incomparable skill, in all possible lights and from all possible sides, and is able withal to meet the demands of thoroughness, without, however, being over-severe in his method"? Now, all the negative traits mentioned in this passage might be applied to Strauss. No one would contend, I suppose, that Strauss is original, or that he is over-severe in his method; but the question is whether we can regard him as "master of his subject," and grant him "incomparable skill"? The confession to the effect that the treatise was intentionally "lightly equipped" leads us to think that it at least aimed at incomparable skill.

It was not the dream of our architect to build a temple, nor yet a house, but a sort of summer-pavilion, surrounded by everything that the art of gardening can provide. Yea, it even seems as if that mysterious feeling for the All were only calculated to produce an aesthetic effect, to be, so to speak, a view of an irrational element, such as the sea, looked at from the most charming and rational of terraces. The walk through the first chapters— that is to say, through the theological catacombs with all their gloominess and their involved and baroque embellishments—was also no more than an aesthetic expedient in order to throw into greater relief the purity, clearness, and common sense of the chapter "What is our Conception of the Universe?" For, immediately after that walk in the gloaming and that peep into the wilderness of Irrationalism, we step into a hall with a skylight to it. Soberly and limpidly it welcomes us: its mural decorations consist of astronomical charts and mathematical figures; it is filled with scientific apparatus, and its cupboards contain skeletons, stuffed apes, and anatomical specimens. But now, really rejoicing for the first time, we direct our steps into the innermost chamber of bliss belonging to our pavilion-dwellers; there we find them with their wives, children, and newspapers, occupied in the commonplace discussion of politics; we listen for a moment to their conversation on marriage, universal suffrage, capital punishment, and workmen's strikes, and we can scarcely believe it to be possible that the rosary of public opinions can be told off so quickly. At length an attempt is made to convince us of the classical taste of the inmates. A moment's halt in the library, and the music-room suffices to show us what we had expected all along, namely, that the best books lay on the shelves, and that the most famous musical compositions were in the music-cabinets. Some one actually played something to us, and even if it were Haydn's music, Haydn could not be blamed because it sounded like Riehl's music for the home. Meanwhile the host had found occasion to announce to us his complete agreement with Lessing and Goethe, although with the latter only up to the second part of Faust. At last our pavilion-owner began to praise himself, and assured us that he who could not be happy under his roof was beyond help and could not be ripe for his standpoint, whereupon he offered us his coach, but with the polite reservation that he could not assert that it would fulfil every requirement, and that, owing to the stones on his road having been newly laid down, we were not to mind if we were very much jolted. Our Epicurean garden-god then took leave of us with the incomparable skill which he praised in Voltaire.

Who could now persist in doubting the existence of this incomparable skill? The complete master of his subject is revealed; the lightly equipped artist-gardener is exposed, and still we hear the voice of the classical author saying, "As a writer I shall for once cease to be a Philistine: I will not be one; I refuse to be one! But a Voltaire—the German Voltaire—or at least the French Lessing."

With this we have betrayed a secret. Our Master does not always know which he prefers to be—Voltaire or Lessing; but on no account will he be a Philistine. At a pinch he would not object to being both Lessing and Voltaire—that the word might be fulfilled that is written, "He had no character, but when he wished to appear as if he had, he assumed one."

X.

If we have understood Strauss the Confessor correctly, he must be a genuine Philistine, with a narrow, parched soul and scholarly and common-place needs; albeit no one would be more indignant at the title than David Strauss the Writer. He would be quite happy to be regarded as mischievous, bold, malicious, daring; but his ideal of bliss would consist in finding himself compared with either Lessing or

Voltaire—because these men were undoubtedly anything but Philistines. In striving after this state of bliss, he often seems to waver between two alternatives—either to mimic the brave and dialectical petulance of Lessing, or to affect the manner of the faun-like and free-spirited man of antiquity that Voltaire was. When taking up his pen to write, he seems to be continually posing for his portrait; and whereas at times his features are drawn to look like Lessing's, anon they are made to assume the Voltairean mould. While reading his praise of Voltaire's manner, we almost seem to see him abjuring the consciences of his contemporaries for not having learned long ago what the modern Voltaire had to offer them. "Even his excellences are wonderfully uniform," he says: "simple naturalness, transparent clearness, vivacious mobility, seductive charm. Warmth and emphasis are also not wanting where they are needed, and Voltaire's innermost nature always revolted against stiltedness and affectation; while, on the other hand, if at times wantonness or passion descend to an unpleasantly low level, the fault does not rest so much with the stylist as with the man." According to this, Strauss seems only too well aware of the importance of simplicity in style; it is ever the sign of genius, which alone has the privilege to express itself naturally and guilelessly. When, therefore, an author selects a simple mode of expression, this is no sign whatever of vulgar ambition; for although many are aware of what such an author would fain be taken for, they are yet kind enough to take him precisely for that. The genial writer, however, not only reveals his true nature in the plain and unmistakable form of his utterance, but his super-abundant strength actually dallies with the material he treats, even when it is dangerous and difficult. Nobody treads stiffly along unknown paths, especially when these are broken throughout their course by thousands of crevices and furrows; but the genius speeds nimbly over them, and, leaping with grace and daring, scorns the wistful and timorous step of caution.

Even Strauss knows that the problems he prances over are dreadfully serious, and have ever been regarded as such by the philosophers who have grappled with them; yet he calls his book lightly equipped! But of this dreadfulness and of the usual dark nature of our meditations when considering such questions as the worth of existence and the duties of man, we entirely cease to be conscious when the genial Master plays his antics before us, "lightly equipped, and intentionally so." Yes, even more lightly equipped than his Rousseau, of whom he tells us it was said that he stripped himself below and adorned himself on top, whereas Goethe did precisely the reverse. Perfectly guileless geniuses do not, it appears, adorn themselves at all; possibly the words "lightly equipped" may simply be a euphemism for "naked." The few who happen to have seen the Goddess of Truth declare that she is naked, and perhaps, in the minds of those who have never seen her, but who implicitly believe those few, nakedness or light equipment is actually a proof, or at least a feature, of truthi Even this vulgar superstition turns to the advantage of the author's ambition. Some one sees something naked, and he exclaims: "What if this were the truth!" Whereupon he grows more solemn than is his wont. By this means, however, the author scores a tremendous advantage; for he compels his reader to approach him with greater solemnity than another and perhaps more heavily equipped writer. This is unquestionably the best way to become a classical author; hence Strauss himself is able to tell us: "I even enjoy the unsought honour of being, in the opinion of many, a classical writer of prose. "He has therefore achieved his aim. Strauss the Genius goes gadding about the streets in the garb of lightly equipped goddesses as a classic, while Strauss the Philistine, to use an original expression of this genius's, must, at all costs, be "declared to be on the decline," or "irrevocably dismissed."

But, alas! in spite of all declarations of decline and dismissal, the Philistine still returns, and all too frequently. Those features, contorted to resemble Lessing and Voltaire, must relax from time to time to resume their old and original shape. The mask of genius falls from them too often, and the Master's expression is never more sour and his movements never stiffer than when he has just attempted to take the leap, or to glance with the fiery eye, of a genius. Precisely owing to the fact that he is too lightly equipped for our zone, he runs the risk of catching cold more often and more severely than another. It may seem a terrible hardship to him that every one should notice this; but if he wishes to be cured, the following diagnosis of his case ought to be publicly presented to him:— Once upon a time there lived a Strauss, a brave, severe, and stoutly equipped scholar, with whom we sympathised as wholly as with all those in Germany who seek to serve truth with earnestness and energy, and to rule within the limits of their powers. He, however, who is now publicly famous as David Strauss, is another person. The theologians may be to blame for this metamorphosis; but, at any rate, his present toying with the mask of genius inspires us with as much hatred and scorn as his former earnestness commanded respect and sympathy. When, for instance, he tells us, "it would also argue ingratitude towards my genius if I were not to rejoice that to the faculty of an incisive, analytical criticism was added the innocent pleasure in artistic production," it may astonish him to hear that, in spite of this self-praise, there are still men who maintain exactly the reverse, and who say, not only that he has never possessed the gift of artistic production, but that the "innocent" pleasure he mentions is of all things the least innocent, seeing that it succeeded in gradually undermining and ultimately destroying a nature as strongly and deeply scholarly and critical as Strauss's—in fact, the real Straussian Genius. In a moment of unlimited frankness, Strauss himself indeed adds: "Merck was always in my thoughts, calling out, 'Don't produce such child's play again; others can do that too!'" That was the voice of the real Straussian genius, which also asked him what the worth of his newest, innocent, and lightly equipped modern Philistine's testament was. Others can do that too! And many could do it better. And even they who could have done it best, i.e. those thinkers who are more widely endowed than Strauss, could still only have made nonsense of it.

I take it that you are now beginning to understand the value I set on Strauss the Writer. You are beginning to realise that I regard him as a mummer who would parade as an artless genius and classical writer. When Lichtenberg said, "A simple manner of writing is to be recommended, if only in view of the fact that no honest man trims and twists his expressions," he was very far from wishing to imply that a simple style is a proof of literary integrity. I, for my part, only wish that Strauss the Writer had been more upright, for then he would have written more becomingly and have been less famous. Or, if he would be a mummer at all costs, how much more would he not have pleased me if he had been a better mummer—one more able to ape the guileless genius and classical author! For it yet remains to be said that Strauss was not only an inferior actor but a very worthless stylist as well.

XI.

Of course, the blame attaching to Strauss for being a bad writer is greatly mitigated by the fact that it is extremely difficult in Germany to become even a passable or moderately good writer, and that it is more the exception than not, to be a really good one. In this respect the natural soil is wanting, as are also artistic values and the proper method of treating and cultivating oratory. This latter accomplishment, as the various branches of it, i.e. drawing-room, ecclesiastical and Parliamentary parlance, show, has not yet reached the level of a national style; indeed, it has not yet shown even a tendency to attain to a style at all, and all forms of language in Germany do not yet seem to have passed a certain experimental stage. In view of these facts, the writer of to-day, to some extent, lacks an authoritative standard, and he is in some measure excused if, in the matter of language, he attempts to go ahead of his own accord. As to the probable result which the present dilapidated condition of the German language will bring about, Schopenhauer, perhaps, has spoken most forcibly. "If the existing state of affairs continues," he says, "in the year 1900 German classics will cease to be understood, for the simple reason that no other language will be known, save the trumpery jargon of the noble present, the chief characteristic of which is impotence." And, in truth, if one turn to the latest periodicals, one will find German philologists and grammarians already giving expression to the view that our classics can no longer serve us as examples of style, owing to the fact that they constantly use words, modes of speech, and syntactic arrangements which are fast dropping out of currency. Hence the need of collecting specimens of the finest prose that has been produced by our best modern writers, and of offering them as examples to be followed, after the style of Sander's pocket dictionary of bad language. In this book, that repulsive monster of style Gutzkow appears as a classic, and, according to its injunctions, we seem to be called upon to accustom ourselves to quite a new and wondrous crowd of classical authors, among which the first, or one of the first, is David Strauss: he whom we cannot describe more aptly than we have already—that is to say, as a worthless stylist. Now, the notion which the Culture-Philistine has of a classic and standard author speaks eloquently for his pseudo-culture—he who only shows his strength by opposing a really artistic and severe style, and who, thanks to the persistence of his opposition, finally arrives at a certain uniformity of expression, which again almost appears to possess unity of genuine style. In view, therefore, of the right which is granted to every one to experiment with the language, how is it possible at all for individual authors to discover a generally agreeable tone? What is so generally interesting in them? In the first place, a negative quality—the total lack of offensiveness: but every really productive thing is offensive. The greater part of a German's daily reading matter is undoubtedly sought either in the pages of newspapers, periodicals, or reviews. The language of these journals gradually stamps itself on his brain, by means of its steady drip, drip, drip of similar phrases and similar words. And, since he generally devotes to reading those hours of the day during which his exhausted brain is in any case not inclined to offer resistance, his ear for his native tongue so slowly but surely accustoms itself to this everyday German that it ultimately cannot endure its absence without pain. But the manufacturers of these newspapers are, by virtue of their trade, most thoroughly inured to the effluvia of this journalistic jargon; they have literally lost all taste, and their palate is rather gratified than not by the most corrupt and arbitrary innovations. Hence the tutti unisono with which, despite the general lethargy and sickliness, every fresh solecism is greeted; it is with such impudent corruptions of the language that her hirelings are avenged against her for the incredible boredom she imposes ever more and more upon them. I remember having read "an appeal to the German nation," by Berthold Auerbach, in which every sentence was un-German, distorted and false, and which, as a whole, resembled a soulless mosaic of words cemented together with international syntax. As to the disgracefully slipshod German with which Edward Devrient solemnised the death of Mendelssohn, I do not even wish to do more than refer to it. A grammatical error—and this is the most extraordinary feature of the case—does not therefore seem an offence in any sense to our Philistine, but a most delightful restorative in the barren wilderness of everyday German. He still, however, considers all really productive things to be offensive. The wholly bombastic, distorted, and threadbare syntax of the modern standard author—yea, even his ludicrous neologisms—are not only tolerated, but placed to his credit as the spicy element in his works. But woe to the stylist with character, who seeks as earnestly and perseveringly to avoid the trite phrases of everyday parlance, as the "yester-night monster blooms of modern ink-flingers," as Schopenhauer says! When platitudes, hackneyed, feeble, and vulgar phrases are the rule, and the bad and the corrupt become refreshing exceptions, then all that is strong, distinguished, and beautiful perforce acquires an evil odour. From which it follows that, in Germany, the well-known experience which befell the normally built traveller in the land of hunchbacks is constantly being repeated. It will be remembered that he was so shamefully insulted there, owing to his quaint figure and lack of dorsal convexity, that a priest at last had to harangue the people on his behalf as follows: "My brethren, rather pity this poor stranger, and present thank-offerings unto the gods, that ye are blessed with such attractive gibbosities."

If any one attempted to compose a positive grammar out of the international German style of to-day, and wished to trace the unwritten and unspoken laws followed by every one, he would get the most extraordinary notions of style and rhetoric. He would meet with laws which are probably nothing more than reminiscences of bygone schooldays, vestiges of impositions for Latin prose, and results perhaps of choice readings from French novelists, over whose incredible crudeness every decently educated Frenchman would have the right to laugh. But no conscientious native of Germany seems to have given a thought to these extraordinary notions under the yoke of which almost every German lives and writes.

As an example of what I say, we may find an injunction to the effect that a metaphor or a simile must be introduced from time to time, and that it must be new; but, since to the mind of the shallow-pated writer newness and modernity are identical, he proceeds forthwith to rack his

brain for metaphors in the technical vocabularies of the railway, the
telegraph, the steamship, and the Stock Exchange, and is proudly
convinced that such metaphors must be new because they are modern.
In Strauss's confession-book we find liberal tribute paid to modern
metaphor. He treats us to a simile, covering a page and a half, drawn
from modern road-improvement work; a few pages farther back he
likens the world to a machine, with its wheels, stampers, hammers, and
"soothing oil" (p. 432); "A repast that begins with champagne" (p.
384); "Kant is a cold-water cure" (p. 309); "The Swiss constitution is to
that of England as a watermill is to a steam-engine, as a waltz-tune or
a song to a fugue or symphony" (p. 301); "In every appeal, the
sequence of procedure must be observed. Now the mean tribunal
between the individual and humanity is the nation" (p. 165); "If we
would know whether there be still any life in an organism which
appears dead to us, we are wont to test it by a powerful, even painful
stimulus, as for example a stab" (p. 161); "The religious domain in the
human soul resembles the domain of the Red Indian in America" (p.
160); "Virtuosos in piety, in convents"(p. 107); "And place the
sum-total of the foregoing in round numbers under the account" (p.
205); "Darwin's theory resembles a railway track that is just marked
out... where the flags are fluttering joyfully in the breeze." In this really
highly modern way, Strauss has met the Philistine injunction to the
effect that a new simile must be introduced from time to time.

Another rhetorical rule is also very widespread, namely, that didactic
passages should be composed in long periods, and should be drawn
out into lengthy abstractions, while all persuasive passages should
consist of short sentences followed by striking contrasts. On page 154
in Strauss's book we find a standard example of the didactic and
scholarly style—a passage blown out after the genuine Schleiermacher
manner, and made to stumble along at a true tortoise pace: "The
reason why, in the earlier stages of religion, there appear many instead
of this single Whereon, a plurality of gods instead of the one, is
explained in this deduction of religion, from the fact that the various
forces of nature, or relations of life, which inspire man with the
sentiment of unqualified dependence, still act upon him in the
commencement with the full force of their distinctive characteristics;

that he has not as yet become conscious how, in regard to his unmitigated dependence upon them, there is no distinction between them, and that therefore the Whereon of this dependence, or the Being to which it conducts in the last instance, can only be one."

On pages 7 and 8 we find an example of the other kind of style, that of the short sentences containing that affected liveliness which so excited certain readers that they cannot mention Strauss any more without coupling his name with Lessing's. "I am well aware that what I propose to delineate in the following pages is known to multitudes as well as to myself, to some even much better. A few have already spoken out on the subject. Am I therefore to keep silence? I think not. For do we not all supply each other's deficiencies? If another is better informed as regards some things, I may perhaps be so as regards others; while yet others are known and viewed by me in a different light. Out with it, then! let my colours be displayed that it may be seen whether they are genuine or not.'"

It is true that Strauss's style generally maintains a happy medium between this sort of merry quick-march and the other funereal and indolent pace; but between two vices one does not invariably find a virtue; more often rather only weakness, helpless paralysis, and impotence. As a matter of fact, I was very disappointed when I glanced through Strauss's book in search of fine and witty passages; for, not having found anything praiseworthy in the Confessor, I had actually set out with the express purpose of meeting here and there with at least some opportunities of praising Strauss the Writer. I sought and sought, but my purpose remained unfulfilled. Meanwhile, however, another duty seemed to press itself strongly on my mind—that of enumerating the solecisms, the strained metaphors, the obscure abbreviations, the instances of bad taste, and the distortions which I encountered; and these were of such a nature that I dare do no more than select a few examples of them from among a collection which is too bulky to be given in full. By means of these examples I may succeed in showing what it is that inspires, in the hearts of modern Germans, such faith in this great and seductive stylist Strauss: I refer to his eccentricities of expression, which, in the barren waste and dryness of his whole book, jump out at one, not perhaps as pleasant but as painfully stimulating, surprises. When perusing such passages, we are at least assured, to use a Straussian metaphor, that we are not quite dead, but still respond to the test of a stab. For the rest of the book is entirely lacking in offensiveness —that quality which alone, as we have seen, is productive, and which our classical author has himself reckoned among the positive virtues. When the educated masses meet with exaggerated dulness and dryness, when they are in the presence of really vapid commonplaces, they now seem to believe that such things are the signs of health; and in this respect the words of the author of the dialogus de oratoribus are very much to the point: "illam ipsam quam jactant sanitatem non firmitate sed jejunio consequuntur." That is why they so unanimously hate every firmitas, because it bears testimony to a kind of health quite different from theirs; hence their one wish to throw suspicion upon all austerity and terseness, upon all fiery and energetic movement, and upon every full and delicate play of muscles. They have conspired to twist nature and the names of things completely round, and for the future to speak of health only there where we see weakness, and to speak of illness and excitability where for our part we see genuine vigour. From which it follows that David Strauss is to them a classical author.

If only this dulness were of a severely logical order! but simplicity and austerity in thought are precisely what these weaklings have lost, and in their hands even our language has become illogically tangled. As a proof of this, let any one try to translate Strauss's style into Latin: in the case of Kant, be it remembered, this is possible, while with Schopenhauer it even becomes an agreeable exercise. The reason why this test fails with Strauss's German is not owing to the fact that it is more Teutonic than theirs, but because his is distorted and illogical, whereas theirs is lofty and simple. Moreover, he who knows how the ancients exerted themselves in order to learn to write and speak correctly, and how the moderns omit to do so, must feel, as Schopenhauer says, a positive relief when he can turn from a German book like the one under our notice, to dive into those other works, those ancient works which seem to him still to be written in a new language. "For in these books," says Schopenhauer, "I find a regular and fixed language which, throughout, faithfully follows the laws of grammar and orthography, so that I can give up my thoughts completely to their matter; whereas in German I am constantly being disturbed by the author's impudence and his continual attempts to establish his own orthographical freaks and absurd ideas— the swaggering foolery of which disgusts me. It is really a painful sight to see a fine old language, possessed of classical literature, being botched by asses and ignoramuses!"

Thus Schopenhauer's holy anger cries out to us, and you cannot say that you have not been warned. He who turns a deaf ear to such warnings, and who absolutely refuses to relinquish his faith in Strauss the classical author, can only be given this last word of advice—to imitate his hero. In any case, try it at your own risk; but you will repent it, not only in your style but in your head, that it may be fulfilled which was spoken by the Indian prophet, saying, "He who gnaweth a cow's horn gnaweth in vain and shorteneth his life; for he grindeth away his teeth, yet his belly is empty."

XII.

By way of concluding, we shall proceed to give our classical prose-writer the promised examples of his style which we have collected. Schopenhauer would probably have classed the whole lot as "new documents serving to swell the trumpery jargon of the present day"; for David Strauss may be comforted to hear (if what follows can be regarded as a comfort at all) that everybody now writes as he does; some, of course, worse, and that among the blind the one-eyed is king. Indeed, we allow him too much when we grant him one eye; but we do this willingly, because Strauss does not write so badly as the most infamous of all corrupters of German—the Hegelians and their crippled offspring. Strauss at least wishes to extricate himself from the mire, and he is already partly out of it; still, he is very far from being on dry land, and he still shows signs of having stammered Hegel's prose in youth. In those days, possibly, something was sprained in him, some muscle must have been overstrained. His ear, perhaps, like that of a boy brought up amid the beating of drums, grew dull, and became incapable of detecting those artistically subtle and yet mighty laws of sound, under the guidance of which every writer is content to remain who has been strictly trained in the study of good models. But in this way, as a stylist, he has lost his most valuable possessions, and stands condemned to remain reclining, his life long, on the dangerous and barren shifting sand of newspaper style—that is, if he do not wish to fall back into the Hegelian mire. Nevertheless, he has succeeded in making himself famous for a couple of hours in our time, and perhaps in another couple of hours people will remember that he was once famous; then, however, night will come, and with her oblivion; and already at this moment, while we are entering his sins against style in the black book, the sable mantle of twilight is falling upon his fame. For he who has sinned against the German language has desecrated the mystery of all our Germanity. Throughout all the confusion and the changes of races and of customs, the German language alone, as though possessed of some supernatural charm, has saved herself; and with her own salvation she has wrought that of the spirit of Germany. She alone holds the warrant for this spirit in future ages, provided she be not destroyed at the sacrilegious hands of the modern world. "But Di meliora! Avaunt, ye pachyderms, avaunt! This is the German language, by means of which men express themselves, and in which great poets have sung and great thinkers have written. Hands off!" *

[Footnote * : Translator's note.—Nietzsche here proceeds to quote those passages he has culled from The Old and the New Faith with which he undertakes to substantiate all he has said relative to Strauss's style; as, however, these passages, with his comments upon them, lose most of their point when rendered into English, it was thought best to omit them altogether.]

To put it in plain words, what we have seen have been feet of clay, and what appeared to be of the colour of healthy flesh was only applied paint. Of course, Culture-Philistinism in Germany will be very angry when it hears its one living God referred to as a series of painted idols. He, however, who dares to overthrow its idols will not shrink, despite all indignation, from telling it to its face that it has forgotten how to distinguish between the quick and the dead, the genuine and the counterfeit, the original and the imitation, between a God and a host of idols; that it has completely lost the healthy and manly instinct for what is real and right. It alone deserves to be destroyed; and already the manifestations of its power are sinking; already are its purple honours falling from it; but when the purple falls, its royal wearer soon follows.

Here I come to the end of my confession of faith. This is the confession of an individual; and what can such an one do against a whole world, even supposing his voice were heard everywhere! In order for the last time to use a precious Straussism, his judgment only possesses "that amount of subjective truth which is compatible with a complete lack of objective demonstration"—is not that so, my dear friends? Meanwhile, be of good cheer. For the time being let the matter rest at this "amount which is compatible with a complete lack"! For the time being! That is to say, for as long as that is held to be out of season which in reality is always in season, and is now more than ever pressing; I refer to...speaking the truth. [Footnote: All quotations from The Old Faith and the New which appear in the above translation have either been taken bodily out of Mathilde Blind's translation (Asher and Co., 1873), or are adaptations from that translation.]

Richard Wagner in Bayreuth.

I.

FOR an event to be great, two things must be united—the lofty sentiment of those who accomplish it, and the lofty sentiment of those who witness it. No event is great in itself, even though it be the disappearance of whole constellations, the destruction of several nations, the establishment of vast empires, or the prosecution of wars at the cost of enormous forces: over things of this sort the breath of history blows as if they were flocks of wool. But it often happens, too, that a man of might strikes a blow which falls without effect upon a stubborn stone; a short, sharp report is heard, and all is over. History is able to record little or nothing of such abortive efforts. Hence the anxiety which every one must feel who, observing the approach of an event, wonders whether those about to witness it will be worthy of it. This reciprocity between an act and its reception is always taken into account when anything great or small is to be accomplished; and he who would give anything away must see to it that he find recipients who will do justice to the meaning of his gift. This is why even the work of a great man is not necessarily great when it is short, abortive, or fruitless; for at the moment when he performed it he must have failed to perceive that it was really necessary; he must have been careless in his aim, and he cannot have chosen and fixed upon the time with sufficient caution. Chance thus became his master; for there is a very intimate relation between greatness and the instinct which discerns the proper moment at which to act.

We therefore leave it to those who doubt Wagner's power of discerning the proper time for action, to be concerned and anxious as to whether what is now taking place in Bayreuth is really opportune and necessary. To us who are more confident, it is clear that he believes as strongly in the greatness of his feat as in the greatness of feeling in those who are to witness it. Be their number great or small, therefore, all those who inspire this faith in Wagner should feel extremely honoured; for that it was not inspired by everybody, or by the whole age, or even by the whole German people, as they are now constituted, he himself told us in his dedicatory address of the 22nd of May 1872, and not one amongst us could, with any show of conviction, assure him of the contrary. "I had only you to turn to," he said, "when I sought those who I thought would be in sympathy with my plans,— you who are the most personal friends of my own particular art, my work and activity: only you could I invite to help me in my work, that it might be presented pure and whole to those who manifest a genuine interest in my art, despite the fact that it has hitherto made its appeal to them only in a disfigured and adulterated form."

It is certain that in Bayreuth even the spectator is a spectacle worth seeing. If the spirit of some observant sage were to return, after the absence of a century, and were to compare the most remarkable movements in the present world of culture, he would find much to interest him there. Like one swimming in a lake, who encounters a current of warm water issuing from a hot spring, in Bayreuth he would certainly feel as though he had suddenly plunged into a more temperate element, and would tell himself that this must rise out of a distant and deeper source: the surrounding mass of water, which at all events is more common in origin, does not account for it. In this way, all those who assist at the Bayreuth festival will seem like men out of season; their raison-d'etre and the forces which would seem to account for them are elsewhere, and their home is not in the present age. I realise ever more clearly that the scholar, in so far as he is entirely the man of his own day, can only be accessible to all that Wagner does and thinks by means of parody,—and since everything is parodied nowadays, he will even get the event of Bayreuth reproduced for him, through the very un-magic lanterns of our facetious art-critics. And one ought to be thankful if they stop at parody; for by means of it a spirit of aloofness and animosity finds a vent which might otherwise hit upon a less desirable mode of expression. Now, the observant sage already mentioned could not remain blind to this unusual sharpness and tension of contrasts. They who hold by gradual development as a kind of moral law must be somewhat shocked at the sight of one who, in the course of a single lifetime, succeeds in producing something absolutely new. Being dawdlers themselves, and insisting upon slowness as a principle, they are very naturally vexed by one who strides rapidly ahead, and they wonder how on earth he does it. No omens, no periods of transition, and no concessions preceded the enterprise at Bayreuth; no one except Wagner knew either the goal or the long road that was to lead to it. In the realm of art it signifies, so to speak, the first circumnavigation of the world, and by this voyage not only was there discovered an apparently new art, but Art itself. In view of this, all modern arts, as arts of luxury which have degenerated through having been insulated, have become almost worthless. And the same applies to the nebulous and inconsistent reminiscences of a genuine art, which we as modern Europeans derive from the Greeks; let them rest in peace, unless they are now able to shine of their own accord in the light of a new interpretation. The last hour has come for a good many things; this new art is a clairvoyante that sees ruin approaching—not for art alone. Her warning voice must strike the whole of our prevailing civilisation with terror the instant the laughter which its parodies have provoked subsides. Let it laugh and enjoy itself for yet a while longer!

And as for us, the disciples of this revived art, we shall have time and inclination for thoughtfulness, deep thoughtfulness. All the talk and noise about art which has been made by civilisation hitherto must seem like shameless obtrusiveness; everything makes silence a duty with us—the quinquennial silence of the Pythagoreans. Which of us has not soiled his hands and heart in the disgusting idolatry of modern culture? Which of us can exist without the waters of purification? Who does not hear the voice which cries, "Be silent and cleansed"? Be silent and cleansed! Only the merit of being included among those who give ear to this voice will grant even us the lofty look necessary to view the event at Bayreuth; and only upon this look depends the great future of the event.

When on that dismal and cloudy day in May 1872, after the foundation stone had been laid on the height of Bayreuth, amid torrents of rain, and while Wagner was driving back to the town with a small party of us, he was exceptionally silent, and there was that indescribable look in his eyes as of one who has turned his gaze deeply inwards. The day happened to be the first of his sixtieth year, and his whole past now appeared as but a long preparation for this great moment. It is almost a recognised fact that in times of exceptional danger, or at all decisive and culminating points in their lives, men see the remotest and most recent events of their career with singular vividness, and in one rapid inward glance obtain a sort of panorama of a whole span of years in which every event is faithfully depicted. What, for instance, must Alexander the Great have seen in that instant when he caused Asia and Europe to be drunk out of the same goblet? But what went through Wagner's mind on that day—how he became what he is, and what he will be—we only can imagine who are nearest to him, and can follow him, up to a certain point, in his self-examination; but through his eyes alone is it possible for us to understand his grand work, and by the help of this understanding vouch for its fruitfulness.

II.

It were strange if what a man did best and most liked to do could not be traced in the general outline of his life, and in the case of those who are remarkably endowed there is all the more reason for supposing that their life will present not only the counterpart of their character, as in the case of every one else, but that it will present above all the counterpart of their intellect and their most individual tastes. The life of the epic poet will have a dash of the Epos in it—as from all accounts was the case with Goethe, whom the Germans very wrongly regarded only as a lyrist—and the life of the dramatist will probably be dramatic.

The dramatic element in Wagner's development cannot be ignored, from the time when his ruling passion became self-conscious and took possession of his whole being. From that time forward there is an end to all groping, straying, and sprouting of offshoots, and over his most tortuous deviations and excursions, over the often eccentric disposition of his plans, a single law and will are seen to rule, in which we have the explanation of his actions, however strange this explanation may sometimes appear. There was, however, an ante-dramatic period in Wagner's life—his childhood and youth— which it is impossible to approach without discovering innumerable problems. At this period there seems to be no promise yet of himself, and what one might now, in a retrospect, regard as a pledge for his future greatness, amounts to no more than a juxtaposition of traits which inspire more dismay than hope; a restless and excitable spirit, nervously eager to undertake a hundred things at the same time, passionately fond of almost morbidly exalted states of mind, and ready at any moment to veer completely round from calm and profound meditation to a state of violence and uproar. In his case there were no hereditary or family influences at work to constrain him to the sedulous study of one particular art. Painting, versifying, acting, and music were just as much within his reach as the learning and the career of a scholar; and the superficial inquirer into this stage of his life might even conclude that he was born to be a dilettante. The small world within the bounds of which he grew up was not of the kind we should choose to be the home of an artist. He ran the constant risk of becoming infected by that dangerously dissipated attitude of mind in which a person will taste of everything, as also by that condition of slackness resulting from the fragmentary knowledge of all things, which is so characteristic of University towns. His feelings were easily roused and but indifferently satisfied; wherever the boy turned he found himself surrounded by a wonderful and would-be learned activity, to which the garish theatres presented a ridiculous contrast, and the entrancing strains of music a perplexing one. Now, to the observer who sees things relatively, it must seem strange that the modern man who happens to be gifted with exceptional talent should as a child and a youth so seldom be blessed with the quality of ingenuousness and of simple individuality, that he is so little able to have these qualities at all. As a matter of fact, men of rare talent, like Goethe and Wagner, much more often attain to ingenuousness in manhood than during the more tender years of childhood and youth. And this is especially so with the artist, who, being born with a more than usual capacity for imitating, succumbs to the morbid multiformity of modern life as to a virulent disease of infancy. As a child he will more closely resemble an old man. The wonderfully accurate and original picture of youth which Wagner gives us in the Siegfried of the Nibelungen Ring could only have been conceived by a man, and by one who had discovered his youthfulness but late in life. Wagner's maturity, like his adolesence, was also late in making its appearance, and he is thus, in this respect alone, the very reverse of the precocious type.

The appearance of his moral and intellectual strength was the prelude to the drama of his soul. And how different it then became! His nature seems to have been simplified at one terrible stroke, and divided against itself into two instincts or spheres. From its innermost depths there gushes forth a passionate will which, like a rapid mountain torrent, endeavours to make its way through all paths, ravines, and crevices, in search of light and power. Only a force completely free and pure was strong enough to guide this will to all that is good and beneficial. Had it been combined with a narrow intelligence, a will with such a tyrannical and boundless desire might have become fatal; in any case, an exit into the open had to be found for it as quickly as possible, whereby it could rush into pure air and sunshine. Lofty aspirations, which continually meet with failure, ultimately turn to evil. The inadequacy of means for obtaining success may, in certain circumstances, be the result of an inexorable fate, and not necessarily of a lack of strength; but he who under such circumstances cannot abandon his aspirations, despite the inadequacy of his means, will only become embittered, and consequently irritable and intolerant. He may possibly seek the cause of his failure in other people; he may even, in a fit of passion, hold the whole world guilty; or he may turn defiantly down secret byways and secluded lanes, or resort to violence. In this way, noble natures, on their road to the most high, may turn savage. Even among those who seek but their own personal moral purity, among monks and anchorites, men are to be found who, undermined and devoured by failure, have become barbarous and hopelessly morbid. There was a spirit full of love and calm belief, full of goodness and infinite tenderness, hostile to all violence and self-deterioration, and abhorring the sight of a soul in bondage. And it was this spirit which manifested itself to Wagner. It hovered over him as a consoling angel, it covered him with its wings, and showed him the true path. At this stage we bring the other side of Wagner's nature into view: but how shall we describe this other side?

The characters an artist creates are not himself, but the succession of these characters, to which it is clear he is greatly attached, must at all events reveal something of his nature. Now try and recall Rienzi, the Flying Dutchman and Senta, Tannhauser and Elizabeth, Lohengrin and Elsa, Tristan and Marke, Hans Sachs, Woden and Brunhilda,—all these characters are correlated by a secret current of ennobling and broadening morality which flows through them and becomes ever purer and clearer as it progresses. And at this point we enter with respectful reserve into the presence of the most hidden development in Wagner's own soul. In what other artist do we meet with the like of this, in the same proportion? Schiller's characters, from the Robbers to Wallenstein and Tell, do indeed pursue an ennobling course, and likewise reveal something of their author's development; but in Wagner the standard is higher and the distance covered is much greater. In the Nibelungen Ring, for instance, where Brunhilda is awakened by Siegfried, I perceive the most moral music I have ever heard. Here Wagner attains to such a high level of sacred feeling that our mind unconsciously wanders to the glistening ice-and snow-peaks of the Alps, to find a likeness there;— so pure, isolated, inaccessible, chaste, and bathed in love-beams does Nature here display herself, that clouds and tempests—yea, and even the sublime itself—seem to lie beneath her. Now, looking down from this height upon Tannhauser and the Flying Dutchman, we begin to perceive how the man in Wagner was evolved: how restlessly and darkly he began; how tempestuously he strove to gratify his desires, to acquire power and to taste those rapturous delights from which he often fled in disgust; how he wished to throw off a yoke, to forget, to be negative, and to renounce everything. The whole torrent plunged, now into this valley, now into that, and flooded the most secluded chinks and crannies. In the night of these semi-subterranean convulsions a star appeared and glowed high above him with melancholy vehemence; as soon as he recognised it, he named it Fidelity—unselfish fidelity. Why did this star seem to him the brightest and purest of all? What secret meaning had the word "fidelity" to his whole being? For he has graven its image and problems upon all his thoughts and compositions. His works contain almost a complete series of the rarest and most beautiful examples of fidelity: that of brother to sister, of friend to friend, of servant to master; of Elizabeth to Tannhauser, of Senta to the Dutchman, of Elsa to Lohengrin, of Isolde, Kurvenal, and Marke to Tristan, of Brunhilda to the most secret vows of Woden—and many others. It is Wagner's most personal and most individual experience, which he reveres like a religious mystery, and which he calls Fidelity; he never wearies of breathing it into hundreds of different characters, and of endowing it with the sublimest that in him lies, so overflowing is his gratitude. It is, in short, the recognition of the fact that the two sides of his nature remained faithful to each other, that out of free and unselfish love, the creative, ingenuous, and brilliant side kept loyally abreast of the dark, the intractable, and the tyrannical side.

III.

The relation of the two constituent forces to each other, and the yielding of the one to the other, was the great requisite by which alone he could remain wholly and truly himself. At the same time, this was the only thing he could not control, and over which he could only keep a watch, while the temptations to infidelity and its threatening dangers beset him more and more. The uncertainty derived therefrom is an overflowing source of suffering for those in process of development. Each of his instincts made constant efforts to attain to unmeasured heights, and each of the capacities he possessed for enjoying life seemed to long to tear itself away from its companions in order to seek satisfaction alone; the greater their exuberance the more terrific was the tumult, and the more bitter the competition between them. In addition, accident and life fired the desire for power and splendour in him; but he was more often tormented by the cruel necessity of having to live at all, while all around him lay obstacles and snares. How is it possible for any one to remain faithful here, to be completely steadfast? This doubt often depressed him, and he expresses it, as an artist expressed his doubt, in artistic forms. Elizabeth, for instance, can only suffer, pray, and die; she saves the fickle and intemperate man by her loyalty, though not for this life. In the path of every true artist, whose lot is cast in these modern days, despair and danger are strewn. He has many means whereby he can attain to honour and might; peace and plenty persistently offer themselves to him, but only in that form recognised by the modern man, which to the straightforward artist is no better than choke-damp. In this temptation, and in the act of resisting it, lie the dangers that threaten him—dangers arising from his disgust at the means modernity offers him of acquiring pleasure and esteem, and from the indignation provoked by the selfish ease of modern society. Imagine Wagner's filling an official position, as for instance that of bandmaster at public and court theatres, both of which positions he has held: think how he, a serious artist, must have struggled in order to enforce seriousness in those very places which, to meet the demands of modern conventions, are designed with almost systematic frivolity to appeal only to the frivolous. Think how he must have partially succeeded, though only to fail on the whole. How constantly disgust must have been at his heels despite his repeated attempts to flee it, how he failed to find the haven to which he might have repaired, and how he had ever to return to the Bohemians and outlaws of our society, as one of them. If he himself broke loose from any post or position, he rarely found a better one in its stead, while more than once distress was all that his unrest brought him. Thus Wagner changed his associates, his dwelling-place and country, and when we come to comprehend the nature of the circles into which he gravitated, we can hardly realise how he was able to tolerate them for any length of time. The greater half of his past seems to be shrouded in heavy mist; for a long time he appears to have had no general hopes, but only hopes for the morrow, and thus, although he reposed no faith in the future, he was not driven to despair. He must have felt like a nocturnal traveller, broken with fatigue, exasperated from want of sleep, and tramping wearily along beneath a heavy burden, who, far from fearing the sudden approach of death, rather longs for it as something exquisitely charming. His burden, the road and the night—all would disappear! The thought was a temptation to him. Again and again, buoyed up by his temporary hopes, he plunged anew into the turmoil of life, and left all apparatus behind him. But his method of doing this, his lack of moderation in the doing, betrayed what a feeble hold his hopes had upon him; how they were only stimulants to which he had recourse in an extremity. The conflict between his aspirations and his partial or total inability to realise them, tormented him like a thorn in the flesh. Infuriated by constant privations, his imagination lapsed into the dissipated, whenever the state of want was momentarily relieved. Life grew ever more and more complicated for him; but the means and artifices that he discovered in his art as a dramatist became evermore resourceful and daring. Albeit, these were little more than palpable dramatic makeshifts and expedients, which deceived, and were invented, only for the moment. In a flash such means occurred to his mind and were used up. Examined closely and without prepossession, Wagner's life, to recall one of Schopenhauer's expressions, might be said to consist largely of comedy, not to mention burlesque. And what the artist's feelings must have been, conscious as he was, during whole periods of his life, of this undignified element in it,—he who more than any one else, perhaps, breathed freely only in sublime and more than sublime spheres,— the thinker alone can form any idea.

In the midst of this mode of life, a detailed description of which is necessary in order to inspire the amount of pity, awe, and admiration which are its due, he developed a talent for acquiring knowledge, which even in a German—a son of the nation learned above all others—was really extraordinary. And with this talent yet another danger threatened Wagner—a danger more formidable than that involved in a life which was apparently without either a stay or a rule, borne hither and thither by disturbing illusions. From a novice trying his strength, Wagner became a thorough master of music and of the theatre, as also a prolific inventor in the preliminary technical conditions for the execution of art. No one will any longer deny him the glory of having given us the supreme model for lofty artistic execution on a large scale. But he became more than this, and in order so to develop, he, no less than any one else in like circumstances, had to reach the highest degree of culture by virtue of his studies. And wonderfully he achieved this end! It is delightful to follow his progress. From all sides material seemed to come unto him and into him, and the larger and heavier the resulting structure became, the more rigid was the arch of the ruling and ordering thought supporting it. And yet access to the sciences and arts has seldom been made more difficult for any man than for Wagner; so much so that he had almost to break his own road through to them. The reviver of the simple drama, the discoverer of the position due to art in true human society, the poetic interpreter of bygone views of life, the philosopher, the historian, the aesthete and the critic, the master of languages, the mythologist and the myth poet, who was the first to include all these wonderful and beautiful products of primitive times in a single Ring, upon which he engraved the runic characters of his thoughts— what a wealth of knowledge must Wagner have accumulated and commanded, in order to have become all that! And yet this mass of material was just as powerless to impede the action of his will as a matter of detail—however attractive—was to draw his purpose from its path. For the exceptional character of such conduct to be appreciated fully, it should be compared with that of Goethe,— he who, as a student and as a sage, resembled nothing so much as a huge river-basin, which does not pour all its water into the sea, but spends as much of it on its way there, and at its various twists and turns, as it ultimately disgorges at its mouth. True, a nature like Goethe's not only has, but also engenders, more pleasure than any other; there is more mildness and noble profligacy in it; whereas the tenor and tempo of Wagner's power at times provoke both fear and flight. But let him fear who will, we shall only be the more courageous, in that we shall be permitted to come face to face with a hero who, in regard to modern culture, "has never learned the meaning of fear."

But neither has he learned to look for repose in history and philosophy, nor to derive those subtle influences from their study which tend to paralyse action or to soften a man unduly. Neither the creative nor the militant artist in him was ever diverted from his purpose by learning and culture. The moment his constructive powers direct him, history becomes yielding clay in his hands. His attitude towards it then differs from that of every scholar, and more nearly resembles the relation of the ancient Greek to his myths; that is to say, his subject is something he may fashion, and about which he may write verses. He will naturally do this with love and a certain becoming reverence, but with the sovereign right of the creator notwithstanding. And precisely because history is more supple and more variable than a dream to him, he can invest the most individual case with the characteristics of a whole age, and thus attain to a vividness of narrative of which historians are quite incapable. In what work of art, of any kind, has the body and soul of the Middle Ages ever been so thoroughly depicted as in Lohengrin? And will not the Meistersingers continue to acquaint men, even in the remotest ages to come, with the nature of Germany's soul? Will they not do more than acquaint men of it? Will they not represent its very ripest fruit—the fruit of that spirit which ever wishes to reform and not to overthrow, and which, despite the broad couch of comfort on which it lies, has not forgotten how to endure the noblest discomfort when a worthy and novel deed has to be accomplished?

And it is just to this kind of discomfort that Wagner always felt himself drawn by his study of history and philosophy: in them he not only found arms and coats of mail, but what he felt in their presence above all was the inspiring breath which is wafted from the graves of all great fighters, sufferers, and thinkers. Nothing distinguishes a man more from the general pattern of the age than the use he makes of history and philosophy. According to present views, the former seems to have been allotted the duty of giving modern man breathing-time, in the midst of his panting and strenuous scurry towards his goal, so that he may, for a space, imagine he has slipped his leash. What Montaigne was as an individual amid the turmoil of the Reformation—that is to say, a creature inwardly coming to peace with himself, serenely secluded in himself and taking breath, as his best reader, Shakespeare, understood him, —this is what history is to the modern spirit today. The fact that the Germans, for a whole century, have devoted themselves more particularly to the study of history, only tends to prove that they are the stemming, retarding, and becalming force in the activity of modern society—a circumstance which some, of course, will place to their credit. On the whole, however, it is a dangerous symptom when the mind of a nation turns with preference to the study of the past. It is a sign of flagging strength, of decline and degeneration; it denotes that its people are perilously near to falling victims to the first fever that may happen to be rife —the political fever among others. Now, in the history of modern thought, our scholars are an example of this condition of weakness as opposed to all reformative and revolutionary activity. The mission they have chosen is not of the noblest; they have rather been content to secure smug happiness for their kind, and little more. Every independent and manly step leaves them halting in the background, although it by no means outstrips history. For the latter is possessed of vastly different powers, which only natures like Wagner have any notion of; but it requires to be written in a much more earnest and severe spirit, by much more vigorous students, and with much less optimism than has been the case hitherto. In fact, it requires to be treated quite differently from the way German scholars have treated it until now. In all their works there is a continual desire to embellish, to submit and to be content, while the course of events invariably seems to have their approbation. It is rather the exception for one of them to imply that he is satisfied only because things might have turned out worse; for most of them believe, almost as a matter of course, that everything has been for the best simply because it has only happened once. Were history not always a disguised Christian theodicy, were it written with more justice and fervent feeling, it would be the very last thing on earth to be made to serve the purpose it now serves, namely, that of an opiate against everything subversive and novel. And philosophy is in the same plight: all that the majority demand of it is, that it may teach them to understand approximate facts—very approximate facts—in order that they may then become adapted to them. And even its noblest exponents press its soporific and comforting powers so strongly to the fore, that all lovers of sleep and of loafing must think that their aim and the aim of philosophy are one. For my part, the most important question philosophy has to decide seems to be, how far things have acquired an unalterable stamp and form, and, once this question has been answered, I think it the duty of philosophy unhesitatingly and courageously to proceed with the task of improving that part of the world which has been recognised as still susceptible to change. But genuine philosophers do, as a matter of fact, teach this doctrine themselves, inasmuch as they work at endeavouring to alter the very changeable views of men, and do not keep their opinions to themselves. Genuine disciples of genuine philosophies also teach this doctrine; for, like Wagner, they understand the art of deriving a more decisive and inflexible will from their master's teaching, rather than an opiate or a sleeping draught. Wagner is most philosophical where he is most powerfully active and heroic. It was as a philosopher that he went, not only through the fire of various philosophical systems without fear, but also through the vapours of science and scholarship, while remaining ever true to his highest self. And it was this highest self which exacted from his versatile spirit works as complete as his were, which bade him suffer and learn, that he might accomplish such works.

IV.

The history of the development of culture since the time of the Greeks is short enough, when we take into consideration the actual ground it covers, and ignore the periods during which man stood still, went backwards, hesitated or strayed. The Hellenising of the world—and to make this possible, the Orientalising of Hellenism—that double mission of Alexander the Great, still remains the most important event: the old question whether a foreign civilisation may be transplanted is still the problem that the peoples of modern times are vainly endeavouring to solve. The rhythmic play of those two factors against each other is the force that has determined the course of history heretofore. Thus Christianity appears, for instance, as a product of Oriental antiquity, which was thought out and pursued to its ultimate conclusions by men, with almost intemperate thoroughness. As its influence began to decay, the power of Hellenic culture was revived, and we are now experiencing phenomena so strange that they would hang in the air as unsolved problems, if it were not possible, by spanning an enormous gulf of time, to show their relation to analogous phenomena in Hellenistic culture. Thus, between Kant and the Eleatics, Schopenhauer and Empedocles, Aeschylus and Wagner, there is so much relationship, so many things in common, that one is vividly impressed with the very relative nature of all notions of time. It would even seem as if a whole diversity of things were really all of a piece, and that time is only a cloud which makes it hard for our eyes to perceive the oneness of them. In the history of the exact sciences we are perhaps most impressed by the close bond uniting us with the days of Alexander and ancient Greece. The pendulum of history seems merely to have swung back to that point from which it started when it plunged forth into unknown and mysterious distance.

The picture represented by our own times is by no means a new one: to the student of history it must always seem as though he were merely in the presence of an old familiar face, the features of which he recognises. In our time the spirit of Greek culture is scattered broadcast. While forces of all kinds are pressing one upon the other, and the fruits of modern art and science are offering themselves as a means of exchange, the pale outline of Hellenism is beginning to dawn faintly in the distance. The earth which, up to the present, has been more than adequately Orientalised, begins to yearn once more for Hellenism. He who wishes to help her in this respect will certainly need to be gifted for speedy action and to have wings on his heels, in order to synthetise the multitudinous and still undiscovered facts of science and the many conflicting divisions of talent so as to reconnoitre and rule the whole enormous field. It is now necessary that a generation of anti-Alexanders should arise, endowed with the supreme strength necessary for gathering up, binding together, and joining the individual threads of the fabric, so as to prevent their being scattered to the four winds. The object is not to cut the Gordian knot of Greek culture after the manner adopted by Alexander, and then to leave its frayed ends fluttering in all directions; it is rather to bind it after it has been loosed. That is our task to-day. In the person of Wagner I recognise one of these anti-Alexanders: he rivets and locks together all that is isolated, weak, or in any way defective; if I may be allowed to use a medical expression, he has an astringent power. And in this respect he is one of the greatest civilising forces of his age. He dominates art, religion, and folklore, yet he is the reverse of a polyhistor or of a mere collecting and classifying spirit; for he constructs with the collected material, and breathes life into it, and is a Simplifier of the Universe. We must not be led away from this idea by comparing the general mission which his genius imposed upon him with the much narrower and more immediate one which we are at present in the habit of associating with the name of Wagner. He is expected to effect a reform in the theatre world; but even supposing he should succeed in doing this, what would then have been done towards the accomplishment of that higher, more distant mission?

But even with this lesser theatrical reform, modern man would also be altered and reformed; for everything is so intimately related in this world, that he who removes even so small a thing as a rivet from the framework shatters and destroys the whole edifice. And what we here assert, with perhaps seeming exaggeration, of Wagner's activity would hold equally good of any other genuine reform. It is quite impossible to reinstate the art of drama in its purest and highest form without effecting changes everywhere in the customs of the people, in the State, in education, and in social intercourse. When love and justice have become powerful in one department of life, namely in art, they must, in accordance with the law of their inner being, spread their influence around them, and can no more return to the stiff stillness of their former pupal condition. In order even to realise how far the attitude of the arts towards life is a sign of their decline, and how far our theatres are a disgrace to those who build and visit them, everything must be learnt over again, and that which is usual and commonplace should be regarded as something unusual and complicated. An extraordinary lack of clear judgment, a badly-concealed lust of pleasure, of entertainment at any cost, learned scruples, assumed airs of importance, and trifling with the seriousness of art on the part of those who represent it; brutality of appetite and money-grubbing on the part of promoters; the empty-mindedness and thoughtlessness of society, which only thinks of the people in so far as these serve or thwart its purpose, and which attends theatres and concerts without giving a thought to its duties,—all these things constitute the stifling and deleterious atmosphere of our modern art conditions: when, however, people like our men of culture have grown accustomed to it, they imagine that it is a condition of their healthy existence, and would immediately feel unwell if, for any reason, they were compelled to dispense with it for a while. In point of fact, there is but one speedy way of convincing oneself of the vulgarity, weirdness, and confusion of our theatrical institutions, and that is to compare them with those which once flourished in ancient Greece. If we knew nothing about the Greeks, it would perhaps be impossible to assail our present conditions at all, and objections made on the large scale conceived for the first time by Wagner would have been regarded as the dreams of people who could only be at home in outlandish places. "For men as we now find them," people would have retorted, "art of this modern kind answers the purpose and is fitting— and men have never been different." But they have been very different, and even now there are men who are far from satisfied with the existing state of affairs—the fact of Bayreuth alone demonstrates this point. Here you will find prepared and initiated spectators, and the emotion of men conscious of being at the very zenith of their happiness, who concentrate their whole being on that happiness in order to strengthen themselves for a higher and more far-reaching purpose. Here you will find the most noble self-abnegation on the part of the artist, and the finest of all spectacles —that of a triumphant creator of works which are in themselves an overflowing treasury of artistic triumphs. Does it not seem almost like a fairy tale, to be able to come face to face with such a personality? Must not they who take any part whatsoever, active or passive, in the proceedings at Bayreuth, already feel altered and rejuvenated, and ready to introduce reforms and to effect renovations in other spheres of life? Has not a haven been found for all wanderers on high and desert seas, and has not peace settled over the face of the waters? Must not he who leaves these spheres of ruling profundity and loneliness for the very differently ordered world with its plains and lower levels, cry continually like Isolde: "Oh, how could I bear it? How can I still bear it?" And should he be unable to endure his joy and his sorrow, or to keep them egotistically to himself, he will avail himself from that time forward of every opportunity of making them known to all. "Where are they who are suffering under the yoke of modern institutions?" he will inquire. "Where are my natural allies, with whom I may struggle against the ever waxing and ever more oppressive pretensions of modern erudition? For at present, at least, we have but one enemy—at present!—and it is that band of aesthetes, to whom the word Bayreuth means the completest rout—they have taken no share in the arrangements, they were rather indignant at the whole movement, or else availed themselves effectively of the deaf-ear policy, which has now become the trusty weapon of all very superior opposition. But this proves that their animosity and knavery were ineffectual in destroying Wagner's spirit or in hindering the accomplishment of his plans; it proves even more, for it betrays their weakness and the fact that all those who are at present in possession of power will not be able to withstand many more attacks. The time is at hand for those who would conquer and triumph; the vastest empires lie at their mercy, a note of interrogation hangs to the name of all present possessors of power, so far as possession may be said to exist in this respect. Thus educational institutions are said to be decaying, and everywhere individuals are to be found who have secretly deserted them. If only it were possible to invite those to open rebellion and public utterances, who even now are thoroughly dissatisfied with the state of affairs in this quarter! If only it were possible to deprive them of their faint heart and lukewarmness! I am convinced that the whole spirit of modern culture would receive its deadliest blow if the tacit support which these natures give it could in any way be cancelled. Among scholars, only those would remain loyal to the old order of things who had been infected with the political mania or who were literary hacks in any form whatever. The repulsive organisation which derives its strength from the violence and injustice upon which it relies—that is to say, from the State and Society—and which sees its advantage in making the latter ever more evil and unscrupulous,—this structure which without such support would be something feeble and effete, only needs to be despised in order to perish. He who is struggling to spread justice and love among mankind must regard this organisation as the least significant of the obstacles in his way; for he will only encounter his real opponents once he has successfully stormed and conquered modern culture, which is nothing more than their outworks.

For us, Bayreuth is the consecration of the dawn of the combat. No greater injustice could be done to us than to suppose that we are concerned with art alone, as though it were merely a means of healing or stupefying us, which we make use of in order to rid our consciousness of all the misery that still remains in our midst. In the image of this tragic art work at Bayreuth, we see, rather, the struggle of individuals against everything which seems to oppose them with invincible necessity, with power, law, tradition, conduct, and the whole order of things established. Individuals cannot choose a better life than that of holding themselves ready to sacrifice themselves and to die in their fight for love and justice. The gaze which the mysterious eye of tragedy vouchsafes us neither lulls nor paralyses. Nevertheless, it demands silence of us as long as it keeps us in view; for art does not serve the purposes of war, but is merely with us to improve our hours of respite, before and during the course of the contest,—to improve those few moments when, looking back, yet dreaming of the future, we seem to understand the symbolical, and are carried away into a refreshing reverie when fatigue overtakes us. Day and battle dawn together, the sacred shadows vanish, and Art is once more far away from us; but the comfort she dispenses is with men from the earliest hour of day, and never leaves them. Wherever he turns, the individual realises only too clearly his own shortcomings, his insufficiency and his incompetence; what courage would he have left were he not previously rendered impersonal by this consecration! The greatest of all torments harassing him, the conflicting beliefs and opinions among men, the unreliability of these beliefs and opinions, and the unequal character of men's abilities—all these things make him hanker after art. We cannot be happy so long as everything about us suffers and causes suffering; we cannot be moral so long as the course of human events is determined by violence, treachery, and injustice; we cannot even be wise, so long as the whole of mankind does not compete for wisdom, and does not lead the individual to the most sober and reasonable form of life and knowledge. How, then, would it be possible to endure this feeling of threefold insufficiency if one were not able to recognise something sublime and valuable in one's struggles, strivings, and defeats, if one did not learn from tragedy how to delight in the rhythm of the great passions, and in their victim? Art is certainly no teacher or educator of practical conduct: the artist is never in this sense an instructor or adviser; the things after which a tragic hero strives are not necessarily worth striving after. As in a dream so in art, the valuation of things only holds good while we are under its spell. What we, for the time being, regard as so worthy of effort, and what makes us sympathise with the tragic hero when he prefers death to renouncing the object of his desire, this can seldom retain the same value and energy when transferred to everyday life: that is why art is the business of the man who is recreating himself. The strife it reveals to us is a simplification of life's struggle; its problems are abbreviations of the infinitely complicated phenomena of man's actions and volitions. But from this very fact—that it is the reflection, so to speak, of a simpler world, a more rapid solution of the riddle of life—art derives its greatness and indispensability. No one who suffers from life can do without this reflection, just as no one can exist without sleep. The more difficult the science of natural laws becomes, the more fervently we yearn for the image of this simplification, if only for an instant; and the greater becomes the tension between each man's general knowledge of things and his moral and spiritual faculties. Art is with us to prevent the bow from snapping.

The individual must be consecrated to something impersonal—that is the aim of tragedy: he must forget the terrible anxiety which death and time tend to create in him; for at any moment of his life, at any fraction of time in the whole of his span of years, something sacred may cross his path which will amply compensate him for all his struggles and privations. This means having a sense for the tragic. And if all mankind must perish some day—and who could question this! —it has been given its highest aim for the future, namely, to increase and to live in such unity that it may confront its final extermination as a whole, with one spirit-with a common sense of the tragic: in this one aim all the ennobling influences of man lie locked; its complete repudiation by humanity would be the saddest blow which the soul of the philanthropist could receive. That is how I feel in the matter! There is but one hope and guarantee for the future of man, and that is that his sense for the tragic may not die out. If he ever completely lost it, an agonised cry, the like of which has never been heard, would have to be raised all over the world; for there is no more blessed joy than that which consists in knowing what we know—how tragic thought was born again on earth. For this joy is thoroughly impersonal and general: it is the wild rejoicing of humanity, anent the hidden relationship and progress of all that is human.

V.

Wagner concentrated upon life, past and present, the light of an intelligence strong enough to embrace the most distant regions in its rays. That is why he is a simplifier of the universe; for the simplification of the universe is only possible to him whose eye has been able to master the immensity and wildness of an apparent chaos, and to relate and unite those things which before had lain hopelessly asunder. Wagner did this by discovering a connection between two objects which seemed to exist apart from each other as though in separate spheres—that between music and life, and similarly between music and the drama. Not that he invented or was the first to create this relationship, for they must always have existed and have been noticeable to all; but, as is usually the case with a great problem, it is like a precious stone which thousands stumble over before one finally picks it up. Wagner asked himself the meaning of the fact that an art such as music should have become so very important a feature of the lives of modern men. It is not necessary to think meanly of life in order to suspect a riddle behind this question. On the contrary, when all the great forces of existence are duly considered, and struggling life is regarded as striving mightily after conscious freedom and independence of thought, only then does music seem to be a riddle in this world. Should one not answer: Music could not have been born in our time? What then does its presence amongst us signify? An accident? A single great artist might certainly be an accident, but the appearance of a whole group of them, such as the history of modern music has to show, a group only once before equalled on earth, that is to say in the time of the Greeks,—a circumstance of this sort leads one to think that perhaps necessity rather than accident is at the root of the whole phenomenon. The meaning of this necessity is the riddle which Wagner answers.

He was the first to recognise an evil which is as widespread as civilisation itself among men; language is everywhere diseased, and the burden of this terrible disease weighs heavily upon the whole of man's development. Inasmuch as language has retreated ever more and more from its true province—the expression of strong feelings, which it was once able to convey in all their simplicity—and has always had to strain after the practically impossible achievement of communicating the reverse of feeling, that is to say thought, its strength has become so exhausted by this excessive extension of its duties during the comparatively short period of modern civilisation, that it is no longer able to perform even that function which alone justifies its existence, to wit, the assisting of those who suffer, in communicating with each other concerning the sorrows of existence. Man can no longer make his misery known unto others by means of language; hence he cannot really express himself any longer. And under these conditions, which are only vaguely felt at present, language has gradually become a force in itself which with spectral arms coerces and drives humanity where it least wants to go. As soon as they would fain understand one another and unite for a common cause, the craziness of general concepts, and even of the ring of modern words, lays hold of them. The result of this inability to communicate with one another is that every product of their co-operative action bears the stamp of discord, not only because it fails to meet their real needs, but because of the very emptiness of those all-powerful words and notions already mentioned. To the misery already at hand, man thus adds the curse of convention—that is to say, the agreement between words and actions without an agreement between the feelings. Just as, during the decline of every art, a point is reached when the morbid accumulation of its means and forms attains to such tyrannical proportions that it oppresses the tender souls of artists and converts these into slaves, so now, in the period of the decline of language, men have become the slaves of words. Under this yoke no one is able to show himself as he is, or to express himself artlessly, while only few are able to preserve their individuality in their fight against a culture which thinks to manifest its success, not by the fact that it approaches definite sensations and desires with the view of educating them, but by the fact that it involves the individual in the snare of "definite notions," and teaches him to think correctly: as if there were any value in making a correctly thinking and reasoning being out of man, before one has succeeded in making him a creature that feels correctly. If now the strains of our German masters' music burst upon a mass of mankind sick to this extent, what is really the meaning of these strains? Only correct feeling, the enemy of all convention, of all artificial estrangement and misunderstandings between man and man: this music signifies a return to nature, and at the same time a purification and remodelling of it; for the need of such a return took shape in the souls of the most loving of men, and, through their art, nature transformed into love makes its voice heard.

Let us regard this as one of Wagner's answers to the question, What does music mean in our time? for he has a second. The relation between music and life is not merely that existing between one kind of language and another; it is, besides, the relation between the perfect world of sound and that of sight. Regarded merely as a spectacle, and compared with other and earlier manifestations of human life, the existence of modern man is characterised by indescribable indigence and exhaustion, despite the unspeakable garishness at which only the superficial observer rejoices. If one examines a little more closely the impression which this vehement and kaleidoscopic play of colours makes upon one, does not the whole seem to blaze with the shimmer and sparkle of innumerable little stones borrowed from former civilisations? Is not everything one sees merely a complex of inharmonious bombast, aped gesticulations, arrogant superficiality?—a ragged suit of motley for the naked and the shivering? A seeming dance of joy enjoined upon a sufferer? Airs of overbearing pride assumed by one who is sick to the backbone? And the whole moving with such rapidity and confusion that it is disguised and masked— sordid impotence, devouring dissension, assiduous ennui, dishonest distress! The appearance of present-day humanity is all appearance, and nothing else: in what he now represents man himself has become obscured and concealed; and the vestiges of the creative faculty in art, which still cling to such countries as France and Italy, are all concentrated upon this one task of concealing. Wherever form is still in demand in society, conversation, literary style, or the relations between governments, men have unconsciously grown to believe that it is adequately met by a kind of agreeable dissimulation, quite the reverse of genuine form conceived as a necessary relation between the proportions of a figure, having no concern whatever with the notions "agreeable" or "disagreeable," simply because it is necessary and not optional. But even where form is not openly exacted by civilised people, there is no greater evidence of this requisite relation of proportions; a striving after the agreeable dissimulation, already referred to, is on the contrary noticeable, though it is never so successful even if it be more eager than in the first instance. How far this dissimulation is agreeable at times, and why it must please everybody to see how modern men at least endeavour to dissemble, every one is in a position to judge, according to, the extent to which he himself may happen to be modern. "Only galley slaves know each other," says Tasso, "and if we mistake others, it is only out of courtesy, and with the hope that they, in their turn, should mistake us."

Now, in this world of forms and intentional misunderstandings, what purpose is served by the appearance of souls overflowing with music? They pursue the course of grand and unrestrained rhythm with noble candour—with a passion more than personal; they glow with the mighty and peaceful fire of music, which wells up to the light of day from their unexhausted depths—and all this to what purpose?

By means of these souls music gives expression to the longing that it feels for the company of its natural ally, gymnastics—that is to say, its necessary form in the order of visible phenomena. In its search and craving for this ally, it becomes the arbiter of the whole visible world and the world of mere lying appearance of the present day. This is Wagner's second answer to the question, What is the meaning of music in our times? "Help me," he cries to all who have ears to hear, "help me to discover that culture of which my music, as the rediscovered language of correct feeling, seems to foretell the existence. Bear in mind that the soul of music now wishes to acquire a body, that, by means of you all, it would find its way to visibleness in movements, deeds, institutions, and customs!" There are some men who understand this summons, and their number will increase; they have also understood, for the first time, what it means to found the State upon music. It is something that the ancient Hellenes not only understood but actually insisted upon; and these enlightened creatures would just as soon have sentenced the modern State to death as modern men now condemn the Church. The road to such a new though not unprecedented goal would lead to this: that we should be compelled to acknowledge where the worst faults of our educational system lie, and why it has failed hitherto to elevate us out of barbarity: in reality, it lacks the stirring and creative soul of music; its requirements and arrangements are moreover the product of a period in which the music, to which We seem to attach so much importance, had not yet been born. Our education is the most antiquated factor of our present conditions, and it is so more precisely in regard to the one new educational force by which it makes men of to-day in advance of those of bygone centuries, or by which it would make them in advance of their remote ancestors, provided only they did not persist so rashly in hurrying forward in meek response to the scourge of the moment. Through not having allowed the soul of music to lodge within them, they have no notion of gymnastics in the Greek and Wagnerian sense; and that is why their creative artists are condemned to despair, as long as they wish to dispense with music as a guide in a new world of visible phenomena. Talent may develop as much as may be desired: it either comes too late or too soon, and at all events out of season; for it is in the main superfluous and abortive, just as even the most perfect and the highest products of earlier times which serve modern artists as models are superfluous and abortive, and add not a stone to the edifice already begun. If their innermost consciousness can perceive no new forms, but only the old ones belonging to the past, they may certainly achieve something for history, but not for life; for they are already dead before having expired. He, however, who feels genuine and fruitful life in him, which at present can only be described by the one term "Music," could he allow himself to be deceived for one moment into nursing solid hopes by this something which exhausts all its energy in producing figures, forms, and styles? He stands above all such vanities, and as little expects to meet with artistic wonders outside his ideal world of sound as with great writers bred on our effete and discoloured language. Rather than lend an ear to illusive consolations, he prefers to turn his unsatisfied gaze stoically upon our modern world, and if his heart be not warm enough to feel pity, let it at least feel bitterness and hate! It were better for him to show anger and scorn than to take cover in spurious contentment or steadily to drug himself, as our "friends of art" are wont to do. But if he can do more than condemn and despise, if he is capable of loving, sympathising, and assisting in the general work of construction, he must still condemn, notwithstanding, in order to prepare the road for his willing soul. In order that music may one day exhort many men to greater piety and make them privy to her highest aims, an end must first be made to the whole of the pleasure-seeking relations which men now enjoy with such a sacred art. Behind all our artistic pastimes— theatres, museums, concerts, and the like—that aforementioned "friend of art" is to be found, and he it is who must be suppressed: the favour he now finds at the hands of the State must be changed into oppression; public opinion, which lays such particular stress upon the training of this love of art, must be routed by better judgment. Meanwhile we must reckon the declared enemy of art as our best and most useful ally; for the object of his animosity is precisely art as understood by the "friend of art,"—he knows of no other kind! Let him be allowed to call our "friend of art" to account for the nonsensical waste of money occasioned by the building of his theatres and public monuments, the engagement of his celebrated singers and actors, and the support of his utterly useless schools of art and picture-galleries—to say nothing of all the energy, time, and money which every family squanders in pretended "artistic interests." Neither hunger nor satiety is to be noticed here, but a dead-and-alive game is played—with the semblance of each, a game invented by the idle desire to produce an effect and to deceive others. Or, worse still, art is taken more or less seriously, and then it is itself expected to provoke a kind of hunger and craving, and to fulfil its mission in this artificially induced excitement. It is as if people were afraid of sinking beneath the weight of their loathing and dulness, and invoked every conceivable evil spirit to scare them and drive them about like wild cattle. Men hanker after pain, anger, hate, the flush of passion, sudden flight, and breathless suspense, and they appeal to the artist as the conjurer of this demoniacal host. In the spiritual economy of our cultured classes art has become a spurious or ignominious and undignified need—a nonentity or a something evil. The superior and more uncommon artist must be in the throes of a bewildering nightmare in order to be blind to all this, and like a ghost, diffidently and in a quavering voice, he goes on repeating beautiful words which he declares descend to him from higher spheres, but whose sound he can hear only very indistinctly. The artist who happens to be moulded according to the modern pattern, however, regards the dreamy gropings and hesitating speech of his nobler colleague with contempt, and leads forth the whole brawling mob of assembled passions on a leash in order to let them loose upon modern men as he may think fit. For these modern creatures wish rather to be hunted down, wounded, and torn to shreds, than to live alone with themselves in solitary calm. Alone with oneself!—this thought terrifies the modern soul; it is his one anxiety, his one ghastly fear.

When I watch the throngs that move and linger about the streets of a very populous town, and notice no other expression in their faces than one of hunted stupor, I can never help commenting to myself upon the misery of their condition. For them all, art exists only that they may be still more wretched, torpid, insensible, or even more flurried and covetous. For incorrect feeling governs and drills them unremittingly, and does not even give them time to become aware of their misery. Should they wish to speak, convention whispers their cue to them, and this makes them forget what they originally intended to say; should they desire to understand one another, their comprehension is maimed as though by a spell: they declare that to be their joy which in reality is but their doom, and they proceed to collaborate in wilfully bringing about their own damnation. Thus they have become transformed into perfectly and absolutely different creatures, and reduced to the state of abject slaves of incorrect feeling.

VI.

I shall only give two instances showing how utterly the sentiment of our time has been perverted, and how completely unconscious the present age is of this perversion. Formerly financiers were looked down upon with honest scorn, even though they were recognised as needful; for it was generally admitted that every society must have its viscera. Now, however, they are the ruling power in the soul of modern humanity, for they constitute the most covetous portion thereof. In former times people were warned especially against taking the day or the moment too seriously: the nil admirari was recommended and the care of things eternal. Now there is but one kind of seriousness left in the modern mind, and it is limited to the news brought by the newspaper and the telegraph. Improve each shining hour, turn it to some account and judge it as quickly as possible!—one would think modern men had but one virtue left—presence of mind. Unfortunately, it much more closely resembles the omnipresence of disgusting and insatiable cupidity, and spying inquisitiveness become universal. For the question is whether mind is present at all to-day;—but we shall leave this problem for future judges to solve; they, at least, are bound to pass modern men through a sieve. But that this age is vulgar, even we can see now, and it is so because it reveres precisely what nobler ages contemned. If, therefore, it loots all the treasures of bygone wit and wisdom, and struts about in this richest of rich garments, it only proves its sinister consciousness of its own vulgarity in so doing; for it does not don this garb for warmth, but merely in order to mystify its surroundings. The desire to dissemble and to conceal himself seems stronger than the need of protection from the cold in modern man. Thus scholars and philosophers of the age do not have recourse to Indian and Greek wisdom in order to become wise and peaceful: the only purpose of their work seems to be to earn them a fictitious reputation for learning in their own time. The naturalists endeavour to classify the animal outbreaks of violence, ruse and revenge, in the present relations between nations and individual men, as immutable laws of nature. Historians are anxiously engaged in proving that every age has its own particular right and special conditions,— with the view of preparing the groundwork of an apology for the day that is to come, when our generation will be called to judgment. The science of government, of race, of commerce, and of jurisprudence, all have that preparatorily apologetic character now; yea, it even seems as though the small amount of intellect which still remains active to-day, and is not used up by the great mechanism of gain and power, has as its sole task the defending—and excusing of the present

Against what accusers? one asks, surprised.

Against its own bad conscience.

And at this point we plainly discern the task assigned to modern art—that of stupefying or intoxicating, of lulling to sleep or bewildering. By hook or by crook to make conscience unconscious! To assist the modern soul over the sensation of guilt, not to lead it back to innocence! And this for the space of moments only! To defend men against themselves, that their inmost heart may be silenced, that they may turn a deaf ear to its voice! The souls of those few who really feel the utter ignominy of this mission and its terrible humiliation of art, must be filled to the brim with sorrow and pity, but also with a new and overpowering yearning. He who would fain emancipate art, and reinstall its sanctity, now desecrated, must first have freed himself from all contact with modern souls; only as an innocent being himself can he hope to discover the innocence of art, for he must be ready to perform the stupendous tasks of self-purification and self-consecration. If he succeeded, if he were ever able to address men from out his enfranchised soul and by means of his emancipated art, he would then find himself exposed to the greatest of dangers and involved in the most appalling of struggles. Man would prefer to tear him and his art to pieces, rather than acknowledge that he must die of shame in presence of them. It is just possible that the emancipation of art is the only ray of hope illuminating the future, an event intended only for a few isolated souls, while the many remain satisfied to gaze into the flickering and smoking flame of their art and can endure to do so. For they do not want to be enlightened, but dazzled. They rather hate light —more particularly when it is thrown on themselves.

That is why they evade the new messenger of light; but he follows them—the love which gave him birth compels him to follow them and to reduce them to submission. "Ye must go through my mysteries," he cries to them; "ye need to be purified and shaken by them. Dare to submit to this for your own salvation, and abandon the gloomily lighted corner of life and nature which alone seems familiar to you. I lead you into a kingdom which is also real, and when I lead you out of my cell into your daylight, ye will be able to judge which life is more real, which, in fact, is day and which night. Nature is much richer, more powerful, more blessed and more terrible below the surface; ye cannot divine this from the way in which ye live. O that ye yourselves could learn to become natural again, and then suffer yourselves to be transformed through nature, and into her, by the charm of my ardour and love!"

It is the voice of Wagner's art which thus appeals to men. And that we, the children of a wretched age, should be the first to hear it, shows how deserving of pity this age must be: it shows, moreover, that real music is of a piece with fate and primitive law; for it is quite impossible to attribute its presence amongst us precisely at the present time to empty and meaningless chance. Had Wagner been an accident, he would certainly have been crushed by the superior strength of the other elements in the midst of which he was placed, out in the coming of Wagner there seems to have been a necessity which both justifies it and makes it glorious. Observed from its earliest beginnings, the development of his art constitutes a most magnificent spectacle, and—even though it was attended with great suffering—reason, law, and intention mark its course throughout. Under the charm of such a spectacle the observer will be led to take pleasure even in this painful development itself, and will regard it as fortunate. He will see how everything necessarily contributes to the welfare and benefit of talent and a nature foreordained, however severe the trials may be through which it may have to pass. He will realise how every danger gives it more heart, and every triumph more prudence; how it partakes of poison and sorrow and thrives upon them. The mockery and perversity of the surrounding world only goad and spur it on the more. Should it happen to go astray, it but returns from its wanderings and exile loaded with the most precious spoil; should it chance to slumber, "it does but recoup its strength." It tempers the body itself and makes it tougher; it does not consume life, however long it lives; it rules over man like a pinioned passion, and allows him to fly just in the nick of time, when his foot has grown weary in the sand or has been lacerated by the stones on his way. It can do nought else but impart; every one must share in its work, and it is no stinted giver. When it is repulsed it is but more prodigal in its gifts; ill used by those it favours, it does but reward them with the richest treasures it possesses,—and, according to the oldest and most recent experience, its favoured ones have never been quite worthy of its gifts. That is why the nature foreordained, through which music expresses itself to this world of appearance, is one of the most mysterious things under the sun—an abyss in which strength and goodness lie united, a bridge between self and non-self. Who would undertake to name the object of its existence with any certainty?—even supposing the sort of purpose which it would be likely to have could be divined at all. But a most blessed foreboding leads one to ask whether it is possible for the grandest things to exist for the purpose of the meanest, the greatest talent for the benefit of the smallest, the loftiest virtue and holiness for the sake of the defective and faulty? Should real music make itself heard, because mankind of all creatures least deserves to hear it, though it perhaps need it most? If one ponder over the transcendental and wonderful character of this possibility, and turn from these considerations to look back on life, a light will then be seen to ascend, however dark and misty it may have seemed a moment before.

VII.

It is quite impossible otherwise: the observer who is confronted with a nature such as Wagner's must, willy-nilly, turn his eyes from time to time upon himself, upon his insignificance and frailty, and ask himself, What concern is this of thine? Why, pray, art thou there at all? Maybe he will find no answer to these questions, in which case he will remain estranged and confounded, face to face with his own personality. Let it then suffice him that he has experienced this feeling; let the fact that he has felt strange and embarrassed in the presence of his own soul be the answer to his question For it is precisely by virtue of this feeling that he shows the most powerful manifestation of life in Wagner—the very kernel of his strength—that demoniacal magnetism and gift of imparting oneself to others, which is peculiar to his nature, and by which it not only conveys itself to other beings, but also absorbs other beings into itself; thus attaining to its greatness by giving and by taking. As the observer is apparently subject to Wagner's exuberant and prodigally generous nature, he partakes of its strength, and thereby becomes formidable through him and to him. And every one who critically examines himself knows that a certain mysterious antagonism is necessary to the process of mutual study. Should his art lead us to experience all that falls to the lot of a soul engaged upon a journey, i.e. feeling sympathy with others and sharing their fate, and seeing the world through hundreds of different eyes, we are then able, from such a distance, and under such strange influences, to contemplate him, once we have lived his life. We then feel with the utmost certainty that in Wagner the whole visible world desires to be spiritualised, absorbed, and lost in the world of sounds. In Wagner, too, the world of sounds seeks to manifest itself as a phenomenon for the sight; it seeks, as it were, to incarnate itself. His art always leads him into two distinct directions, from the world of the play of sound to the mysterious and yet related world of visible things, and vice versa. He is continually forced—and the observer with him—to re-translate the visible into spiritual and primeval life, and likewise to perceive the most hidden interstices of the soul as something concrete and to lend it a visible body. This constitutes the nature of the dithyrambic dramatist, if the meaning given to the term includes also the actor, the poet, and the musician; a conception necessarily borrowed from Æschylus and the contemporary Greek artists—the only perfect examples of the dithyrambic dramatist before Wagner. If attempts have been made to trace the most wonderful developments to inner obstacles or deficiencies, if, for instance, in Goethe's case, poetry was merely the refuge of a foiled talent for painting; if one may speak of Schiller's dramas as of vulgar eloquence directed into uncommon channels; if Wagner himself tries to account for the development of music among the Germans by showing that, inasmuch as they are devoid of the entrancing stimulus of a natural gift for singing, they were compelled to take up instrumental music with the same profound seriousness as that with which their reformers took up Christianity,—if, on the same principle, it were sought to associate Wagner's development with an inner barrier of the same kind, it would then be necessary to recognise in him a primitive dramatic talent, which had to renounce all possibility of satisfying its needs by the quickest and most methods, and which found its salvation and its means of expression in drawing all arts to it for one great dramatic display. But then one would also have to assume that the most powerful musician, owing to his despair at having to appeal to people who were either only semi-musical or not musical at all, violently opened a road for himself to the other arts, in order to acquire that capacity for diversely communicating himself to others, by which he compelled them to understand him, by which he compelled the masses to understand him. However the development of the born dramatist may be pictured, in his ultimate expression he is a being free from all inner barriers and voids: the real, emancipated artist cannot help himself, he must think in the spirit of all the arts at once, as the mediator and intercessor between apparently separated spheres, the one who reinstalls the unity and wholeness of the artistic faculty, which cannot be divined or reasoned out, but can only be revealed by deeds themselves. But he in whose presence this deed is performed will be overcome by its gruesome and seductive charm: in a flash he will be confronted with a power which cancels both resistance and reason, and makes every detail of life appear irrational and incomprehensible. Carried away from himself, he seems to be suspended in a mysterious fiery element; he ceases to understand himself, the standard of everything has fallen from his hands; everything stereotyped and fixed begins to totter; every object seems to acquire a strange colour and to tell us its tale by means of new symbols;—one would need to be a Plato in order to discover, amid this confusion of delight and fear, how he accomplishes the feat, and to say to the dramatist: "Should a man come into our midst who possessed sufficient knowledge to simulate or imitate anything, we would honour him as something wonderful and holy; we would even anoint him and adorn his brow with a sacred diadem; but we would urge him to leave our circle for another, notwithstanding." It may be that a member of the Platonic community would have been able to chasten himself to such conduct: we, however, who live in a very different community, long for, and earnestly desire, the charmer to come to us, although we may fear him already,—and we only desire his presence in order that our society and the mischievous reason and might of which it is the incarnation may be confuted. A state of human civilisation, of human society, morality, order, and general organisation which would be able to dispense with the services of an imitative artist or mimic, is not perhaps so utterly inconceivable; but this Perhaps is probably the most daring that has ever been posited, and is equivalent to the gravest expression of doubt. The only man who ought to be at liberty to speak of such a possibility is he who could beget, and have the presentiment of, the highest phase of all that is to come, and who then, like Faust, would either be obliged to turn blind, or be permitted to become so. For we have no right to this blindness; whereas Plato, after he had cast that one glance into the ideal Hellenic, had the right to be blind to all

Hellenism. For this reason, we others are in much greater need of art; because it was in the presence of the realistic that our eyes began to see, and we require the complete dramatist in order that he may relieve us, if only for an hour or so, of the insufferable tension arising from our knowledge of the chasm which lies between our capabilities and the duties we have to perform. With him we ascend to the highest pinnacle of feeling, and only then do we fancy we have returned to nature's unbounded freedom, to the actual realm of liberty. From this point of vantage we can see ourselves and our fellows emerge as something sublime from an immense mirage, and we see the deep meaning in our struggles, in our victories and defeats; we begin to find pleasure in the rhythm of passion and in its victim in the hero's every footfall we distinguish the hollow echo of death, and in its proximity we realise the greatest charm of life: thus transformed into tragic men, we return again to life with comfort in our souls. We are conscious of a new feeling of security, as if we had found a road leading out of the greatest dangers, excesses, and ecstasies, back to the limited and the familiar: there where our relations with our fellows seem to partake of a superior benevolence, and are at all events more noble than they were. For here, everything seemingly serious and needful, which appears to lead to a definite goal, resembles only detached fragments when compared with the path we ourselves have trodden, even in our dreams,— detached fragments of that complete and grand experience whereof we cannot even think without a thrill. Yes, we shall even fall into danger and be tempted to take life too easily, simply because in art we were in such deadly earnest concerning it, as Wagner says somewhere anent certain incidents in his own life. For if we who are but the spectators and not the creators of this display of dithyrambic dramatic art, can almost imagine a dream to be more real than the actual experiences of our wakeful hours, how much more keenly must the creator realise this contrast! There he stands amid all the clamorous appeals and importunities of the day, and of the necessities of life; in the midst of Society and State—and as what does he stand there? Maybe he is the only wakeful one, the only being really and truly conscious, among a host of confused and tormented sleepers, among a multitude of deluded and suffering people. He may even feel like a victim of chronic insomnia, and fancy himself obliged to bring his clear, sleepless, and conscious life into touch with somnambulists and ghostly well-intentioned creatures. Thus everything that others regard as commonplace strikes him as weird, and he is tempted to meet the whole phenomenon with haughty mockery. But how peculiarly this feeling is crossed, when another force happens to join his quivering pride, the craving of the heights for the depths, the affectionate yearning for earth, for happiness and for fellowship—then, when he thinks of all he misses as a hermit-creator, he feels as though he ought to descend to the earth like a god, and bear all that is weak, human, and lost, "in fiery arms up to heaven," so as to obtain love and no longer worship only, and to be able to lose himself completely in his love. But it is just this contradiction which is the miraculous fact in the soul of the dithyrambic dramatist, and if his nature can be understood at all, surely it must be here. For his creative moments in art occur when the antagonism between his feelings is at its height and when his proud astonishment and wonder at the world combine with the ardent desire to approach that same world as a lover. The glances he then bends towards the earth are always rays of sunlight which "draw up water," form mist, and gather storm-clouds. Clear-sighted and prudent, loving and unselfish at the same time, his glance is projected downwards; and all things that are illumined by this double ray of light, nature conjures to discharge their strength, to reveal their most hidden secret, and this through bashfulness. It is more than a mere figure of speech to say that he surprised Nature with that glance, that he caught her naked; that is why she would conceal her shame by seeming precisely the reverse. What has hitherto been invisible, the inner life, seeks its salvation in the region of the visible; what has hitherto been only visible, repairs to the dark ocean of sound: thus Nature, in trying to conceal herself, unveils the character of her contradictions. In a dance, wild, rhythmic and gliding, and with ecstatic movements, the born dramatist makes known something of what is going on within him, of what is taking place in nature: the dithyrambic quality of his movements speaks just as eloquently of quivering comprehension and of powerful penetration as of the approach of love and self-renunciation. Intoxicated speech follows the course of this rhythm; melody resounds coupled with speech, and in its turn melody projects its sparks into the realm of images and ideas. A dream-apparition, like and unlike the image of Nature and her wooer, hovers forward; it condenses into more human shapes; it spreads out in response to its heroically triumphant will, and to a most delicious collapse and cessation of will:—thus tragedy is born; thus life is presented with its grandest knowledge— that of tragic thought; thus, at last, the greatest charmer and benefactor among mortals—the dithyrambic dramatist—is evolved.

VIII.

Wagner's actual life—that is to say, the gradual evolution of the dithyrambic dramatist in him— was at the same time an uninterrupted struggle with himself, a struggle which never ceased until his evolution was complete. His fight with the opposing world was grim and ghastly, only because it was this same world—this alluring enemy—which he heard speaking out of his own heart, and because he nourished a violent demon in his breast—the demon of resistance. When the ruling idea of his life gained ascendancy over his mind—the idea that drama is, of all arts, the one that can exercise the greatest amount of influence over the world—it aroused the most active emotions in his whole being. It gave him no very clear or luminous decision, at first, as to what was to be done and desired in the future; for the idea then appeared merely as a form of temptation—that is to say, as the expression of his gloomy, selfish, and insatiable will, eager for power and glory. Influence—the greatest amount of influence—how? over whom?—these were henceforward the questions and problems which did not cease to engage his head and his heart. He wished to conquer and triumph as no other artist had ever done before, and, if possible, to reach that height of tyrannical omnipotence at one stroke for which all his instincts secretly craved. With a jealous and cautious eye, he took stock of everything successful, and examined with special care all that upon which this influence might be brought to bear. With the magic sight of the dramatist, which scans souls as easily as the most familiar book, he scrutinised the nature of the spectator and the listener, and although he was often perturbed by the discoveries he made, he very quickly found means wherewith he could enthral them. These means were ever within his reach: everything that moved him deeply he desired and could also produce; at every stage in his career he understood just as much of his predecessors as he himself was able to create, and he never doubted that he would be able to do what they had done. In this respect his nature is perhaps more presumptuous even than Goethe's, despite the fact that the latter said of himself: "I always thought I had mastered everything; and even had I been crowned king, I should have regarded the honour as thoroughly deserved." Wagner's ability. his taste and his aspirations—all of which have ever been as closely related as key to lock—grew and attained to freedom together; but there was a time when it was not so. What did he care about the feeble but noble and egotistically lonely feeling which that friend of art fosters, who, blessed with a literary and aesthetic education, takes his stand far from the common mob! But those violent spiritual tempests which are created by the crowd when under the influence of certain climactic passages of dramatic song, that sudden bewildering ecstasy of the emotions, thoroughly honest and selfless—they were but echoes of his own experiences and sensations, and filled him with glowing hope for the greatest possible power and effect. Thus he recognised grand opera as the means whereby he might express his ruling thoughts; towards it his passions impelled him; his eyes turned in the direction of its home. The larger portion of his life, his most daring wanderings, and his plans, studies, sojourns, and acquaintances are only to be explained by an appeal to these passions and the opposition of the outside world, which the poor, restless, passionately ingenuous German artist had to face. Another artist than he knew better how to become master of this calling, and now that it has gradually become known by means of what ingenious artifices of all kinds Meyerbeer succeeded in preparing and achieving every one of his great successes, and how scrupulously the sequence of "effects" was taken into account in the opera itself, people will begin to understand how bitterly Wagner was mortified when his eyes were opened to the tricks of the metier which were indispensable to a great public success. I doubt whether there has ever been another great artist in history who began his career with such extraordinary illusions and who so unsuspectingly and sincerely fell in with the most revolting form of artistic trickery. And yet the way in which he proceeded partook of greatness and was therefore extraordinarily fruitful. For when he perceived his error, despair made him understand the meaning of modern success, of the modern public, and the whole prevaricating spirit of modern art. And while becoming the critic of "effect," indications of his own purification began to quiver through him. It seems as if from that time forward the spirit of music spoke to him with an unprecedented spiritual charm. As though he had just risen from a long illness and had for the first time gone into the open, he scarcely trusted his hand and his eye, and seemed to grope along his way. Thus it was an almost delightful surprise to him to find that he was still a musician and an artist, and perhaps then only for the first time.

Every subsequent stage in Wagner's development may be distinguished thus, that the two fundamental powers of his nature drew ever more closely together: the aversion of the one to the other lessened, the higher self no longer condescended to serve its more violent and baser brother; it loved him and felt compelled to serve him. The tenderest and purest thing is ultimately—that is to say, at the highest stage of its evolution— always associated with the mightiest; the storming instincts pursue their course as before, but along different roads, in the direction of the higher self; and this in its turn descends to earth and finds its likeness in everything earthly. If it were possible, on this principle, to speak of the final aims and unravelments of that evolution, and to remain intelligible, it might also be possible to discover the graphic terms with which to describe the long interval preceding that last development; but I doubt whether the first achievement is possible at all, and do not therefore attempt the second. The limits of the interval separating the preceding and the subsequent ages will be described historically in two sentences: Wagner was the revolutionist of society; Wagner recognised the only artistic element that ever existed hitherto—the poetry of the people. The ruling idea which in a new form and mightier than it had ever been, obsessed Wagner, after he had overcome his share of despair and repentance, led him to both conclusions. Influence, the greatest possible amount of influence to be exercised by means of the stage! —but over whom? He shuddered when he thought of those whom he had, until then, sought to influence. His experience led him to realise the utterly ignoble position which art and the artist adorn; how a callous and hard-hearted community that calls itself the good, but which is really the evil, reckons art and the artist among its slavish retinue, and keeps them both in order to minister to its need of deception. Modern art is a luxury; he saw this, and understood that it must stand or fall with the luxurious society of which it forms but a part. This society had but one idea, to use its power as hard-heartedly and as craftily as possible in order to render the impotent—the people—ever more and more serviceable, base and unpopular, and to rear the modern workman out of them. It also robbed them of the greatest and purest things which their deepest needs led them to create, and through which they meekly expressed the genuine and unique art within their soul: their myths, songs, dances, and their discoveries in the department of language, in order to distil therefrom a voluptuous antidote against the fatigue and boredom of its existence— modern art. How this society came into being, how it learned to draw new strength for itself from the seemingly antagonistic spheres of power, and how, for instance, decaying Christianity allowed itself to be used, under the cover of half measures and subterfuges, as a shield against the masses and as a support of this society and its possessions, and finally how science and men of learning pliantly consented to become its drudges—all this Wagner traced through the ages, only to be convulsed with loathing at the end of his researches. Through his compassion for the people, he became a revolutionist. From that time forward he loved them and longed for them, as he longed for his art; for, alas! in them alone, in this fast disappearing, scarcely recognisable body, artificially held aloof, he now saw the only spectators and listeners worthy and fit for the power of his masterpieces, as he pictured them. Thus his thoughts concentrated themselves upon the question, How do the people come into being? How are they resuscitated?

He always found but one answer: if a large number of people were afflicted with the sorrow that afflicted him, that number would constitute the people, he said to himself. And where the same sorrow leads to the same impulses and desires, similar satisfaction would necessarily be sought, and the same pleasure found in this satisfaction. If he inquired into what it was that most consoled him and revived his spirits in his sorrow, what it was that succeeded best in counteracting his affliction, it was with joyful certainty that he discovered this force only in music and myth, the latter of which he had already recognised as the people's creation and their language of distress. It seemed to him that the origin of music must be similar, though perhaps more mysterious. In both of these elements he steeped and healed his soul; they constituted his most urgent need:—in this way he was able to ascertain how like his sorrow was to that of the people, when they came into being, and how they must arise anew if many Wagners are going to appear. What part did myth and music play in modern society, wherever they had not been actually sacrificed to it? They shared very much the same fate, a fact which only tends to prove their close relationship: myth had been sadly debased and usurped by idle tales and stories; completely divested of its earnest and sacred virility, it was transformed into the plaything and pleasing bauble of children and women of the afflicted people. Music had kept itself alive among the poor, the simple, and the isolated; the German musician had not succeeded in adapting himself to the luxurious traffic of the arts; he himself had become a fairy tale full Of monsters and mysteries, full of the most touching omens and auguries—a helpless questioner, something bewitched and in need of rescue. Here the artist distinctly heard the command that concerned him alone—to recast myth and make it virile, to break the spell lying over music and to make music speak: he felt his strength for drama liberated at one stroke, and the foundation of his sway established over the hitherto undiscovered province lying between myth and music. His new masterpiece, which included all the most powerful, effective, and entrancing forces that he knew, he now laid before men with this great and painfully cutting question: "Where are ye all who suffer and think as I do? Where is that number of souls that I wish to see become a people, that ye may share the same joys and comforts with me? In your joy ye will reveal your misery to me." These were his questions in Tannhauser and

Lohengrin, in these operas he looked about him for his equals —the anchorite yearned for the number.

But what were his feelings withal? Nobody answered him. Nobody had understood his question. Not that everybody remained silent: on the contrary, answers were given to thousands of questions which he had never put; people gossipped about the new masterpieces as though they had only been composed for the express purpose of supplying subjects for conversation. The whole mania of aesthetic scribbling and small talk overtook the Germans like a pestilence, and ith that lack of modesty which characterises both German scholars and German journalists, people began measuring, and generally meddling with, these masterpieces, as well as with the person of the artist. Wagner tried to help the comprehension of his question by writing about it; but this only led to fresh confusion and more uproar, —for a musician who writes and thinks was, at that time, a thing unknown. The cry arose: "He is a theorist who wishes to remould art with his far-fetched notions—stone him!" Wagner was stunned: his question was not understood, his need not felt; his masterpieces seemed a message addressed only to the deaf and blind; his people— an hallucination. He staggered and vacillated. The feasibility of a complete upheaval of all things then suggested itself to him, and he no longer shrank from the thought: possibly, beyond this revolution and dissolution, there might be a chance of a new hope; on the other hand, there might not. But, in any case, would not complete annihilation be better than the wretched existing state of affairs? Not very long afterwards, he was a political exile in dire distress.

And then only, with this terrible change in his environment and in his soul, there begins that period of the great man's life over which as a golden reflection there is stretched the splendour of highest mastery. Now at last the genius of dithyrambic drama doffs its last disguise. He is isolated; the age seems empty to him; he ceases to hope; and his all-embracing glance descend once more into the deep, and finds the bottom, there he sees suffering in the nature of things, and henceforward, having become more impersonal, he accepts his portion of sorrow more calmly. The desire for great power which was but the inheritance of earlier conditions is now directed wholly into the channel of creative art; through his art he now speaks only to himself, and no longer to a public or to a people, and strives to lend this intimate conversation all the distinction and other qualities in keeping with such a mighty dialogue. During the preceding period things had been different with his art; then he had concerned himself, too, albeit with refinement and subtlety, with immediate effects: that artistic production was also meant as a question, and it ought to have called forth an immediate reply. And how often did Wagner not try to make his meaning clearer to those he questioned! In view of their inexperience in having questions put to them, he tried to meet them half way and to conform with older artistic notions and means of expression. When he feared that arguments couched in his own terms would only meet with failure, he had tried to persuade and to put his question in a language half strange to himself though familiar to his listeners. Now there was nothing to induce him to continue this indulgence: all he desired now was to come to terms with himself, to think of the nature of the world in dramatic actions, and to philosophise in music; what desires he still possessed turned in the direction of the latest philosophical views. He who is worthy of knowing what took place in him at that time or what questions were thrashed out in the darkest holy of holies in his soul—and not many are worthy of knowing all this—must hear, observe, and experience Tristan and Isolde, the real *opus metaphysicum* of all art, a work upon which rests the broken look of a dying man with his insatiable and sweet craving for the secrets of night and death, far away from life which throws a horribly spectral morning light, sharply, upon all that is evil, delusive, and sundering: moreover, a drama austere in the severity of its form, overpowering in its simple grandeur, and in harmony with the secret of which it treats—lying dead in the midst of life, being one in two. And yet there is something still more wonderful than this work, and that is the artist himself, the man who, shortly after he had accomplished it, was able to create a picture of life so full of clashing colours as the Meistersingers of Nurnberg, and who in both of these compositions seems merely to have refreshed and equipped himself for the task of completing at his ease that gigantic edifice in four parts which he had long ago planned and begun—the ultimate result of all his meditations and poetical flights for over twenty years, his Bayreuth masterpiece, the Ring of the Nibelung! He who marvels at the rapid succession of the two operas, Tristan and the Meistersingers, has failed to understand one important side of the life and nature of all great Germans: he does not know the peculiar soil out of which that essentially German gaiety, which characterised Luther, Beethoven, and Wagner, can grow, the gaiety which other nations quite fail to understand and which even seems to be missing in the Germans of to-day—that clear golden and thoroughly fermented mixture of simplicity, deeply discriminating love, observation, and roguishness which Wagner has dispensed, as the most precious of drinks, to all those who have suffered deeply through life, but who nevertheless return to it with the smile of convalescents. And, as he also turned upon the world the eyes of one reconciled, he was more filled with rage and disgust than with sorrow, and more prone to renounce the love of power than to shrink in awe from it. As he thus silently furthered his greatest work and gradually laid score upon score, something happened which caused him to stop and listen: friends were coming, a kind of subterranean movement of many souls approached with a message for him—it was still far from being the people that constituted this movement and which wished to bear him news, but it may have been the nucleus and first living source of a really human community which would reach perfection in some age still remote. For the present they only brought him the warrant that his great work could be entrusted to the care and charge of faithful men, men who would watch and be worthy to watch over this most magnificent of all legacies to posterity. In the love of friends his outlook began to glow with brighter colours; his noblest care—the care that his work should be accomplished and should find a refuge before the evening of his life—was not his only preoccupation. something occurred which he could only understand as a symbol: it was as much as a new comfort and a new token of happiness to him. A great German war caused him to open his eyes, and he observed that those very Germans whom he considered so thoroughly degenerate and so inferior to the high standard of real Teutonism, of which he had formed an ideal both from self-knowledge and the conscientious study of other great Germans in history; he observed that those very Germans were, in the midst of terrible circumstances, exhibiting two virtues of the highest order—simple bravery and prudence; and with his heart bounding with delight he conceived the hope that he might not be the last German, and that some day a greater power would perhaps stand by his works than that devoted yet meagre one consisting of his little band of friends—a power able to guard it during that long period preceding its future glory, as the masterpiece of this future. Perhaps it was not possible to steel this belief permanently against doubt, more particularly when it sought to rise to hopes of immediate results: suffice it that he derived a tremendous spur from his environment, which constantly reminded him of a lofty duty ever to be fulfilled.

His work would not have been complete had he handed it to the world only in the form of silent manuscript. He must make known to the world what it could not guess in regard to his productions, what was his alone to reveal—the new style for the execution and presentation of his works, so that he might set that example which nobody else could set, and thus establish a tradition of style, not on paper, not by means of signs, but through impressions made upon the very souls of men. This duty had become all the more pressing with him, seeing that precisely in regard to the style of their execution his other works had meanwhile succumbed to the most insufferable and absurd of fates: they were famous and admired, yet no one manifested the slightest sign of indignation when they were mishandled. For, strange to say, whereas he renounced ever more and more the hope of success among his contemporaries, owing to his all too thorough knowledge of them, and disclaimed all desire for power, both "success" and "power" came to him, or at least everybody told him so. It was in vain that he made repeated attempts to expose, with the utmost clearness, how worthless and humiliating such successes were to him: people were so unused to seeing an artist able to differentiate at all between the effects of his works that even his most solemn protests were never entirely trusted. Once he had perceived the relationship existing between our system of theatres and their success, and the men of his time, his soul ceased to be attracted by the stage at all. He had no further concern with aesthetic ecstasies and the exultation of excited crowds, and he must even have felt angry to see his art being gulped down indiscriminately by the yawning abyss of boredom and the insatiable love of distraction. How flat and pointless every effect proved under these circumstances— more especially as it was much more a case of having to minister to one quite insatiable than of cloying the hunger of a starving man— Wagner began to perceive from the following repeated experience: everybody, even the performers and promoters, regarded his art as nothing more nor less than any other kind of stage-music, and quite in keeping with the repulsive style of traditional opera; thanks to the efforts of cultivated conductors, his works were even cut and hacked about, until, after they had been bereft of all their spirit, they were held to be nearer the professional singer's plane. But when people tried to follow Wagner's instructions to the letter, they proceeded so clumsily and timidly that they were not incapable of representing the midnight riot in the second act of the Meistersingers by a group of ballet-dancers. They seemed to do all this, however, in perfectly good faith—without the smallest evil intention. Wagner's devoted efforts to show, by means of his own example, the correct and complete way of performing his works, and his attempts at training individual singers in the new style, were foiled time after time, owing only to the thoughtlessness and iron tradition that ruled all around him. Moreover, he was always induced to concern himself with that class of theatricals which he most thoroughly loathed. Had not even Goethe, m his time, once grown tired of attending the rehearsals of his Iphigenia? "I suffer unspeakably," he explained, "when I have to tumble about Wlth these spectres, which never seem to act as they should." Meanwhile Wagner's "success" in the kind of drama which he most disliked steadily increased; so much so, indeed, that the largest theatres began to subsist almost entirely upon the receipts which Wagner's art, in the guise of operas, brought into them. This growing passion on the part of the theatre-going public bewildered even some of Wagner's friends; but this man who had endured so much, had still to endure the bitterest pain of all—he had to see his friends intoxicated with his "successes" and "triumphs" everywhere where his highest ideal was openly belied and shattered. It seemed almost as though a people otherwise earnest and reflecting had decided to maintain an attitude of systematic levity only towards its most serious artist, and to make him the privileged recipient of all the vulgarity, thoughtlessness, clumsiness, and malice of which the German nature is capable. When, therefore, during the German War, a current of greater magnanimity and freedom seemed to run through every one, Wagner remembered the duty to which he had pledged himself, namely, to rescue his greatest work from those successes and affronts which were so largely due to misunderstandings, and to present it in his most personal rhythm as an example for all times. Thus he conceived the idea of Bayreuth. In the wake of that current of better feeling already referred to, he expected to notice an enhanced sense of duty even among those with whom he wished to entrust his most precious possession. Out of this two-fold duty, that event took shape which, like a glow of strange sunlight, will illumine the few years that lie behind and before us, and was designed to bless that distant and problematic future which to our time and to the men of our time can be little more than a riddle or a horror, but which to the fevv who are allowed to assist in its realisation is a foretaste of coming joy, a foretaste of love in a higher sphere, through which they know themselves to be blessed, blessing and fruitful, far beyond their span of years; and which to Wagner himself is but a cloud of distress, care, meditation, and grief, a fresh passionate outbreak of antagonistic elements, but all bathed in the starlight of selfless fidelity, and changed by this light into indescribable joy.

It scarcely need be said that it is the breath of tragedy that fills the lungs of the world. And every one whose innermost soul has a presentiment of this, every one unto whom the yoke of tragic deception concerning the aim of life, the distortion and shattering of intentions, renunciation and purification through love, are not unknown things, must be conscious of a vague reminiscence of Wagner's own heroic life, in the masterpieces with which the great man now presents us. We shall feel as though Siegfried from some place far away were relating his deeds to us: the most blissful of touching recollections are always draped in the deep mourning of waning summer, when all nature lies still in the sable twilight.

IX.

All those to whom the thought of Wagner's development as a man may have caused pain will find it both restful and healing to reflect upon what he was as an artist, and to observe how his ability and daring attained to such a high degree of independence. If art mean only the faculty of communicating to others what one has oneself experienced, and if every work of art confutes itself which does not succeed in making itself understood, then Wagner's greatness as an artist would certainly lie in the almost demoniacal power of his nature to communicate with others, to express itself in all languages at once, and to make known its most intimate and personal experience with the greatest amount of distinctness possible. His appearance in the history of art resembles nothing so much as a volcanic eruption of the united artistic faculties of Nature herself, after mankind had grown to regard the practice of a special art as a necessary rule. It is therefore a somewhat moot point whether he ought to be classified as a poet, a painter, or a musician, even using each these words in its widest sense, or whether a new word ought not to be invented in order to describe him.

Wagner's poetic ability is shown by his thinking in visible and actual facts, and not in ideas; that is to say, he thinks mythically, as the people have always done. No particular thought lies at the bottom of a myth, as the children of an artificial ulture would have us believe; but it is in itself a thought: it conveys an idea of the world, but through the medium of a chain of events, actions, and pains. The Ring of the Nihelung is a huge system of thought without the usual abstractness of the latter. It were perhaps possible for a philosopher to present us with its exact equivalent in pure thought, and to purge it of all pictures drawn from life, and of all living actions, in which case we should be in possession of the same thing portrayed in two completely different forms—the one for the people, and the other for the very reverse of the people; that is to say, men of theory. But Wagner makes no appeal to this last class, for the man of theory can know as little of poetry or myth as the deaf man can know of music; both of them being conscious only of movements which seem meaningless to them. It is impossible to appreciate either one of these completely different forms from the standpoint of the other: as long as the poet's spell is upon one, one thinks with him just as though one were merely a feeling, seeing, and hearing creature; the conclusions thus reached are merely the result of the association of the phenomena one sees, and are therefore not logical but actual causalities.

If, therefore, the heroes and gods of mythical dramas, as understood by Wagner, were to express themselves plainly in words, there would be a danger (inasmuch as the language of words might tend to awaken the theoretical side in us) of our finding ourselves transported from the world of myth to the world of ideas, and the result would be not only that we should fail to understand with greater ease, but that we should probably not understand at all. Wagner thus forced language back to a more primeval stage in its development a stage at which it was almost free of the abstract element, and was still poetry, imagery, and feeling; the fearlessness with which Wagner undertook this formidable mission shows how imperatively he was led by the spirit of poetry, as one who must follow whithersoever his phantom leader may direct him. Every word in these dramas ought to allow of being sung, and gods and heroes should make them their own—that was the task which Wagner set his literary faculty. Any other person in like circumstances would have given up all hope; for our language seems almost too old and decrepit to allow of one's exacting what Wagner exacted from it; and yet, when he smote the rock, he brought forth an abundant flow. Precisely owing to the fact that he loved his language and exacted a great deal from it, Wagner suffered more than any other German through its decay and enfeeblement, from its manifold losses and mutilations of form, from its unwieldy particles and clumsy construction, and from its unmusical auxiliary verbs. All these are things which have entered the language through sin and depravity. On the other hand, he was exceedingly proud to record the number of primitive and vigorous factors still extant in the current speech; and in the tonic strength of its roots he recognised quite a wonderful affinity and relation to real music, a quality which distinguished it from the highly volved and artificially rhetorical Latin languages. Wagner's poetry is eloquent of his affection for the German language, and there is a heartiness and candour in his treatment of it which are scarcely to be met with in any other German writer, save perhaps Goethe. Forcibleness of diction, daring brevity, power and variety in rhythm, a remarkable wealth of strong and striking words, simplicity in construction, an almost unique inventive faculty in regard to fluctuations of feeling and presentiment, and therewithal a perfectly pure and overflowing stream of colloquialisms—these are the qualities that have to be enumerated, and even then the greatest and most wonderful of all is omitted. Whoever reads two such poems as Tristan and the Meistersingers consecutively will be just as astonished and doubtful in regard to the language as to the music; for he will wonder how it could have been possible for a creative spirit to dominate so perfectly two worlds as different in form, colour, and arrangement, as in soul. This is the most wonderful achievement of Wagner's talent; for the ability to give every work its own linguistic stamp and to find a fresh body and a new sound for every thought is a task which only the great master can successfully accomplish. Where this rarest of all powers manifests itself, adverse criticism can be but petty and fruitless which confines itself to attacks upon certain excesses and eccentricities in the treatment, or upon the more frequent obscurities of expression and ambiguity of thought. Moreover, what seemed to electrify and scandalise those who were most bitter in their criticism was not so much the language as the spirit of the Wagnerian operas—that is to say, his whole manner of feeling and suffering. It were well to wait until these very critics have acquired another spirit themselves; they will then also speak a different tongue, and, by that time, it seems to me things will go better with the German language than they do at present.

In the first place, however, no one who studies Wagner the poet and word-painter should forget that none of his dramas were meant to be read, and that it would therefore be unjust to judge them from the same standpoint as the spoken drama. The latter plays upon the feelings by means of words and ideas, and in this respect it is under the dominion of the laws of rhetoric. But in real life passion is seldom eloquent: in spoken drama it perforce must be, in order to be able to express itself at all. When, however, the language of a people is already in a state of decay and deterioration, the word-dramatist is tempted to impart an undue proportion of new colour and form both to his medium and to his thoughts; he would elevate the language in order to make it a vehicle capable of conveying lofty feelings, and by so doing he runs the risk of becoming abstruse. By means of sublime phrases and conceits he likewise tries to invest passion with some nobility, and thereby runs yet another risk, that of appearing false and artificial. For in real life passions do not speak in sentences, and the poetical element often draws suspicion upon their genuineness when it departs too palpably from reality. Now Wagner, who was the first to detect the essential feeling in spoken drama, presents every dramatic action threefold: in a word, in a gesture, and in a sound. For, as a matter of fact, music succeeds in conveying the deepest emotions of the dramatic performers direct to the spectators, and while these see the evidence of the actors' states of soul in their bearing and movements, a third though more feeble confirmation of these states, translated into conscious will, quickly follows in the form of the spoken word. All these effects fulfil their purpose simultaneously, without disturbing one another in the least, and urge the spectator to a completely new understanding and sympathy, just as if his senses had suddenly grown more spiritual and his spirit more sensual, and as if everything which seeks an outlet in him, and which makes him thirst for knowledge, were free and joyful in exultant perception. Because every essential factor in a Wagnerian drama is conveyed to the spectator with the utmost clearness, illumined and permeated throughout by music as by an internal flame, their author can dispense with the expedients usually employed by the writer of the spoken play in order to lend light and warmth to the action. The whole of the dramatist's stock in trade could be more simple, and the architect's sense of rhythm could once more dare to manifest itself in the general proportions of the edifice; for there was no more need of "the deliberate confusion and involved variety of tyles, whereby the ordinary playwright strove in the interests of his work to produce that feeling of wonder and thrilling suspense which he ultimately enhanced to one of delighted amazement. The impression of ideal distance and height was no more to be induced by means of tricks and artifices. Language withdrew itself from the length and breadth of rhetoric into the strong confines of the speech of the feelings, and although the actor spoke much less about all he did and felt in the performance, his innermost sentiments, which the ordinary playwright had hitherto ignored for fear of being undramatic, was now able to drive the spectators to passionate sympathy, while the accompanying language of gestures could be restricted to the most delicate modulations. Now, when passions are rendered in song, they require rather more time than when conveyed by speech; music prolongs, so to speak, the duration of the feeling, from which it follows, as a rule, that the actor who is also a singer must overcome the extremely unplastic animation from which spoken drama suffers. He feels himself incited all the more to a certain nobility of bearing, because music envelopes his feelings in a purer atmosphere, and thus brings them closer to beauty.

The extraordinary tasks which Wagner set his actors and singers will provoke rivalry between them for ages to come, in the personification of each of his heroes with the greatest possible amount of clearness, perfection, and fidelity, according to that perfect incorporation already typified by the music of drama. Following this leader, the eye of the plastic artist will ultimately behold the marvels of another visible world, which, previous to him, was seen for the first time only by the creator of such works as the Ring of the Nibelung —that creator of highest rank, who, like AEschylus, points the way to a coming art. Must not jealousy awaken the greatest talent, if the plastic artist ever compares the effect of his productions with that of Wagnerian music, in which there is so much pure and sunny happiness that he who hears it feels as though all previous music had been but an alien, faltering, and constrained language; as though in the past it had been but a thing to sport with in the presence of those who were not deserving of serious treatment, or a thing with which to train and instruct those who were not even deserving of play? In the case of this earlier kind of music, the joy we always experience while listening to Wagner's compositions is ours only for a short space of time, and it would then seem as though it were overtaken by certain rare moments of forgetfulness, during which it appears to be communing with its inner self and directing its eyes upwards, like Raphael's Cecilia, away from the listeners and from all those who demand distraction, happiness, or instruction from it.

In general it may be said of Wagner the Musician, that he endowed everything in nature which hitherto had had no wish to speak with the power of speech: he refuses to admit that anything must be dumb, and, resorting to the dawn, the forest, the mist, the cliffs, the hills, the thrill of night and the moonlight, he observes a desire common to them all—they too wish to sing their own melody. If the philosopher says it is will that struggles for existence in animate and inanimate nature, the musician adds: And this will wherever it manifests itself, yearns for a melodious existence.

Before Wagner's time, music for the most part moved in narrow limits: it concerned itself with the permanent states of man, or with what the Greeks call ethos. And only with Beethoven did it begin to find the language of pathos, of passionate will, and of the dramatic occurrences in the souls of men. Formerly, what people desired was to interpret a mood, a stolid, merry, reverential, or penitential state of mind, by means of music; the object was, by means of a certain striking uniformity of treatment and the prolonged duration of this uniformity, to compel the listener to grasp the meaning of the music and to impose its mood upon him. To all such interpretations of mood or atmosphere, distinct and particular forms of treatment were necessary: others were established by convention. The question of length was left to the discretion of the musician, whose aim was not only to put the listener into a certain mood, but also to avoid rendering that mood monotonous by unduly protracting it. A further stage was reached when the interpretations of contrasted moods were made to follow one upon the other, and the charm of light and shade was discovered; and yet another step was made when the same piece of music was allowed to contain a contrast of the ethos—for instance, the contest between a male and a female theme. All these, however, are crude and primitive stages in the development of music. The fear of passion suggested the first rule, and the fear of monotony the second; all depth of feeling and any excess thereof were regarded as "unethical." Once, however, the art of the ethos had repeatedly been made to ring all the changes on the moods and situations which convention had decreed as suitable, despite the most astounding resourcefulness on the part of its masters, its powers were exhausted. Beethoven was the first to make music speak a new language—till then forbidden—the language of passion; but as his art was based upon the laws and conventions of the ETHOS, and had to attempt to justify itself in regard to them, his artistic development was beset with peculiar difficulties and obscurities. An inner dramatic factor—and every passion pursues a dramatic course—struggled to obtain a new form, but the traditional scheme of "mood music" stood in its way, and protested—almost after the manner in which morality opposes innovations and immorality. It almost seemed, therefore, as if Beethoven had set himself the contradictory task of expressing pathos in the terms of the ethos. This view does not, however, apply to Beethoven's latest and greatest works; for he really did succeed in discovering a novel method of expressing the grand and vaulting arch of passion. He merely selected certain portions of its curve; imparted these with the utmost clearness to his listeners, and then left it to them to divine its whole span. Viewed superficially, the new form seemed rather like an aggregation of several musical compositions, of which every one appeared to represent a sustained situation, but was in reality but a momentary stage in the dramatic course of a passion. The listener might think that he was hearing the old "mood" music over again, except that he failed to grasp the relation of the various parts to one another, and these no longer conformed with the canon of the law. Even among minor musicians, there flourished a certain contempt for the rule which enjoined harmony in the general construction of a composition and the sequence of the parts in their works still remained arbitrary. Then, owing to a misunderstanding, the discovery of the majestic treatment of passion led back to the use of the single movement with an optional setting, and the tension between the parts thus ceased completely. That is why the symphony, as Beethoven understood it, is such a wonderfully obscure production, more especially when, here and there, it makes faltering attempts at rendering Beethoven's pathos. The means ill befit the intention, and the intention is, on the whole, not sufficiently clear to the listener, because it was never really clear, even in the mind of the composer. But the very injunction that something definite must be imparted, and that this must be done as distinctly as possible, becomes ever more and more essential, the higher, more difficult, and more exacting the class of work happens to be.

That is why all Wagner's efforts were concentrated upon the one object of discovering those means which best served the purpose of distinctness, and to this end it was above all necessary for him to emancipate himself from all the prejudices and claims of the old "mood" music, and to give his compositions—the musical interpretations of feelings and passion—a perfectly unequivocal mode of expression. If we now turn to what he has achieved, we see that his services to music are practically equal in rank to those which that sculptor-inventor rendered to sculpture who introduced "sculpture in the round." All previous music seems stiff and uncertain when compared with Wagner's, just as though it were ashamed and did not wish to be inspected from all sides. With the most consummate skill and precision, Wagner avails himself of every degree and colour in the realm of feeling; without the slightest hesitation or fear of its escaping him, he seizes upon the most delicate, rarest, and mildest emotion, and holds it fast, as though it had hardened at his touch, despite the fact that it may seem like the frailest butterfly to every one else. His music is never vague or dreamy; everything that is allowed to speak through it, whether it be of man or of nature, has a strictly individual passion; storm and fire acquire the ruling power of a personal will in his hands. Over all the clamouring characters and the clash of their passions, over the whole torrent of contrasts, an almighty and symphonic understanding hovers with perfect serenity, and continually produces concord out of war. Taken as a whole, Wagner's music is a reflex of the world as it was understood by the great Ephesian poet—that is to say, a harmony resulting from strife, as the union of justice and enmity. I admire the ability which could describe the grand line of universal passion out of a confusion of passions which all seem to be striking out in different directions: the fact that this was a possible achievement I find demonstrated in every individual act of a Wagnerian drama, which describes the individual history of various characters side by side with a general history of the whole company. Even at the very beginning we know we are watching a host of cross currents dominated by one great violent stream; and though at first this stream moves unsteadily over hidden reefs, and the torrent seems to be torn asunder as if it were travelling towards different points, gradually we perceive the central and general movement growing stronger and more rapid, the convulsive fury of the contending waters is converted into one broad, steady, and terrible flow in the direction of an unknown goal; and suddenly, at the end, the whole flood in all its breadth plunges into the depths, rejoicing demoniacally over the abyss and all its uproar. Wagner is never more himself than when he is overwhelmed with difficulties and can exercise power on a large scale with all the joy of a lawgiver. To bring restless and contending masses into simple rhythmic movement, and to exercise one will over a bewildering host of claims and desires—these are the tasks for which he feels he was born, and in the performance of which he finds freedom. And he never loses his breath withal, nor does he ever reach his goal panting. He strove just as persistently to impose the severest laws upon himself as to lighten the burden of others in this respect. Life and art weigh heavily upon him when he cannot play wit their most difficult questions. If one considers the relation between the melody of song and that of speech, one will perceive how he sought to adopt as his natural model the pitch, strength, and tempo of the passionate man's voice in order to transform it into art; and if one further considers the task of introducing this singing passion into the general symphonic order of music, one gets some idea of the stupendous difficulties he had to overcome. In this behalf, his inventiveness in small things as in great, his omniscience and industry are such, that at the sight of one of Wagner's scores one is almost led to believe that no real work or effort had ever existed before his time. It seems almost as if he too could have said, in regard to the hardships of art, that the real virtue of the dramatist lies in self-renunciation. But he would probably have added, There is but one kind of hardship— that of the artist who is not yet free: virtue and goodness are trivial accomplishments.

Viewing him generally as an artist, and calling to mind a more famous type, we see that Wagner is not at all unlike Demosthenes: in him also we have the terrible earnestness of purpose and that strong prehensile mind which always obtains a complete grasp of a thing; in him, too, we have the hand's quick clutch and the grip as of iron. Like

Demosthenes, he conceals his art or compels one to forget it by the peremptory way he calls attention to the subject he treats; and yet, like his great predecessor, he is the last and greatest of a whole line of artist-minds, and therefore has more to conceal than his forerunners: his art acts like nature, like nature recovered and restored. Unlike all previous musicians, there is nothing bombastic about him; for the former did not mind playing at times with their art, and making an exhibition of their virtuosity. One associates Wagner's art neither with interest nor with diversion, nor with Wagner himself and art in general. All one is conscious of is of the great necessity of it all. No one will ever be able to appreciate what severity evenness of will, and self-control the artist required during his development, in order, at his zenith, to be able to do the necessary thing joyfully and freely. Let it suffice if we can appreciate how, in some respects, his music, with a certain cruelty towards itself, determines to subserve the course of the drama, which is as unrelenting as fate, whereas in reality his art was ever thirsting for a free ramble in the open and over the wilderness.

X.

An artist who has this empire over himself subjugates all other artists, even though he may not particularly desire to do so. For him alone there lies no danger or stemming-force in those he has subjugated—his friends and his adherents; whereas the weaker natures who learn to rely on their friends pay for this reliance by forfeiting their independence. It is very wonderful to observe how carefully, throughout his life, Wagner avoided anything in the nature of heading a party, notwithstanding the fact that at the close of every phase in his career a circle of adherents formed, presumably with the view of holding him fast to his latest development He always succeeded, however, in wringing himself free from them, and never allowed himself to be bound; for not only was the ground he covered too vast for one alone to keep abreast of him with any ease, but his way was so exceptionally steep that the most devoted would have lost his breath. At almost every stage in Wagner's progress his friends would have liked to preach to him, and his enemies would fain have done so too—but for other reasons. Had the purity of his artist's nature been one degree less decided than it was, he would have attained much earlier than he actually did to the leading position in the artistic and musical world of his time. True, he has reached this now, but in a much higher sense, seeing that every performance to be witnessed in any department of art makes its obeisance, so to speak, before the judgment-stool of his genius and of his artistic temperament. He has overcome the most refractory of his contemporaries; there is not one gifted musician among them but in his innermost heart would willingly listen to him, and find Wagner's compositions more worth listening to than his own and all other musical productions taken together. Many who wish, by hook or by crook, to make their mark, even wrestle with Wagner's secret charm, and unconsciously throw in their lot with the older masters, preferring to ascribe their "independence" to Schubert or Handel rather than to Wagner. But in vain! Thanks to their very efforts in contending against the dictates of their own consciences, they become ever meaner and smaller artists; they ruin their own natures by forcing themselves to tolerate undesirable allies and friends And in spite of all these sacrifices, they still find perhaps in their dreams, that their ear turns attentively to Wagner. These adversaries are to be pitied: they imagine they lose a great deal when they lose themselves, but here they are mistaken.

Albeit it is obviously all one to Wagner whether musicians compose in his style, or whether they compose at all, he even does his utmost to dissipate the belief that a school of composers should now necessarily follow in his wake; though, in so far as he exercises a direct influence upon musicians, he does indeed try to instruct them concerning the art of grand execution. In his opinion, the evolution of art seems to have reached that stage when the honest endeavour to become an able and masterly exponent or interpreter is ever so much more worth talking about than the longing to be a creator at all costs. For, at the present stage of art, universal creating has this fatal result, that inasmuch as it encourages a much larger output, it tends to exhaust the means and artifices of genius by everyday use, and thus to reduce the real grandeur of its effect. Even that which is good in art is superfluous and detrimental when it proceeds from the imitation of what is best. Wagnerian ends and means are of one piece: to perceive this, all that is required is honesty in art matters, and it would be dishonest to adopt his means in order to apply them to other and less significant ends.

If, therefore, Wagner declines to live on amid a multitude of creative musicians, he is only the more desirous of imposing upon all men of talent the new duty of joining him in seeking the law of style for dramatic performances. He deeply feels the need of establishing a traditional style for his art, by means of which his work may continue to live from one age to another in a pure form, until it reaches that future which its creator ordained for it.

Wagner is impelled by an undaunted longing to make known everything relating to that foundation of a style, mentioned above, and, accordingly, everything relating to the continuance of his art. To make his work—as Schopenhauer would say— a sacred depository and the real fruit of his life, as well as the inheritance of mankind, and to store it for the benefit of a posterity better able to appreciate it,—these were the supreme objects of his life, and for these he bore that crown of thorns which, one day, will shoot forth leaves of bay. Like the insect which, in its last form, concentrates all its energies upon the one object of finding a safe depository for its eggs and of ensuring the future welfare of its posthumous brood,—then only to die content, so Wagner strove with equal determination to find a place of security for his works.

This subject, which took precedence of all others with him, constantly incited him to new discoveries; and these he sought ever more and more at the spring of his demoniacal gift of communicability, the more distinctly he saw himself in conflict with an age that was both perverse and unwilling to lend him its ear. Gradually however, even this same age began to mark his indefatigable efforts, to respond to his subtle advances, and to turn its ear to him. Whenever a small or a great opportunity arose, however far away, which suggested to Wagner a means wherewith to explain his thoughts, he availed himself of it: he thought his thoughts anew into every fresh set of circumstances, and would make them speak out of the most paltry bodily form. Whenever a soul only half capable of comprehending him opened itself to him, he never failed to implant his seed in it. He saw hope in things which caused the average dispassionate observer merely to shrug his shoulders; and he erred again and again, only so as to be able to carry his point against that same observer. Just as the sage, in reality, mixes with living men only for the purpose of increasing his store of knowledge, so the artist would almost seem to be unable to associate with his contemporaries at all, unless they be such as can help him towards making his work eternal. He cannot be loved otherwise than with the love of this eternity, and thus he is conscious only of one kind of hatred directed at him, the hatred which would demolish the bridges bearing his art into the future. The pupils Wagner educated for his own purpose, the individual musicians and actors whom he advised and whose ear he corrected and improved, the small and large orchestras he led, the towns which witnessed him earnestly fulfilling the duties of ws calling, the princes and ladies who half boastfully and half lovingly participated in the framing of his plans, the various European countries to which he temporarily belonged as the judge and evil conscience of their arts,—everything gradually became the echo of his thought and of his indefatigable efforts to attain to fruitfulness in the future. Although this echo often sounded so discordant as to confuse him, still the tremendous power of his voice repeatedly crying out into the world must in the end call forth reverberations, and it will soon be impossible to be deaf to him or to misunderstand him. It is this reflected sound which even now causes the art-institutions of modern men to shake: every time the breath of his spirit blew into these coverts, all that was overripe or withered fell to the ground; but the general increase of scepticism in all directions speaks more eloquently than all this trembling. Nobody any longer dares to predict where Wagner's influence may not unexpectedly break out. He is quite unable to divorce the salvation of art from any other salvation or damnation: wherever modern life conceals a danger, he, with the discriminating eye of mistrust, perceives a danger threatening art. In his imagination he pulls the edifice of modern civilisation to pieces, and allows nothing rotten, no unsound timber-work to escape: if in the process he should happen to encounter weather-tight walls or anything like solid foundations, he immediately casts about for means wherewith he can convert them into bulwarks and shelters for his art. He lives like a fugitive, whose will is not to preserve his own life, but to keep a secret— like an unhappy woman who does not wish to save her own soul, but that of the child lying in her lap: in short, he lives like Sieglinde, "for the sake of love."

For life must indeed be full of pain and shame to one who can find neither rest nor shelter in this world, and who must nevertheless appeal to it, exact things from it, contemn it, and still be unable to dispense with the thing contemned, —this really constitutes the wretchedness of the artist of the future, who, unlike the philosopher, cannot prosecute his work alone in the seclusion of a study, but who requires human souls as messengers to this future, public institutions as a guarantee of it, and, as it were, bridges between now and hereafter. His art may not, like the philosopher's, be put aboard the boat of written documents: art needs capable men, not letters and notes, to transmit it. Over whole periods in Wagner's life rings a murmur of distress—his distress at not being able to meet with these capable interpreters before whom he longed to execute examples of his work, instead of being confined to written symbols; before whom he yearned to practise his art, instead of showing a pallid reflection of it to those who read books, and who, generally speaking, therefore are not artists.

In Wagner the man of letters we see the struggle of a brave fighter, whose right hand has, as it were, been lopped off, and who has continued the contest with his left. In his writings he is always the sufferer, because a temporary and insuperable destiny deprives him of his own and the correct way of conveying his thoughts—that is to say, in the form of apocalyptic and triumphant examples. His writings contain nothing canonical or severe: the canons are to be found in his works as a whole. Their literary side represents his attempts to understand the instinct which urged him to create his works and to get a glimpse of himself through them. If he succeeded in transforming his instincts into terms of knowledge, it was always with the hope that the reverse process might take place in the souls of his readers—it was with this intention that he wrote. Should it ultimately be proved that, in so doing, Wagner attempted the impossible, he would still only share the lot of all those who have meditated deeply on art; and even so he would be ahead of most of them in this, namely, that the strongest instinct for all arts harboured in him. I know of no written aesthetics that give more light than those of Wagner; all that can possibly be learnt concerning the origin of a work of art is to be found in them. He is one of the very great, who appeared amongst us a witness, and who is continually improving his testimony and making it ever clearer and freer; even when he stumbles as a scientist, sparks rise from the ground. Such tracts as "Beethoven," "Concerning the Art of Conducting," "Concerning Actors and Singers," "State and Religion," silence all contradiction, and, like sacred reliquaries, impose upon all who approach them a calm, earnest, and reverential regard. Others, more particularly the earlier ones, including "Opera and Drama," excite and agitate one; their rhythm is so uneven that, as prose they are bewildering. Their dialectics is constantly interrupted, and their course is more retarded than accelerated by outbursts of feeling; a certain reluctance on the part of the writer seems to hang over them like a pall, just as though the artist were somewhat ashamed of speculative discussions. What the reader who is only imperfectly initiated will probably find most oppressive is the general tone of authoritative dignity which is peculiar to Wagner, and which is very difficult to describe: it always strikes me as though Wagner were continually addressing enemies; for the style of all these tracts more resembles that of the spoken than of the written language, hence they will seem much more intelligible if heard read aloud, in the presence of his enemies, with whom he cannot be on familiar terms, and towards whom he must therefore show some reserve and aloofness, The entrancing passion of his feelings, however, constantly pierces this intentional disguise, and then the stilted and heavy periods, swollen with accessary words, vanish, and his pen dashes off sentences, and even whole pages, which belong to the best in German prose. But even admitting that while he wrote such passages he was addressing friends, and that the shadow of his enemies had been removed for a while, all the friends and enemies that Wagner, as a man of letters, has, possess one factor in common, which differentiates them fundamentally from the "people" for whom he worked as an artist. Owing to the refining and fruitless nature of their education, they are quite devoid of the essential traits of the national character, and he who would appeal to them must speak in a way which is not of the people—that is to say, after the manner of our best prose-writers and Wagner himself; though that he did violence to himself in writing thus is evident. But the strength of that almost maternal instinct of prudence in him, which is ready to make any sacrifice, rather tends to reinstall him among the scholars and men of learning, to whom as a creator he always longed to bid farewell. He submits to the language of culture and all the laws governing its use, though he was the first to recognise its profound insufficiency as a means of communication.

For if there is anything that distinguishes his art from every other art of modern times, it is that it no longer speaks the language of any particular caste, and refuses to admit the distinctions "literate" and "illiterate." It thus stands as a contrast to every culture of the Renaissance, which to this day still bathes us modern men in its light and shade. Inasmuch as Wagner's art bears us, from time to time, beyond itself, we are enabled to get a general view of its uniform character: we see Goethe and Leopardi as the last great stragglers of the Italian philologist-poets, Faust as the incarnation of a most unpopular problem, in the form of a man of theory thirsting for life; even Goethe's song is an imitation of the song of the people rather than a standard set before them to which they are expected to attain, and the poet knew very well how truly he spoke when he seriously assured his adherents: "My compositions cannot become popular; he who hopes and strives to make them so is mistaken."

That an art could arise which would be so clear and warm as to flood the base and the poor in spirit with its light, as well as to melt the haughtiness of the learned—such a phenomenon had to be experienced though it could not be guessed. But even in the mind of him who experiences it to-day it must upset all preconceived notions concerning education and culture; to such an one the veil will seem to have been rent in twain that conceals a future in which no highest good or highest joys exist that are not the common property of all. The odium attaching to the word "common" will then be abolished.

If presentiment venture thus into the remote future, the discerning eye of all will recognise the dreadful social insanity of our present age, and will no longer blind itself to the dangers besetting an art which seems to have roots only in the remote and distant future, and which allows its burgeoning branches to spread before our gaze when it has not yet revealed the ground from which it draws its sap. How can we protect this homeless art through the ages until that remote future is reached? How can we so dam the flood of a revolution seemingly inevitable everywhere, that the blessed prospect and guarantee of a better future—of a freer human life—shall not also be washed away with all that is destined to perish and deserves to perish?

He who asks himself this question shares Wagner's care: he will feel himself impelled with Wagner to seek those established powers that have the goodwill to protect the noblest passions of man during the period of earthquakes and upheavals. In this sense alone Wagner questions the learned through his writings, whether they intend storing his legacy to them—the precious Ring of his art—among their other treasures. And even the wonderful confidence which he reposes in the German mind and the aims of German politics seems to me to arise from the fact that he grants the people of the Reformation that strength, mildness, and bravery which is necessary in order to divert "the torrent of revolution into the tranquil river-bed of a calmly flowing stream of humanity": and I could almost believe that this and only this is what he meant to express by means of the symbol of his Imperial march.

As a rule, though, the generous impulses of the creative artist and the extent of his philanthropy are too great for his gaze to be confined within the limits of a single nation. His thoughts, like those of every good and great German, are more than German, and the language of his art does not appeal to particular races but to mankind in general.

But to the men of the future.

This is the belief that is proper to him; this is his torment and his distinction. No artist, of what past soever, has yet received such a remarkable portion of genius; no one, save him, has ever been obliged to mix this bitterest of ingredients with the drink of nectar to which enthusiasm helped him. It is not as one might expect, the misunderstood and mishandled artist, the fugitive of his age, who adopted this faith in self-defence: success or failure at the hands of his contemporaries was unable either to create or to destroy it Whether it glorified or reviled him, he did not belong to this generation: that was the conclusion to which his instincts led him. And the possibility of any generation's ever belonging to him is something which he who disbelieves in Wagner can never be made to admit. But even this unbeliever may at least ask, what kind of generation it will be in which Wagner will recognise his "people," and in which he will see the type of all those who suffer a common distress, and who wish to escape from it by means of an art common to them all. Schiller was certainly more hopeful and sanguine; he did not ask what a future must be like if the instinct of the artist that predicts it prove true; his command to every artist was rather—

Soar aloft in daring flight Out of sight of thine own years! In thy mirror, gleaming bright, Glimpse of distant dawn appears.

XI.

May blessed reason preserve us from ever thinking that mankind will at any time discover a final and ideal order of things, and that happiness will then and ever after beam down upon us uniformly, like the rays of the sun in the tropics. Wagner has nothing to do with such a hope; he is no Utopian. If he was unable to dispense with the belief in a future, it only meant that he observed certain properties in modern men which he did not hold to be essential to their nature, and which did not seem to him to form any necessary part of their constitution; in fact, which were changeable and transient; and that precisely owing to these properties art would find no home among them, and he himself had to be the precursor and prophet of another epoch. No golden age, no cloudless sky will fall to the portion of those future generations, which his instinct led him to expect, and whose approximate characteristics may be gleaned from the cryptic characters of his art, in so far as it is possible to draw conclusions concerning the nature of any pain from the kind of relief it seeks. Nor will superhuman goodness and justice stretch like an everlasting rainbow over this future land. Belike this coming generation will, on the whole, seem more evil than the present one—for in good as in evil it will be more straightforward. It is even possible, if its soul were ever able to speak out in full and unembarrassed tones, that it might convulse and terrify us, as though the voice of some hitherto concealed and evil spirit had suddenly cried out in our midst. Or how do the following propositions strike our ears?—That passion is better than stocism or hypocrisy; that straightforwardness, even in evil, is better than losing oneself in trying to observe traditional morality; that the free man is just as able to be good as evil, but that the unemancipated man is a disgrace to nature, and has no share in heavenly or earthly bliss; finally, that all who wish to be free must become so through themselves, and that freedom falls to nobody's lot as a gift from Heaven. However harsh and strange these propositions may sound, they are nevertheless reverberations from that future world, which is verily in need of art, and which expects genuine pleasure from its presence; they are the language of nature—reinstated even in mankind; they stand for what I have already termed correct feeling as opposed to the incorrect feeling that reigns to-day.

But real relief or salvation exists only for nature not for that which is contrary to nature or which arises out of incorrect feeling. When all that is unnatural becomes self-conscious, it desires but one thing—nonentity; the natural thing, on the other hand, yearns to be transfigured through love: the former would fain not be, the latter would fain be otherwise. Let him who has understood this recall, in the stillness of his soul, the simple themes of Wagner's art, in order to be able to ask himself whether it were nature or nature's opposite which sought by means of them to achieve the aims just described.

The desperate vagabond finds deliverance from his distress in the compassionate love of a woman who would rather die than be unfaithful to him: the theme of the Flying Dutchman. The sweet-heart, renouncing all personal happiness, owing to a divine transformation of Love into Charity, becomes a saint, and saves the soul of her loved one: the theme of Tannhauser. The sublimest and highest thing descends a suppliant among men, and will not be questioned whence it came; when, however, the fatal question is put, it sorrowfully returns to its higher life: the theme of Lohengrin. The loving soul of a wife, and the people besides, joyfully welcome the new benevolent genius, although the retainers of tradition and custom reject and revile him: the theme of the Meistersingers. Of two lovers, that do not know they are loved, who believe rather that they are deeply wounded and contemned, each demands of the other that he or she should drink a cup of deadly poison, to all intents and purposes as an expiation of the insult; in reality, however, as the result of an impulse which neither of them understands: through death they wish to escape all possibility of separation or deceit. The supposed approach of death loosens their fettered souls and allows them a short moment of thrilling happiness, just as though they had actually escaped from the present, from illusions and from life: the theme of Tristan and Isolde.

In the Ring of the Nibelung the tragic hero is a god whose heart yearns for power, and who, since he travels along all roads in search of it, finally binds himself to too many undertakings, loses his freedom, and is ultimately cursed by the curse inseparable from power. He becomes aware of his loss of freedom owing to the fact that he no longer has the means to take possession of the golden Ring—that symbol of all earthly power, and also of the greatest dangers to himself as long as it lies in the hands of his enemies. The fear of the end and the twilight of all gods overcomes him, as also the despair at being able only to await the end without opposing it. He is in need of the free and fearless man who, without his advice or assistance—even in a struggle against gods—can accomplish single-handed what is denied to the powers of a god. He fails to see him, and just as a new hope finds shape within him, he must obey the conditions to which he is bound: with his own hand he must murder the thing he most loves, and purest pity must be punished by his sorrow. Then he begins to loathe power, which bears evil and bondage in its lap; his will is broken, and he himself begins to hanker for the end that threatens him from afar off. At this juncture something happens which had long been the subject of his most ardent desire: the free and fearless man appears, he rises in opposition to everything accepted and established, his parents atone for having been united by a tie which was antagonistic to the order of nature and usage; they perish, but Siegfried survives. And at the sight of his magnificent development and bloom, the loathing leaves otan's soul, and he follows the hero's history with the eye of fatherly love and anxiety. How he forges his sword, kills the dragon, gets possession of the ring, escapes the craftiest ruse, awakens Brunhilda; how the curse abiding in the ring gradually overtakes him; how, faithful in faithfulness, he wounds the thing he most loves, out of love; becomes enveloped in the shadow and cloud of guilt, and, rising out of it more brilliantly than the sun, ultimately goes down, firing the whole heavens with his burning glow and purging the world of the curse,—all this is seen by the god whose sovereign spear was broken in the contest with the freest man, and who lost his power through him, rejoicing greatly over his own defeat: full of sympathy for the triumph and pain of his victor, his eye burning with aching joy looks back upon the last events; he has become free through love, free from himself.

And now ask yourselves, ye generation of to-day, Was all this composed for you? Have ye the courage to point up to the stars of the whole of this heavenly dome of beauty and goodness and to say, This is our life, that Wagner has transferred to a place beneath the stars?

Where are the men among you who are able to interpret the divine image of Wotan in the light of their own lives, and who can become ever greater while, like him, ye retreat? Who among you would renounce power, knowing and having learned that power is evil? Where are they who like Brunhilda abandon their knowledge to love, and finally rob their lives of the highest wisdom, "afflicted love, deepest sorrow, opened my eyes"? and where are the free and fearless, developing and blossoming in innocent egoism? and where are the Siegfrieds, among you?

He who questions thus and does so in vain, will find himself compelled to look around him for signs of the future; and should his eye, on reaching an unknown distance, espy just that "people" which his own generation can read out of the signs contained in Wagnerian art, he will then also understand what Wagner will mean to this people—something that he cannot be to all of us, namely, not the prophet of the future, as perhaps he would fain appear to us, but the interpreter and clarifier of the past.

Part II

Translated by Adrian Collins

The Use and Abuse of History.

Preface.

"I hate everything that merely instructs me without increasing or directly quickening my activity." These words of Goethe, like a sincere ceterum censeo, may well stand at the head of my thoughts on the worth and the worthlessness of history. I will show in them why instruction that does not "quicken," knowledge that slackens the rein of activity, why in fact history, in Goethe's phrase, must be seriously "hated," as a costly and superfluous luxury of the understanding: for we are still in want of the necessaries of life, and the superfluous is an enemy to the necessary. We do need history, but quite differently from the jaded idlers in the garden of knowledge, however grandly they may look down on our rude and unpicturesque requirements. In other words, we need it for life and action, not as a convenient way to avoid life and action, or to excuse a selfish life and a cowardly or base action. We would serve history only so far as it serves life; but to value its study beyond a certain point mutilates and degrades life: and this is a fact that certain marked symptoms of our time make it as necessary as it may be painful to bring to the test of experience.

I have tried to describe a feeling that has often troubled me: I revenge myself on it by giving it publicity. This may lead some one to explain to me that he has also had the feeling, but that I do not feel it purely and elementally enough, and cannot express it with the ripe certainty of experience. A few may say so; but most people will tell me that it is a perverted, unnatural, horrible, and altogether unlawful feeling to have, and that I show myself unworthy of the great historical movement which is especially strong among the German people for the last two generations.

I am at all costs going to venture on a description of my feelings; which will be decidedly in the interests of propriety, as I shall give plenty of opportunity for paying compliments to such a "movement." And I gain an advantage for myself that is more valuable to me than propriety—the attainment of a correct point of view, through my critics, with regard to our age.

These thoughts are "out of season," because I am trying to represent something of which the age is rightly proud—its historical culture—as a fault and a defect in our time, believing as I do that we are all suffering from a malignant historical fever and should at least recognise the fact. But even if it be a virtue, Goethe may be right in asserting that we cannot help developing our faults at the same time as our virtues; and an excess of virtue can obviously bring a nation to ruin, as well as an excess of vice. In any case I may be allowed my say. But I will first relieve my mind by the confession that the experiences which produced those disturbing feelings were mostly drawn from myself,—and from other sources only for the sake of comparison; and that I have only reached such "unseasonable" experience, so far as I am the nursling of older ages like the Greek, and less a child of this age. I must admit so much in virtue of my profession as a classical scholar: for I do not know what meaning classical scholarship may have for our time except in its being "unseasonable,"—that is, contrary to our time, and yet with an influence on it for the benefit, it may be hoped, of a future time.

I.

Consider the herds that are feeding yonder: they know not the meaning of yesterday or to-day, they graze and ruminate, move or rest, from morning to night, from day to day, taken up with their little loves and hates, at the mercy of the moment, feeling neither melancholy nor satiety. Man cannot see them without regret, for even in the pride of his humanity he looks enviously on the beast's happiness. He wishes simply to live without satiety or pain, like the beast; yet it is all in vain, for he will not change places with it. He may ask the beast—"Why do you look at me and not speak to me of your happiness?" The beast wants to answer—"Because I always forget what I wished to say": but he forgets this answer too, and is silent; and the man is left to wonder.

He wonders also about himself, that he cannot learn to forget, but hangs on the past: however far or fast he run, that chain runs with him. It is matter for wonder: the moment, that is here and gone, that was nothing before and nothing after, returns like a spectre to trouble the quiet of a later moment. A leaf is continually dropping out of the volume of time and fluttering away—and suddenly it flutters back into the man's lap. Then he says, "I remember...," and envies the beast, that forgets at once, and sees every moment really die, sink into night and mist, extinguished for ever. The beast lives unhistorically; for it "goes into" the present, like a number, without leaving any curious remainder. It cannot dissimulate, it conceals nothing; at every moment it seems what it actually is, and thus can be nothing that is not honest. But man is always resisting the great and continually increasing weight of the past; it presses him down, and bows his shoulders; he travels with a dark invisible burden that he can plausibly disown, and is only too glad to disown in converse with his fellows—in order to excite their envy. And so it hurts him, like the thought of a lost Paradise, to see a herd grazing, or, nearer still, a child, that has nothing yet of the past to disown, and plays in a happy blindness between the walls of the past and the future. And yet its play must be disturbed, and only too soon will it be summoned from its little kingdom of oblivion. Then it learns to understand the words "once upon a time," the "open sesame" that lets in battle, suffering and weariness on mankind, and reminds them what their existence really is, an imperfect tense that never becomes a present. And when death brings at last the desired forgetfulness, it abolishes life and being together, and sets the seal on the knowledge that "being" is merely a continual "has been," a thing that lives by denying and destroying and contradicting itself.

If happiness and the chase for new happiness keep alive in any sense the will to live, no philosophy has perhaps more truth than the cynic's: for the beast's happiness, like that of the perfect cynic, is the visible proof of the truth of cynicism. The smallest pleasure, if it be only continuous and make one happy, is incomparably a greater happiness than the more intense pleasure that comes as an episode, a wild freak, a mad interval between ennui, desire, and privation. But in the smallest and greatest happiness there is always one thing that makes it happiness: the power of forgetting, or, in more learned phrase, the capacity of feeling "unhistorically" throughout its duration. One who cannot leave himself behind on the threshold of the moment and forget the past, who cannot stand on a single point, like a goddess of victory, without fear or giddiness, will never know what happiness is; and, worse still, will never do anything to make others happy. The extreme case would be the man without any power to forget, who is condemned to see "becoming" everywhere. Such a man believes no more in himself or his own existence, he sees everything fly past in an eternal succession, and loses himself in the stream of becoming. At last, like the logical disciple of Heraclitus, he will hardly dare to raise his finger. Forgetfulness is a property of all action; just as not only light but darkness is bound up with the life of every organism. One who wished to feel everything historically, would be like a man forcing himself to refrain from sleep, or a beast who had to live by chewing a continual cud. Thus even a happy life is possible without remembrance, as the beast shows: but life in any true sense is absolutely impossible without forgetfulness. Or, to put my conclusion better, there is a degree of sleeplessness, of rumination, of "historical sense," that injures and finally destroys the living thing, be it a man or a people or a system of culture.

To fix this degree and the limits to the memory of the past, if it is not to become the gravedigger of the present, we must see clearly how great is the "plastic power" of a man or a community or a culture; I mean the power of specifically growing out of one's self, of making the past and the strange one body with the near and the present, of healing wounds, replacing what is lost, repairing broken moulds. There are men who have this power so slightly that a single sharp experience, a single pain, often a little injustice, will lacerate their souls like the scratch of a poisoned knife. There are others, who are so little injured by the worst misfortunes, and even by their own spiteful actions, as to feel tolerably comfortable, with a fairly quiet conscience, in the midst of them,—or at any rate shortly afterwards. The deeper the roots of a man's inner nature, the better will he take the past into himself; and the greatest and most powerful nature would be known by the absence of limits for the historical sense to overgrow and work harm. It would assimilate and digest the past, however foreign, and turn it to sap. Such a nature can forget what it cannot subdue; there is no break in the horizon, and nothing to remind it that there are still men, passions, theories and aims on the other side. This is a universal law; a living thing can only be healthy, strong and productive within a certain horizon: if it be incapable of drawing one round itself, or too selfish to lose its own view in another's, it will come to an untimely end. Cheerfulness, a good conscience, belief in the future, the joyful deed, all depend, in the individual as well as the nation, on there being a line that divides the visible and clear from the vague and shadowy: we must know the right time to forget as well as the right time to remember; and instinctively see when it is necessary to feel historically, and when unhistorically. This is the point that the reader is asked to consider; that the unhistorical and the historical are equally necessary to the health of an individual, a community, and a system of culture.

Every one has noticed that a man's historical knowledge and range of feeling may be very limited, his horizon as narrow as that of an Alpine valley, his judgments incorrect and his experience falsely supposed original, and yet in spite of all the incorrectness and falsity he may stand forth in unconquerable health and vigour, to the joy of all who see him; whereas another man with far more judgment and learning will fail in comparison, because the lines of his horizon are continually changing and shifting, and he cannot shake himself free from the delicate network of his truth and righteousness for a downright act of will or desire. We saw that the beast, absolutely "unhistorical," with the narrowest of horizons, has yet a certain happiness, and lives at least without hypocrisy or ennui; and so we may hold the capacity of feeling (to a certain extent) unhistorically, to be the more important and elemental, as providing the foundation of every sound and real growth, everything that is truly great and human. The unhistorical is like the surrounding atmosphere that can alone create life, and in whose annihilation life itself disappears. It is true that man can only become man by first suppressing this unhistorical element in his thoughts, comparisons, distinctions, and conclusions, letting a clear sudden light break through these misty clouds by his power of turning the past to the uses of the present. But an excess of history makes him flag again, while without the veil of the unhistorical he would never have the courage to begin. What deeds could man ever have done if he had not been enveloped in the dust-cloud of the unhistorical? Or, to leave metaphors and take a concrete example, imagine a man swayed and driven by a strong passion, whether for a woman or a theory. His world is quite altered. He is blind to everything behind him, new sounds are muffled and meaningless; though his perceptions were never so intimately felt in all their colour, light and music, and he Seems to grasp them with his five senses together. All his judgments of value are changed for the worse; there is much he can no longer value, as he can scarcely feel it: he wonders that he has so long been the sport of strange words and opinions, that his recollections have run around in one unwearying circle and are yet too weak and weary to make a single step away from it. His whole case is most indefensible; it is narrow, ungrateful to the past, blind to danger, deaf to warnings, a small living eddy in a dead sea of night and forgetfulness. And yet this condition, unhistorical and antihistorical throughout, is the cradle not only of unjust action, but of every just and justifiable action in the world. No artist will paint his picture, no general win his victory, no nation gain its freedom, without having striven and yearned for it under those very "unhistorical" conditions. If the man of action, in Goethe's phrase, is without conscience, he is also without knowledge: he forgets most things in order to do one, he is unjust to what is behind him, and only recognises one law, the law of that which is to be. So he loves his work infinitely more than it deserves to be loved; and the best works are produced in such an ecstasy of love that they must always be unworthy of it, however great their worth otherwise.

Should any one be able to dissolve the unhistorical atmosphere in which every great event happens, and breathe afterwards, he might be capable of rising to the "super-historical" standpoint of consciousness, that Niebuhr has described as the possible result of historical research. "History," he says, "is useful for one purpose, if studied in detail: that men may know, as the greatest and best spirits of our generation do not know, the accidental nature of the forms in which they see and insist on others seeing,—insist, I say, because their consciousness of them is exceptionally intense. Any one who has not grasped this idea in its different applications will fall under the spell of a more powerful spirit who reads a deeper emotion into the given form." Such a standpoint might be called "super-historical," as one who took it could feel no impulse from history to any further life or work, for he would have recognised the blindness and injustice in the soul of the doer as a condition of every deed: he would be cured henceforth of taking history too seriously, and have learnt to answer the question how and why life should be lived,—for all men and all circumstances, Greeks or Turks, the first century or the nineteenth. Whoever asks his friends whether they would live the last ten or twenty years over again, will easily see which of them is born for the "super-historical standpoint": they will all answer no, but will give different reasons for their answer. Some will say they have the consolation that the next twenty will be better: they are the men referred to satirically by David Hume:—

"And from the dregs of life hope to receive,
What the first sprightly running could not give."

We will call them the "historical men." Their vision of the past turns them towards the future, encourages them to persevere with life, and kindles the hope that justice will yet come and happiness is behind the mountain they are climbing. They believe that the meaning of existence will become ever clearer in the course of its evolution, they only look backward at the process to understand the present and stimulate their longing for the future. They do not know how unhistorical their thoughts and actions are in spite of all their history, and how their preoccupation with it is for the sake of life rather than mere science.

But that question to which we have heard the first answer, is capable of another; also a "no," but on different grounds. It is the "no" of the "super-historical" man who sees no salvation in evolution, for whom the world is complete and fulfils its aim in every single moment. How could the next ten years teach what the past ten were not able to teach?

Whether the aim of the teaching be happiness or resignation, virtue or penance, these super-historical men are not agreed; but as against all merely historical ways of viewing the past, they are unanimous in the theory that the past and the present are one and the same, typically alike in all their diversity, and forming together a picture of eternally present imperishable types of unchangeable value and significance. Just as the hundreds of different languages correspond to the same constant and elemental needs of mankind, and one who understood the needs could learn nothing new from the languages; so the "super-historical" philosopher sees all the history of nations and individuals from within. He has a divine insight into the original meaning of the hieroglyphs, and comes even to be weary of the letters that are continually unrolled before him. How should the endless rush of events not bring satiety, surfeit, loathing? So the boldest of us is ready perhaps at last to say from his heart with Giacomo Leopardi: "Nothing lives that were worth thy pains, and the earth deserves not a sigh. Our being is pain and weariness, and the world is mud—nothing else. Be calm."

But we will leave the super-historical men to their loathings and their wisdom: we wish rather to-day to be joyful in our unwisdom and have a pleasant life as active men who go forward, and respect the course of the world. The value we put on the historical may be merely a Western prejudice: let us at least go forward within this prejudice and not stand still. If we could only learn better to study history as a means to life! We would gladly grant the super-historical people their superior wisdom, so long as we are sure of having more life than they: for in that case our unwisdom would have a greater future before it than their wisdom. To make my opposition between life and wisdom clear, I will take the usual road of the short summary.

A historical phenomenon, completely understood and reduced to an item of knowledge, is, in relation to the man who knows it, dead: for he has found out its madness, its injustice, its blind passion, and especially the earthly and darkened horizon that was the source of its power for history. This power has now become, for him who has recognised it, powerless; not yet, perhaps, for him who is alive.

History regarded as pure knowledge and allowed to sway the intellect would mean for men the final balancing of the ledger of life. Historical study is only fruitful for the future if it follow a powerful life-giving influence, for example, a new system of culture; only, therefore, if it be guided and dominated by a higher force, and do not itself guide and dominate.

History, so far as it serves life, serves an unhistorical power, and thus will never become a pure science like mathematics. The question how far life needs such a service is one of the most serious questions affecting the well-being of a man, a people and a culture. For by excess of history life becomes maimed and degenerate, and is followed by the degeneration of history as well.

II.

The fact that life does need the service of history must be as clearly grasped as that an excess of history hurts it; this will be proved later. History is necessary to the living man in three ways: in relation to his action and struggle, his conservatism and reverence, his suffering and his desire for deliverance. These three relations answer to the three kinds of history—so far as they can be distinguished—the monumental, the antiquarian, and the critical.

History is necessary above all to the man of action and power who fights a great fight and needs examples, teachers and comforters; he cannot find them among his contemporaries. It was necessary in this sense to Schiller; for our time is so evil, Goethe says, that the poet meets no nature that will profit him, among living men. Polybius is thinking of the active man when he calls political history the true preparation for governing a state; it is the great teacher, that shows us how to bear steadfastly the reverses of fortune, by reminding us of what others have suffered. Whoever has learned to recognise this meaning in history must hate to see curious tourists and laborious beetle-hunters climbing up the great pyramids of antiquity. He does not wish to meet the idler who is rushing through the picture-galleries of the past for a new distraction or sensation, where he himself is looking for example and encouragement. To avoid being troubled by the weak and hopeless idlers, and those whose apparent activity is merely neurotic, he looks behind him and stays his course towards the goal in order to breathe. His goal is happiness, not perhaps his own, but often the nation's, or humanity's at large: he avoids quietism, and uses history as a weapon against it. For the most part he has no hope of reward except fame, which means the expectation of a niche in the temple of history, where he in his turn may be the consoler and counsellor of posterity. For his orders are that what has once been able to extend the conception "man" and give it a fairer content, must ever exist for the same office. The great moments in the individual battle form a chain, a high road for humanity through the ages, and the highest points of those vanished moments are yet great and living for men; and this is the fundamental idea of the belief in humanity, that finds a voice in the demand for a "monumental" history.

But the fiercest battle is fought round the demand for greatness to be eternal. Every other living thing cries no. "Away with the monuments," is the watch-word. Dull custom fills all the chambers of the world with its meanness, and rises in thick vapour round anything that is great, barring its way to immortality, blinding and stifling it. And the way passes through mortal brains! Through the brains of sick and short-lived beasts that ever rise to the surface to breathe, and painfully keep off annihilation for a little space. For they wish but one thing: to live at any cost. Who would ever dream of any "monumental history" among them, the hard torch-race that alone gives life to greatness? And yet there are always men awakening, who are strengthened and made happy by gazing on past greatness, as though man's life were a lordly thing, and the fairest fruit of this bitter tree were the knowledge that there was once a man who walked sternly and proudly through this world, another who had pity and loving-kindness, another who lived in contemplation,—but all leaving one truth behind them, that his life is the fairest who thinks least about life. The common man snatches greedily at this little span, with tragic earnestness, but they, on their way to monumental history and immortality, knew how to greet it with Olympic laughter, or at least with a lofty scorn; and they went down to their graves in irony—for what had they to bury? Only what they had always treated as dross, refuse, and vanity, and which now falls into its true home of oblivion, after being so long the sport of their contempt. One thing will live, the sign-manual of their inmost being, the rare flash of light, the deed, the creation; because posterity cannot do without it. In this spiritualised form fame is something more than the sweetest morsel for our egoism, in Schopenhauer's phrase: it is the belief in the oneness and continuity of the great in every age, and a protest against the change and decay of generations.

What is the use to the modern man of this "monumental" contemplation of the past, this preoccupation with the rare and classic?

It is the knowledge that the great thing existed and was therefore possible, and so may be possible again. He is heartened on his way; for his doubt in weaker moments, whether his desire be not for the impossible, is struck aside. Suppose one believe that no more than a hundred men, brought up in the new spirit, efficient and productive, were needed to give the deathblow to the present fashion of education in Germany; he will gather strength from the remembrance that the culture of the Renaissance was raised on the shoulders of such another band of a hundred men.

And yet if we really wish to learn something from an example, how vague and elusive do we find the comparison! If it is to give us strength, many of the differences must be neglected, the individuality of the past forced into a general formula and all the sharp angles broken off for the sake of correspondence. Ultimately, of course, what was once possible can only become possible a second time on the Pythagorean theory, that when the heavenly bodies are in the same position again, the events on earth are reproduced to the smallest detail; so when the stars have a certain relation, a Stoic and an Epicurean will form a conspiracy to murder Cæsar, and a different conjunction will show another Columbus discovering America. Only if the earth always began its drama again after the fifth act, and it were certain that the same interaction of motives, the same deus ex machina, the same catastrophe would occur at particular intervals, could the man of action venture to look for the whole archetypic truth in monumental history, to see each fact fully set out in its uniqueness: it would not probably be before the astronomers became astrologers again. Till then monumental history will never be able to have complete truth; it will always bring together things that are incompatible and generalise them into compatibility, will always weaken the differences of motive and occasion. Its object is to depict effects at the expense of the causes—"monumentally," that is, as examples for imitation: it turns aside, as far as it may, from reasons, and might be called with far less exaggeration a collection of "effects in themselves," than of events that will have an effect on all ages. The events of war or religion cherished in our popular celebrations are such "effects in themselves"; it is these that will not let ambition sleep, and lie like amulets on the bolder hearts—not the real historical nexus of cause and effect, which, rightly understood, would only prove that nothing quite similar could ever be cast again from the dice-boxes of fate and the future.

As long as the soul of history is found in the great impulse that it gives to a powerful spirit, as long as the past is principally used as a model for imitation, it is always in danger of being a little altered and touched up, and brought nearer to fiction. Sometimes there is no possible distinction between a "monumental" past and a mythical romance, as the same motives for action can be gathered from the one world as the other. If this monumental method of surveying the past dominate the others,—the antiquarian and the critical,—the past itself suffers wrong. Whole tracts of it are forgotten and despised; they flow away like a dark unbroken river, with only a few gaily coloured islands of fact rising above it. There is something beyond nature in the rare figures that become visible, like the golden hips that his disciples attributed to Pythagoras. Monumental history lives by false analogy; it entices the brave to rashness, and the enthusiastic to fanaticism by its tempting comparisons. Imagine this history in the hands—and the head—of a gifted egoist or an inspired scoundrel; kingdoms will be overthrown, princes murdered, war and revolution let loose, and the number of "effects in themselves"—in other words, effects without sufficient cause—increased. So much for the harm done by monumental history to the powerful men of action, be they good or bad; but what if the weak and the inactive take it as their servant—or their master!

Consider the simplest and commonest example, the inartistic or half artistic natures whom a monumental history provides with sword and buckler. They will use the weapons against their hereditary enemies, the great artistic spirits, who alone can learn from that history the one real lesson, how to live, and embody what they have learnt in noble action. Their way is obstructed, their free air darkened by the idolatrous—and conscientious—dance round the half understood monument of a great past. "See, that is the true and real art," we seem to hear: "of what use are these aspiring little people of to-day?" The dancing crowd has apparently the monopoly of "good taste": for the creator is always at a disadvantage compared with the mere looker-on, who never put a hand to the work; just as the arm-chair politician has ever had more wisdom and foresight than the actual statesman. But if the custom of democratic suffrage and numerical majorities be transferred to the realm of art, and the artist put on his defence before the court of æsthetic dilettanti, you may take your oath on his condemnation; although, or rather because, his judges had proclaimed solemnly the canon of "monumental art," the art that has "had an effect on all ages," according to the official definition. In their eyes no need nor inclination nor historical authority is in favour of the art which is not yet "monumental" because it is contemporary. Their instinct tells them that art can be slain by art: the monumental will never be reproduced, and the weight of its authority is invoked from the past to make it sure. They are connoisseurs of art, primarily because they wish to kill art; they pretend to be physicians, when their real idea is to dabble in poisons. They develop their tastes to a point of perversion, that they may be able to show a reason for continually rejecting all the nourishing artistic fare that is offered them. For they do not want greatness, to arise: their method is to say, "See, the great thing is already here!" In reality they care as little about the great thing that is already here, as that which is about to arise: their lives are evidence of that. Monumental history is the cloak under which their hatred of present power and greatness masquerades as an extreme admiration of the past: the real meaning of this way of viewing history is disguised as its opposite; whether they wish it or no, they are acting as though their motto were, "let the dead bury the—living."

Each of the three kinds of history will only flourish in one ground and climate: otherwise it grows to a noxious weed. If the man who will produce something great, have need of the past, he makes himself its master by means of monumental history: the man who can rest content with the traditional and venerable, uses the past as an "antiquarian historian": and only he whose heart is oppressed by an instant need, and who will cast the burden off at any price, feels the want of "critical history," the history that judges and condemns. There is much harm wrought by wrong and thoughtless planting: the critic without the need, the antiquary without piety, the knower of the great deed who cannot be the doer of it, are plants that have grown to weeds, they are torn from their native soil and therefore degenerate.

III.

Secondly, history is necessary to the man of conservative and reverent nature, who looks back to the origins of his existence with love and trust; through it, he gives thanks for life. He is careful to preserve what survives from ancient days, and will reproduce the conditions of his own upbringing for those who come after him; thus he does life a service. The possession of his ancestors' furniture changes its meaning in his soul: for his soul is rather possessed by it. All that is small and limited, mouldy and obsolete, gains a worth and inviolability of its own from the conservative and reverent soul of the antiquary migrating into it, and building a secret nest there. The history of his town becomes the history of himself; he looks on the walls, the turreted gate, the town council, the fair, as an illustrated diary of his youth, and sees himself in it all—his strength, industry, desire, reason, faults and follies. "Here one could live," he says, "as one can live here now—and will go on living; for we are tough folk, and will not be uprooted in the night." And so, with his "we," he surveys the marvellous individual life of the past and identifies himself with the spirit of the house, the family and the city. He greets the soul of his people from afar as his own, across the dim and troubled centuries: his gifts and his virtues lie in such power of feeling and divination, his scent of a half-vanished trail, his instinctive correctness in reading the scribbled past, and understanding at once its palimpsests—nay, its polypsests. Goethe stood with such thoughts before the monument of Erwin von Steinbach: the storm of his feeling rent the historical cloud-veil that hung between them, and he saw the German work for the first time "coming from the stern, rough, German soul." This was the road that the Italians of the Renaissance travelled, the spirit that reawakened the ancient Italic genius in their poets to "a wondrous echo of the immemorial lyre," as Jacob Burckhardt says. But the greatest value of this antiquarian spirit of reverence lies in the simple emotions of pleasure and content that it lends to the drab, rough, even painful circumstances of a nation's or individual's life: Niebuhr confesses that he could live happily on a moor among free peasants with a history, and would never feel the want of art. How could history serve life better than by anchoring the less gifted races and peoples to the homes and customs of their ancestors, and keeping them from ranging far afield in search of better, to find only struggle and competition? The influence that ties men down to the same companions and circumstances, to the daily round of toil, to their bare mountain-side,—seems to be selfish and unreasonable: but it is a healthy unreason and of profit to the community; as every one knows who has clearly realised the terrible consequences of mere desire for migration and adventure,—perhaps in whole peoples,—or who watches the destiny of a nation that has lost confidence in its earlier days, and is given up to a restless cosmopolitanism and an unceasing desire for novelty. The feeling of the tree that clings to its roots, the happiness of knowing one's growth to be one not merely arbitrary and fortuitous, but the inheritance, the fruit and blossom of a past, that does not merely justify but crown the present—this is what we nowadays prefer to call the real historical sense.

These are not the conditions most favourable to reducing the past to pure science: and we see here too, as we saw in the case of monumental history, that the past itself suffers when history serves life and is directed by its end. To vary the metaphor, the tree feels its roots better than it can see them: the greatness of the feeling is measured by the greatness and strength of the visible branches. The tree may be wrong here; how far more wrong will it be in regard to the whole forest, which it only knows and feels so far as it is hindered or helped by it, and not otherwise! The antiquarian sense of a man, a city or a nation has always a very limited field. Many things are not noticed at all; the others are seen in isolation, as through a microscope. There is no measure: equal importance is given to everything, and therefore too much to anything. For the things of the past are never viewed in their true perspective or receive their just value; but value and perspective change with the individual or the nation that is looking back on its past.

There is always the danger here, that everything ancient will be regarded as equally venerable, and everything without this respect for antiquity, like a new spirit, rejected as an enemy. The Greeks themselves admitted the archaic style of plastic art by the side of the freer and greater style; and later, did not merely tolerate the pointed nose and the cold mouth, but made them even a canon of taste. If the judgment of a people harden in this way, and history's service to the past life be to undermine a further and higher life; if the historical sense no longer preserve life, but mummify it: then the tree dies, unnaturally, from the top downwards, and at last the roots themselves wither. Antiquarian history degenerates from the moment that it no longer gives a soul and inspiration to the fresh life of the present. The spring of piety is dried up, but the learned habit persists without it and revolves complaisantly round its own centre. The horrid spectacle is seen of the mad collector raking over all the dust-heaps of the past. He breathes a mouldy air; the antiquarian habit may degrade a considerable talent, a real spiritual need in him, to a mere insatiable curiosity for everything old: he often sinks so low as to be satisfied with any food, and greedily devour all the scraps that fall from the bibliographical table.

Even if this degeneration do not take place, and the foundation be not withered on which antiquarian history can alone take root with profit to life: yet there are dangers enough, if it become too powerful and invade the territories of the other methods. It only understands how to preserve life, not to create it; and thus always undervalues the present growth, having, unlike monumental history, no certain instinct for it. Thus it hinders the mighty impulse to a new deed and paralyses the doer, who must always, as doer, be grazing some piety or other. The fact that has grown old carries with it a demand for its own immortality. For when one considers the life-history of such an ancient fact, the amount of reverence paid to it for generations—whether it be a custom, a religious creed, or a political principle,—it seems presumptuous, even impious, to replace it by a new fact, and the ancient congregation of pieties by a new piety.

Here we see clearly how necessary a third way of looking at the past is to man, beside the other two. This is the "critical" way; which is also in the service of life. Man must have the strength to break up the past; and apply it too, in order to live. He must bring the past to the bar of judgment, interrogate it remorselessly, and finally condemn it. Every past is worth condemning: this is the rule in mortal affairs, which always contain a large measure of human power and human weakness. It is not justice that sits in judgment here; nor mercy that proclaims the verdict; but only life, the dim, driving force that insatiably desires—itself. Its sentence is always unmerciful, always unjust, as it never flows from a pure fountain of knowledge: though it would generally turn out the same, if Justice herself delivered it. "For everything that is born is worthy of being destroyed: better were it then that nothing should be born." It requires great strength to be able to live and forget how far life and injustice are one. Luther himself once said that the world only arose by an oversight of God; if he had ever dreamed of heavy ordnance, he would never have created it. The same life that needs forgetfulness, needs sometimes its destruction; for should the injustice of something ever become obvious—a monopoly, a caste, a dynasty for example—the thing deserves to fall. Its past is critically examined, the knife put to its roots, and all the "pieties" are grimly trodden under foot. The process is always dangerous, even for life; and the men or the times that serve life in this way, by judging and annihilating the past, are always dangerous to themselves and others. For as we are merely the resultant of previous generations, we are also the resultant of their errors, passions, and crimes: it is impossible to shake off this chain. Though we condemn the errors and think we have escaped them, we cannot escape the fact that we spring from them. At best, it comes to a conflict between our innate, inherited nature and our knowledge, between a stern, new discipline and an ancient tradition; and we plant a new way of life, a new instinct, a second nature, that withers the first. It is an attempt to gain a past a posteriori from which we might spring, as against that from which we do spring; always a dangerous attempt, as it is difficult to find a limit to the denial of the past, and the second natures are generally weaker than the first. We stop too often at knowing the good without doing it, because we also know the better but cannot do it. Here and there the victory is won, which gives a strange consolation to the fighters, to those who use critical history for the sake of life. The consolation is the knowledge that this "first nature" was once a second, and that every conquering "second nature" becomes a first.

IV.

This is how history can serve life. Every man and nation needs a certain knowledge of the past, whether it be through monumental, antiquarian, or critical history, according to his objects, powers, and necessities. The need is not that of the mere thinkers who only look on at life, or the few who desire knowledge and can only be satisfied with knowledge; but it has always a reference to the end of life, and is under its absolute rule and direction. This is the natural relation of an age, a culture and a people to history; hunger is its source, necessity its norm, the inner plastic power assigns its limits. The knowledge of the past is only desired for the service of the future and the present, not to weaken the present or undermine a living future. All this is as simple as truth itself, and quite convincing to any one who is not in the toils of "historical deduction."

And now to take a quick glance at our time! We fly back in astonishment. The clearness, naturalness, and purity of the connection between life and history has vanished; and in what a maze of exaggeration and contradiction do we now see the problem! Is the guilt ours who see it, or have life and history really altered their conjunction and an inauspicious star risen between them? Others may prove we have seen falsely; I am merely saying what we believe we see. There is such a star, a bright and lordly star, and the conjunction is really altered—by science, and the demand for history to be a science. Life is no more dominant, and knowledge of the past no longer its thrall: boundary marks are overthrown everything bursts its limits. The perspective of events is blurred, and the blur extends through their whole immeasurable course. No generation has seen such a panoramic comedy as is shown by the "science of universal evolution," history; that shows it with the dangerous audacity of its motto—"Fiat veritas, pereat vita."

Let me give a picture of the spiritual events in the soul of the modern man. Historical knowledge streams on him from sources that are inexhaustible, strange incoherencies come together, memory opens all its gates and yet is never open wide enough, nature busies herself to receive all the foreign guests, to honour them and put them in their places. But they are at war with each other: violent measures seem necessary, in order to escape destruction one's self. It becomes second nature to grow gradually accustomed to this irregular and stormy home-life, though this second nature is unquestionably weaker, more restless, more radically unsound than the first. The modern man carries inside him an enormous heap of indigestible knowledge-stones that occasionally rattle together in his body, as the fairy-tale has it. And the rattle reveals the most striking characteristic of these modern men, the opposition of something inside them to which nothing external corresponds; and the reverse. The ancient nations knew nothing of this. Knowledge, taken in excess without hunger, even contrary to desire, has no more the effect of transforming the external life; and remains hidden in a chaotic inner world that the modern man has a curious pride in calling his "real personality." He has the substance, he says, and only wants the form; but this is quite an unreal opposition in a living thing. Our modern culture is for that reason not a living one, because it cannot be understood without that opposition. In other words, it is not a real culture but a kind of knowledge about culture, a complex of various thoughts and feelings about it, from which no decision as to its direction can come. Its real motive force that issues in visible action is often no more than a mere convention, a wretched imitation, or even a shameless caricature. The man probably feels like the snake that has swallowed a rabbit whole and lies still in the sun, avoiding all movement not absolutely necessary. The "inner life" is now the only thing that matters to education, and all who see it hope that the education may not fail by being too indigestible. Imagine a Greek meeting it; he would observe that for modern men "education" and "historical education" seem to mean the same thing, with the difference that the one phrase is longer. And if he spoke of his own theory, that a man can be very well educated without any history at all, people would shake their heads and think they had not heard aright. The Greeks, the famous people of a past still near to us, had the "unhistorical sense" strongly developed in the period of the greatest power. If a typical child of this age were transported to that world by some enchantment, he would probably find the Greeks very "uneducated." And that discovery would betray the closely guarded secret of modern culture to the laughter of the world. For we moderns have nothing of our own. We only become worth notice by filling ourselves to overflowing with foreign customs, arts, philosophies, religions and sciences: we are wandering encyclopædias, as an ancient Greek who had strayed into our time would probably call us. But the only value of an encyclopædia lies in the inside, in the contents, not in what is written outside, in the binding or the wrapper. And so the whole of modern culture is essentially internal; the bookbinder prints something like this on the cover: "Manual of internal culture for external barbarians." The opposition of inner and outer makes the outer side still more barbarous, as it would naturally be, when the outward growth of a rude people merely developed its primitive inner needs. For what means has nature of repressing too great a luxuriance from without? Only one,—to be affected by it as little as possible, to set it aside and stamp it out at the first opportunity. And so we have the custom of no longer taking real things seriously, we get the feeble personality on which the real and the permanent make so little impression. Men become at last more careless and accommodating in external matters, and the considerable cleft between substance and form is widened; until they have no longer any feeling for barbarism, if only their memories be kept continually titillated, and there flow a constant stream of new things to be known, that can be neatly packed up in the cupboards of their memory. The culture of a people as against this barbarism, can be, I think, described with justice as the "unity of artistic style in every outward expression of the people's life." This must not be misunderstood, as though it were merely a question of the opposition between barbarism and "fine style." The people that can be called cultured, must be in a real sense a living unity, and not be miserably cleft asunder into form and substance. If one wish to promote a people's culture, let him try to promote this higher unity first, and work for the destruction of the modern educative system for the sake of a true education. Let him dare to consider how the health of a people that has been destroyed by history may be restored, and how it may recover its instincts with its honour.

I am only speaking, directly, about the Germans of the present day, who have had to suffer more than other people from the feebleness of personality and the opposition of substance and form. "Form" generally implies for us some convention, disguise or hypocrisy, and if not hated, is at any rate not loved. We have an extraordinary fear of both the word convention and the thing. This fear drove the German from the French school; for he wished to become more natural, and therefore more German. But he seems to have come to a false conclusion with his "therefore." First he ran away from his school of convention, and went by any road he liked: he has come ultimately to imitate voluntarily in a slovenly fashion, what he imitated painfully and often successfully before. So now the lazy fellow lives under French conventions that are actually incorrect: his manner of walking shows it, his conversation and dress, his general way of life. In the belief that he was returning to Nature, he merely followed caprice and comfort, with the smallest possible amount of self-control. Go through any German town; you will see conventions that are nothing but the negative aspect of the national characteristics of foreign states. Everything is colourless, worn out, shoddy and ill-copied. Every one acts at his own sweet will—which is not a strong or serious will—on laws dictated by the universal rush and the general desire for comfort. A dress that made no head ache in its inventing and wasted no time in the making, borrowed from foreign models and imperfectly copied, is regarded as an important contribution to German fashion. The sense of form is ironically disclaimed by the people—for they have the "sense of substance": they are famous for their cult of "inwardness."

But there is also a famous danger in their "inwardness": the internal substance cannot be seen from the outside, and so may one day take the opportunity of vanishing, and no one notice its absence, any more than its presence before. One may think the German people to be very far from this danger: yet the foreigner will have some warrant for his reproach that our inward life is too weak and ill-organised to provide a form and external expression for itself. It may in rare cases show itself finely receptive, earnest and powerful, richer perhaps than the inward life of other peoples; but, taken as a whole, it remains weak, as all its fine threads are not tied together in one strong knot. The visible action is not the self-manifestation of the inward life, but only a weak and crude attempt of a single thread to make a show of representing the whole. And thus the German is not to be judged on any one action, for the individual may be as completely obscure after it as before. He must obviously be measured by his thoughts and feelings, which are now expressed in his books; if only the books did not, more than ever, raise the doubt whether the famous inward life is still really sitting in its inaccessible shrine. It might one day vanish and leave behind it only the external life,—with its vulgar pride and vain servility,—to mark the German. Fearful thought!—as fearful as if the inward life still sat there, painted and rouged and disguised, become a play-actress or something worse; as his theatrical experience seems to have taught the quiet observer Grillparzer, standing aside as he did from the main press. "We feel by theory," he says. "We hardly know any more how our contemporaries give expression to their feelings: we make them use gestures that are impossible nowadays. Shakespeare has spoilt us moderns."

This is a single example, its general application perhaps too hastily assumed. But how terrible it would be were that generalisation justified before our eyes! There would be then a note of despair in the phrase, "We Germans feel by theory, we are all spoilt by history;"—a phrase that would cut at the roots of any hope for a future national culture. For every hope of that kind grows from the belief in the genuineness and immediacy of German feeling, from the belief in an untarnished inward life. Where is our hope or belief, when its spring is muddied, and the inward quality has learned gestures and dances and the use of cosmetics, has learned to express itself "with due reflection in abstract terms," and gradually lose itself? And how should a great productive spirit exist among a nation that is not sure of its inward unity and is divided into educated men whose inner life has been drawn from the true path of education, and uneducated men whose inner life cannot be approached at all? How should it exist, I say, when the people has lost its own unity of feeling, and knows that the feeling of the part calling itself the educated part and claiming the right of controlling the artistic spirit of the nation, is false and hypocritical? Here and there the judgment and taste of individuals may be higher and finer than the rest, but that is no compensation: it tortures a man to have to speak only to one section and be no longer in sympathy with his people. He would rather bury his treasure now, in disgust at the vulgar patronage of a class, though his heart be filled with tenderness for all. The instinct of the people can no longer meet him half-way; it is useless for them to stretch their arms out to him in yearning. What remains but to turn his quickened hatred against the ban, strike at the barrier raised by the so-called culture, and condemn as judge what blasted and degraded him as a living man and a source of life? He takes a profound insight into fate in exchange for the godlike desire of creation and help, and ends his days as a lonely philosopher, with the wisdom of disillusion. It is the painfullest comedy: he who sees it will feel a sacred obligation on him, and say to himself,—"Help must come: the higher unity in the nature and soul of a people must be brought back, the cleft between inner and outer must again disappear under the hammer of necessity." But to what means can he look? What remains to him now but his knowledge? He hopes to plant the feeling of a need, by speaking from the breadth of that knowledge, giving it freely with both hands. From the strong need the strong action may one day arise. And to leave no doubt of the instance I am taking of the need and the knowledge, my testimony shall stand, that it is German unity in its highest sense which is the goal of our endeavour, far more than political union: it is the unity of the German spirit and life after the annihilation of the antagonism between form and substance, inward life and convention.

V.

An excess of history seems to be an enemy to the life of a time, and dangerous in five ways. Firstly, the contrast of inner and outer is emphasised and personality weakened. Secondly, the time comes to imagine that it possesses the rarest of virtues, justice, to a higher degree than any other time. Thirdly, the instincts of a nation are thwarted, the maturity of the individual arrested no less than that of the whole. Fourthly, we get the belief in the old age of mankind, the belief, at all times harmful, that we are late survivals, mere Epigoni. Lastly, an age reaches a dangerous condition of irony with regard to itself, and the still more dangerous state of cynicism, when a cunning egoistic theory of action is matured that maims and at last destroys the vital strength.

To return to the first point: the modern man suffers from a weakened personality. The Roman of the Empire ceased to be a Roman through the contemplation of the world that lay at his feet; he lost himself in the crowd of foreigners that streamed into Rome, and degenerated amid the cosmopolitan carnival of arts, worships and moralities. It is the same with the modern man, who is continually having a world-panorama unrolled before his eyes by his historical artists. He is turned into a restless, dilettante spectator, and arrives at a condition when even great wars and revolutions cannot affect him beyond the moment. The war is hardly at an end, and it is already converted into thousands of copies of printed matter, and will be soon served up as the latest means of tickling the jaded palates of the historical gourmets. It seems impossible for a strong full chord to be prolonged, however powerfully the strings are swept: it dies away again the next moment in the soft and strengthless echo of history. In ethical language, one never succeeds in staying on a height; your deeds are sudden crashes, and not a long roll of thunder. One may bring the greatest and most marvellous thing to perfection; it must yet go down to Orcus unhonoured and unsung. For art flies away when you are roofing your deeds with the historical awning. The man who wishes to understand everything in a moment, when he ought to grasp the unintelligible as the sublime by a long struggle, can be called intelligent only in the sense of Schiller's epigram on the "reason of reasonable men." There is something the child sees that he does not see; something the child hears that he does not hear; and this something is the most important thing of all. Because he does not understand it, his understanding is more childish than the child's and more simple than simplicity itself; in spite of the many clever wrinkles on his parchment face, and the masterly play of his fingers in unravelling the knots. He has lost or destroyed his instinct; he can no longer trust the "divine animal" and let the reins hang loose, when his understanding fails him and his way lies through the desert. His individuality is shaken, and left without any sure belief in itself; it sinks into its own inner being, which only means here the disordered chaos of what it has learned, which will never express itself externally, being mere dogma that cannot turn to life. Looking further, we see how the banishment of instinct by history has turned men to shades and abstractions: no one ventures to show a personality, but masks himself as a man of culture, a savant, poet or politician.

If one take hold of these masks, believing he has to do with a serious thing and not a mere puppet-show—for they all have an appearance of seriousness—he will find nothing but rags and coloured streamers in his hands. He must deceive himself no more, but cry aloud, "Off with your jackets, or be what you seem!" A man of the royal stock of seriousness must no longer be Don Quixote, for he has better things to do than to tilt at such pretended realities. But he must always keep a sharp look about him, call his "Halt! who goes there?" to all the shrouded figures, and tear the masks from their faces. And see the result! One might have thought that history encouraged men above all to be honest, even if it were only to be honest fools: this used to be its effect, but is so no longer. Historical education and the uniform frock-coat of the citizen are both dominant at the same time. While there has never been such a full-throated chatter about "free personality," personalities can be seen no more (to say nothing of free ones); but merely men in uniform, with their coats anxiously pulled over their ears. Individuality has withdrawn itself to its recesses; it is seen no more from the outside, which makes one doubt if it be possible to have causes without effects. Or will a race of eunuchs prove to be necessary to guard the historical harem of the world? We can understand the reason for their aloofness very well. Does it not seem as if their task were to watch over history to see that nothing comes out except other histories, but no deed that might be historical; to prevent personalities becoming "free," that is, sincere towards themselves and others, both in word and deed? Only through this sincerity will the inner need and misery of the modern man be brought to the light, and art and religion come as true helpers in the place of that sad hypocrisy of convention and masquerade, to plant a common culture which will answer to real necessities, and not teach, as the present "liberal education" teaches, to tell lies about these needs, and thus become a walking lie one's self.

In such an age, that suffers from its "liberal education," how unnatural, artificial and unworthy will be the conditions under which the sincerest of all sciences, the holy naked goddess Philosophy, must exist! She remains, in such a world of compulsion and outward conformity, the subject of the deep monologue of the lonely wanderer or the chance prey of any hunter, the dark secret of the chamber or the daily talk of the old men and children at the university. No one dare fulfil the law of philosophy in himself; no one lives philosophically, with that single-hearted virile faith that forced one of the olden time to bear himself as a Stoic, wherever he was and whatever he did, if he had once sworn allegiance to the Stoa. All modern philosophising is political or official, bound down to be a mere phantasmagoria of learning by our modern governments, churches, universities, moralities and cowardices: it lives by sighing "if only...." and by knowing that "it happened once upon a time...." Philosophy has no place in historical education, if it will be more than the knowledge that lives indoors, and can have no expression in action. Were the modern man once courageous and determined, and not merely such an indoor being even in his hatreds, he would banish philosophy. At present he is satisfied with modestly covering her nakedness. Yes, men think, write, print, speak and teach philosophically: so much is permitted them. It is only otherwise in action, in "life." Only one thing is permitted there, and everything else quite impossible: such are the orders of historical education. "Are these human beings," one might ask, "or only machines for thinking, writing and speaking?"

Goethe says of Shakespeare: "No one has more despised correctness of costume than he: he knows too well the inner costume that all men wear alike. You hear that he describes Romans wonderfully; I do not think so: they are flesh-and-blood Englishmen; but at any rate they are men from top to toe, and the Roman toga sits well on them." Would it be possible, I wonder, to represent our present literary and national heroes, officials and politicians as Romans? I am sure it would not, as they are no men, but incarnate compendia, abstractions made concrete. If they have a character of their own, it is so deeply sunk that it can never rise to the light of day: if they are men, they are only men to a physiologist. To all others they are something else, not men, not "beasts or gods," but historical pictures of the march of civilisation, and nothing but pictures and civilisation, form without any ascertainable substance, bad form unfortunately, and uniform at that. And in this way my thesis is to be understood and considered: "only strong personalities can endure history, the weak are extinguished by it." History unsettles the feelings when they are not powerful enough to measure the past by themselves. The man who dare no longer trust himself, but asks history against his will for advice "how he ought to feel now," is insensibly turned by his timidity into a play-actor, and plays a part, or generally many parts,—very badly therefore and superficially. Gradually all connection ceases between the man and his historical subjects. We see noisy little fellows measuring themselves with the Romans as though they were like them: they burrow in the remains of the Greek poets, as if these were corpora for their dissection—and as vilia as their own well-educated corpora might be. Suppose a man is working at Democritus. The question is always on my tongue, why precisely Democritus? Why not Heraclitus, or Philo, or Bacon, or Descartes? And then, why a philosopher? Why not a poet or orator? And why especially a Greek? Why not an Englishman or a Turk? Is not the past large enough to let you find some place where you may disport yourself without becoming ridiculous? But, as I said, they are a race of eunuchs: and to the eunuch one woman is the same as another, merely a woman, "woman in herself," the Ever-unapproachable. And it is indifferent what they study, if history itself always remain beautifully "objective" to them, as men, in fact, who could never make history themselves. And since the Eternal Feminine could never "draw you upward," you draw it down to you, and being neuter yourselves, regard history as neuter also. But in order that no one may take any comparison of history and the Eternal Feminine too seriously, I will say at once that I hold it, on the contrary, to be the Eternal Masculine: I only add that for those who are "historically trained" throughout, it must be quite indifferent which it is; for they are themselves neither man nor woman, nor even hermaphrodite, but mere neuters, or, in more philosophic language, the Eternal Objective.

If the personality be once emptied of its subjectivity, and come to what men call an "objective" condition, nothing can have any more effect on it. Something good and true may be done, in action, poetry or music: but the hollow culture of the day will look beyond the work and ask the history of the author. If the author have already created something, our historian will set out clearly the past and the probable future course of his development, he will put him with others and compare them, and separate by analysis the choice of his material and his treatment; he will wisely sum the author up and give him general advice for his future path. The most astonishing works may be created; the swarm of historical neuters will always be in their place, ready to consider the authors through their long telescopes. The echo is heard at once: but always in the form of "criticism," though the critic never dreamed of the work's possibility a moment before. It never comes to have an influence, but only a criticism: and the criticism itself has no influence, but only breeds another criticism. And so we come to consider the fact of many critics as a mark of influence, that of few or none as a mark of failure. Actually everything remains in the old condition, even in the presence of such "influence": men talk a little while of a new thing, and then of some other new thing, and in the meantime they do what they have always done. The historical training of our critics prevents their having an influence in the true sense, an influence on life and action. They put their blotting paper on the blackest writing, and their thick brushes over the gracefullest designs; these they call "corrections";—and that is all. Their critical pens never cease to fly, for they have lost power over them; they are driven by their pens instead of driving them. The weakness of modern personality comes out well in the measureless overflow of criticism, in the want of self-mastery, and in what the Romans called impotentia.

VI.

But leaving these weaklings, let us turn rather to a point of strength for which the modern man is famous. Let us ask the painful question whether he has the right in virtue of his historical "objectivity" to call himself strong and just in a higher degree than the man of another age. Is it true that this objectivity has its source in a heightened sense of the need for justice? Or, being really an effect of quite other causes, does it only have the appearance of coming from justice, and really lead to an unhealthy prejudice in favour of the modern man? Socrates thought it near madness to imagine one possessed a virtue without really possessing it. Such imagination has certainly more danger in it than the contrary madness of a positive vice. For of this there is still a cure; but the other makes a man or a time daily worse, and therefore more unjust.

No one has a higher claim to our reverence than the man with the feeling and the strength for justice. For the highest and rarest virtues unite and are lost in it, as an unfathomable sea absorbs the streams that flow from every side. The hand of the just man, who is called to sit in judgment, trembles no more when it holds the scales: he piles the weights inexorably against his own side, his eyes are not dimmed as the balance rises and falls, and his voice is neither hard nor broken when he pronounces the sentence. Were he a cold demon of knowledge, he would cast round him the icy atmosphere of an awful, superhuman majesty, that we should fear, not reverence. But he is a man, and has tried to rise from a careless doubt to a strong certainty, from gentle tolerance to the imperative "thou must"; from the rare virtue of magnanimity to the rarest, of justice. He has come to be like that demon without being more than a poor mortal at the outset; above all, he has to atone to himself for his humanity and tragically shatter his own nature on the rock of an impossible virtue.—All this places him on a lonely height as the most reverend example of the human race. For truth is his aim, not in the form of cold intellectual knowledge, but the truth of the judge who punishes according to law; not as the selfish possession of an individual, but the sacred authority that removes the boundary stones from all selfish possessions; truth, in a word, as the tribunal of the world, and not as the chance prey of a single hunter. The search for truth is often thoughtlessly praised: but it only has anything great in it if the seeker have the sincere unconditional will for justice. Its roots are in justice alone: but a whole crowd of different motives may combine in the search for it, that have nothing to do with truth at all; curiosity, for example, or dread of ennui, envy, vanity, or amusement. Thus the world seems to be full of men who "serve truth":

and yet the virtue of justice is seldom present, more seldom known, and almost always mortally hated. On the other hand a throng of sham virtues has entered in at all times with pomp and honour.

Few in truth serve truth, as only few have the pure will for justice; and very few even of these have the strength to be just. The will alone is not enough: the impulse to justice without the power of judgment has been the cause of the greatest suffering to men. And thus the common good could require nothing better than for the seed of this power to be strewn as widely as possible, that the fanatic may be distinguished from the true judge, and the blind desire from the conscious power. But there are no means of planting a power of judgment: and so when one speaks to men of truth and justice, they will be ever troubled by the doubt whether it be the fanatic or the judge who is speaking to them. And they must be pardoned for always treating the "servants of truth" with special kindness, who possess neither the will nor the power to judge and have set before them the task of finding "pure knowledge without reference to consequences," knowledge, in plain terms, that comes to nothing. There are very many truths which are unimportant; problems that require no struggle to solve, to say nothing of sacrifice. And in this safe realm of indifference a man may very successfully become a "cold demon of knowledge." And yet—if we find whole regiments of learned inquirers being turned to such demons in some age specially favourable to them, it is always unfortunately possible that the age is lacking in a great and strong sense of justice, the noblest spring of the so-called impulse to truth.

Consider the historical virtuoso of the present time: is he the justest man of his age? True, he has developed in himself such a delicacy and sensitiveness that "nothing human is alien to him." Times and persons most widely separated come together in the concords of his lyre. He has become a passive instrument, whose tones find an echo in similar instruments: until the whole atmosphere of a time is filled with such echoes, all buzzing in one soft chord. Yet I think one only hears the overtones of the original historical note: its rough powerful quality can be no longer guessed from these thin and shrill vibrations. The original note sang of action, need, and terror; the overtone lulls us into a soft dilettante sleep. It is as though the heroic symphony had been arranged for two flutes for the use of dreaming opium-smokers. We can now judge how these virtuosi stand towards the claim of the modern man to a higher and purer conception of justice. This virtue has never a pleasing quality; it never charms; it is harsh and strident. Generosity stands very low on the ladder of the virtues in comparison; and generosity is the mark of a few rare historians! Most of them only get as far as tolerance, in other words they leave what cannot be explained away, they correct it and touch it up condescendingly, on the tacit assumption that the novice will count it as justice if the past be narrated without harshness or open expressions of hatred. But only superior strength can really judge; weakness must tolerate, if it do not pretend to be strength and turn justice to a play-actress. There is still a dreadful class of historians remaining—clever, stern and honest, but narrow-minded: who have the "good will" to be just with a pathetic belief in their actual judgments, which are all false; for the same reason, almost, as the verdicts of the usual juries are false. How difficult it is to find a real historical talent, if we exclude all the disguised egoists, and the partisans who pretend to take up an impartial attitude for the sake of their own unholy game! And we also exclude the thoughtless folk who write history in the naïve faith that justice resides in the popular view of their time, and that to write in the spirit of the time is to be just; a faith that is found in all religions, and which, in religion, serves very well. The measurement of the opinions and deeds of the past by the universal opinions of the present is called "objectivity" by these simple people: they find the canon of all truth here: their work is to adapt the past to the present triviality. And they call all historical writing "subjective" that does not regard these popular opinions as canonical.

Might not an illusion lurk in the highest interpretation of the word objectivity? We understand by it a certain standpoint in the historian, who sees the procession of motive and consequence too clearly for it to have an effect on his own personality. We think of the æsthetic phenomenon of the detachment from all personal concern with which the painter sees the picture and forgets himself, in a stormy landscape, amid thunder and lightning, or on a rough sea: and we require the same artistic vision and absorption in his object from the historian.

But it is only a superstition to say that the picture given to such a man by the object really shows the truth of things. Unless it be that objects are expected in such moments to paint or photograph themselves by their own activity on a purely passive medium!

But this would be a myth, and a bad one at that. One forgets that this moment is actually the powerful and spontaneous moment of creation in the artist, of "composition" in its highest form, of which the result will be an artistically, but not an historically, true picture. To think objectively, in this sense, of history is the work of the dramatist: to think one thing with another, and weave the elements into a single whole; with the presumption that the unity of plan must be put into the objects if it be not already there. So man veils and subdues the past, and expresses his impulse to art—but not his impulse to truth or justice. Objectivity and justice have nothing to do with each other. There could be a kind of historical writing that had no drop of common fact in it and yet could claim to be called in the highest degree objective. Grillparzer goes so far as to say that "history is nothing but the manner in which the spirit of man apprehends facts that are obscure to him, links things together whose connection heaven only knows, replaces the unintelligible by something intelligible, puts his own ideas of causation into the external world, which can perhaps be explained only from within: and assumes the existence of chance, where thousands of small causes may be really at work. Each man has his own individual needs, and so millions of tendencies are running together, straight or crooked, parallel or across, forward or backward, helping or hindering each other. They have all the appearance of chance, and make it impossible, quite apart from all natural influences, to establish any universal lines on which past events must have run." But as a result of this so-called "objective" way of looking at things, such a "must" ought to be made clear. It is a presumption that takes a curious form if adopted by the historian as a dogma. Schiller is quite clear about its truly subjective nature when he says of the historian, "one event after the other begins to draw away from blind chance and lawless freedom, and take its place as the member of an harmonious whole—which is of course only apparent in its presentation." But what is one to think of the innocent statement, wavering between tautology and nonsense, of a famous historical virtuoso? "It seems that all human actions and impulses are subordinate to the process of the material world, that works unnoticed, powerfully and irresistibly." In such a sentence one no longer finds obscure wisdom in the form of obvious folly; as in the saying of Goethe's gardener, "Nature may be forced but not compelled," or in the notice on the side-show at a fair, in Swift: "The largest elephant in the world, except himself, to be seen here." For what opposition is there between human action and the process of the world? It seems to me that such historians cease to be instructive as soon as they begin to generalise; their weakness is shown by their obscurity. In other sciences the generalisations are the most important things, as they contain the laws. But if such generalisations as these are to stand as laws, the historian's labour is lost; for the residue of truth, after the obscure and insoluble part is removed, is nothing but the commonest knowledge. The smallest range of experience will teach it. But to worry whole peoples for the purpose, and spend many hard years of work on it, is like crowding one scientific experiment on another long after the law can be deduced from the results already obtained: and this absurd excess of experiment has been the bane of all natural science since Zollner. If the value of a drama lay merely in its final scene, the drama itself would be a very long, crooked and laborious road to the goal: and I hope history will not find its whole significance in general propositions, and regard them as its blossom and fruit. On the contrary, its real value lies in inventing ingenious variations on a probably commonplace theme, in raising the popular melody to a universal symbol and showing what a world of depth, power and beauty exists in it.

But this requires above all a great artistic faculty, a creative vision from a height, the loving study of the data of experience, the free elaborating of a given type,—objectivity in fact, though this time as a positive quality. Objectivity is so often merely a phrase. Instead of the quiet gaze of the artist that is lit by an inward flame, we have an affectation of tranquillity; just as a cold detachment may mask a lack of moral feeling. In some cases a triviality of thought, the everyday wisdom that is too dull not to seem calm and disinterested, comes to represent the artistic condition in which the subjective side has quite sunk out of sight. Everything is favoured that does not rouse emotion, and the driest phrase is the correct one. They go so far as to accept a man who is not affected at all by some particular moment in the past as the right man to describe it. This is the usual relation of the Greeks and the classical scholars. They have nothing to do with each other—and this is called "objectivity"! The intentional air of detachment that is assumed for effect, the sober art of the superficial motive-hunter is most exasperating when the highest and rarest things are in question; and it is the vanity of the historian that drives him to this attitude of indifference. He goes to justify the axiom that a man's vanity corresponds to his lack of wit. No, be honest at any rate! Do not pretend to the artist's strength, that is the real objectivity; do not try to be just, if you are not born to that dread vocation. As if it were the task of every time to be just to everything before it! Ages and generations have never the right to be the judges of all previous ages and generations: only to the rarest men in them can that difficult mission fall. Who compels you to judge? If it is your wish—you must prove first that you are capable of justice. As judges, you must stand higher than that which is to be judged: as it is, you have only come later. The guests that come last to the table should rightly take the last places: and will you take the first? Then do some great and mighty deed: the place may be prepared for you then, even though you do come last.

You can only explain the past by what is highest in the present. Only by straining the noblest qualities you have to their highest power will you find out what is greatest in the past, most worth knowing and preserving. Like by like! otherwise you will draw the past to your own level. Do not believe any history that does not spring from the mind of a rare spirit. You will know the quality of the spirit, by its being forced to say something universal, or to repeat something that is known already; the fine historian must have the power of coining the known into a thing never heard before and proclaiming the universal so simply and profoundly that the simple is lost in the profound, and the profound in the simple. No one can be a great historian and artist, and a shallowpate at the same time. But one must not despise the workers who sift and cast together the material because they can never become great historians. They must, still less, be confounded with them, for they are the necessary bricklayers and apprentices in the service of the master: just as the French used to speak, more naïvely than a German would, of the "historiens de M. Thiers." These workmen should gradually become extremely learned, but never, for that reason, turn to be masters. Great learning and great shallowness go together very well under one hat.

Thus, history is to be written by the man of experience and character. He who has not lived through something greater and nobler than others, will not be able to explain anything great and noble in the past. The language of the past is always oracular: you will only understand it as builders of the future who know the present. We can only explain the extraordinarily wide influence of Delphi by the fact that the Delphic priests had an exact knowledge of the past: and, similarly, only he who is building up the future has a right to judge the past. If you set a great aim before your eyes, you control at the same time the itch for analysis that makes the present into a desert for you, and all rest, all peaceful growth and ripening, impossible. Hedge yourselves with a great, all-embracing hope, and strive on. Make of yourselves a mirror where the future may see itself, and forget the superstition that you are Epigoni. You have enough to ponder and find out, in pondering the life of the future: but do not ask history to show you the means and the instrument to it. If you live yourselves back into the history of great men, you will find in it the high command to come to maturity and leave that blighting system of cultivation offered by your time: which sees its own profit in not allowing you to become ripe, that it may use and dominate you while you are yet unripe. And if you want biographies, do not look for those with the legend "Mr. So-and-so and his times," but for one whose title-page might be inscribed "a fighter against his time." Feast your souls on Plutarch, and dare to believe in yourselves when you believe in his heroes. A hundred such men—educated against the fashion of to-day, made familiar with the heroic, and come to maturity—are enough to give an eternal quietus to the noisy sham education of this time.

VII.

The unrestrained historical sense, pushed to its logical extreme, uproots the future, because it destroys illusions and robs existing things of the only atmosphere in which they can live. Historical justice, even if practised conscientiously, with a pure heart, is therefore a dreadful virtue, because it always undermines and ruins the living thing: its judgment always means annihilation. If there be no constructive impulse behind the historical one, if the clearance of rubbish be not merely to leave the ground free for the hopeful living future to build its house, if justice alone be supreme, the creative instinct is sapped and discouraged. A religion, for example, that has to be turned into a matter of historical knowledge by the power of pure justice, and to be scientifically studied throughout, is destroyed at the end of it all. For the historical audit brings so much to light which is false and absurd, violent and inhuman, that the condition of pious illusion falls to pieces. And a thing can only live through a pious illusion. For man is creative only through love and in the shadow of love's illusions, only through the unconditional belief in perfection and righteousness. Everything that forces a man to be no longer unconditioned in his love, cuts at the root of his strength: he must wither, and be dishonoured. Art has the opposite effect to history: and only perhaps if history suffer transformation into a pure work of art, can it preserve instincts or arouse them. Such history would be quite against the analytical and inartistic tendencies of our time, and even be considered false. But the history that merely destroys without any impulse to construct, will in the long-run make its instruments tired of life; for such men destroy illusions, and "he who destroys illusions in himself and others is punished by the ultimate tyrant, Nature." For a time a man can take up history like any other study, and it will be perfectly harmless. Recent theology seems to have entered quite innocently into partnership with history, and scarcely sees even now that it has unwittingly bound itself to the Voltairean écrasez! No one need expect from that any new and powerful constructive impulse: they might as well have let the so-called Protestant Union serve as the cradle of a new religion, and the jurist Holtzendorf, the editor of the far more dubiously named Protestant Bible, be its John the Baptist.

This state of innocence may be continued for some time by the Hegelian philosophy,—still seething in some of the older heads,—by which men can distinguish the "idea of Christianity" from its various imperfect "manifestations"; and persuade themselves that it is the "self-movement of the Idea" that is ever particularising itself in purer and purer forms, and at last becomes the purest, most transparent, in fact scarcely visible form in the brain of the present theologus liberalis vulgaris. But to listen to this pure Christianity speaking its mind about the earlier impure Christianity, the uninitiated hearer would often get the impression that the talk was not of Christianity at all but of ...—what are we to think? if we find Christianity described by the "greatest theologians of the century" as the religion that claims to "find itself in all real religions and some other barely possible religions," and if the "true church" is to be a thing "which may become a liquid mass with no fixed outline, with no fixed place for its different parts, but everything to be peacefully welded together"—what, I ask again, are we to think?

Christianity has been denaturalised by historical treatment—which in its most complete form means "just" treatment—until it has been resolved into pure knowledge and destroyed in the process. This can be studied in everything that has life. For it ceases to have life if it be perfectly dissected, and lives in pain and anguish as soon as the historical dissection begins. There are some who believe in the saving power of German music to revolutionise the German nature. They angrily exclaim against the special injustice done to our culture, when such men as Mozart and Beethoven are beginning to be spattered with the learned mud of the biographers and forced to answer a thousand searching questions on the rack of historical criticism. Is it not premature death, or at least mutilation, for anything whose living influence is not yet exhausted, when men turn their curious eyes to the little minutiæ of life and art, and look for problems of knowledge where one ought to learn to live, and forget problems? Set a couple of these modern biographers to consider the origins of Christianity or the Lutheran reformation: their sober, practical investigations would be quite sufficient to make all spiritual "action at a distance" impossible: just as the smallest animal can prevent the growth of the mightiest oak by simply eating up the acorn. All living things need an atmosphere, a mysterious mist, around them. If that veil be taken away and a religion, an art, or a genius condemned to revolve like a star without an atmosphere, we must not be surprised if it becomes hard and unfruitful, and soon withers. It is so with all great things "that never prosper without some illusion," as Hans Sachs says in the Meistersinger.

Every people, every man even, who would become ripe, needs such a veil of illusion, such a protecting cloud. But now men hate to become ripe, for they honour history above life. They cry in triumph that "science is now beginning to rule life." Possibly it might; but a life thus ruled is not of much value. It is not such true life, and promises much less for the future than the life that used to be guided not by science, but by instincts and powerful illusions. But this is not to be the age of ripe, alert and harmonious personalities, but of work that may be of most use to the commonwealth. Men are to be fashioned to the needs of the time, that they may soon take their place in the machine. They must work in the factory of the "common good" before they are ripe, or rather to prevent them becoming ripe; for this would be a luxury that would draw away a deal of power from the "labour market." Some birds are blinded that they may sing better; I do not think men sing to-day better than their grandfathers, though I am sure they are blinded early. But light, too clear, too sudden and dazzling, is the infamous means used to blind them. The young man is kicked through all the centuries: boys who know nothing of war, diplomacy, or commerce are considered fit to be introduced to political history. We moderns also run through art galleries and hear concerts in the same way as the young man runs through history. We can feel that one thing sounds differently from another, and pronounce on the different "effects." And the power of gradually losing all feelings of strangeness or astonishment, and finally being pleased at anything, is called the historical sense, or historical culture. The crowd of influences streaming on the young soul is so great, the clods of barbarism and violence flung at him so strange and overwhelming, that an assumed stupidity is his only refuge. Where there is a subtler and stronger self-consciousness we find another emotion too—disgust. The young man has become homeless: he doubts all ideas, all moralities. He knows "it was different in every age, and what you are does not matter." In a heavy apathy he lets opinion on opinion pass by him, and understands the meaning of Hölderlin's words when he read the work of Diogenes Laertius on the lives and doctrines of the Greek philosophers: "I have seen here too what has often occurred to me, that the change and waste in men's thoughts and systems is far more tragic than the fates that overtake what men are accustomed to call the only realities." No, such study of history bewilders and overwhelms. It is not necessary for youth, as the ancients show, but even in the highest degree dangerous, as the moderns show. Consider the historical student, the heir of ennui, that appears even in his boyhood. He has the "methods" for original work, the "correct ideas" and the airs of the master at his fingers' ends. A little isolated period of the past is marked out for sacrifice. He cleverly applies his method, and produces something, or rather, in prouder phrase, "creates" something. He becomes a "servant of truth" and a ruler in the great domain of history. If he was what they call ripe as a boy, he is now over-ripe. You only need shake him and wisdom will rattle down into your lap; but the wisdom is rotten, and every apple has its worm. Believe me, if men work in the factory of science and have to make themselves useful before they are really ripe, science is ruined as much as the slaves who have been employed too soon. I am sorry to use the common jargon about slave-owners and taskmasters in respect of such conditions, that might be thought free from any economic taint: but the words "factory, labour-market, auction-sale, practical use," and all the auxiliaries of egoism, come involuntarily to the lips in describing the younger generation of savants. Successful mediocrity tends to become still more mediocre, science still more "useful." Our modern savants are only wise on one subject, in all the rest they are, to say the least, different from those of the old stamp. In spite of that they demand honour and profit for themselves, as if the state and public opinion were bound to take the new coinage for the same value as the old. The carters have made a trade-compact among themselves, and settled that genius is superfluous, for every carrier is being re-stamped as one. And probably a later age will see that their edifices are only carted together and not built. To those who have ever on their lips the modern cry of battle and sacrifice—"Division of labour! fall into line!" we may say roundly: "If you try to further the progress of science as quickly as possible, you will end by destroying it as quickly as possible; just as the hen is worn out which you force to lay too many eggs." The progress of science has been amazingly rapid in the last decade; but consider the savants, those exhausted hens. They are certainly not "harmonious" natures: they can merely cackle more than before, because they lay eggs oftener: but the eggs are always smaller, though their books are bigger. The natural result of it all is the favourite "popularising" of science (or rather its feminising and infantising), the villainous habit of cutting the cloth of science to fit the figure of the "general public." Goethe saw the abuse in this, and demanded that science should only influence the outer world by way of a nobler ideal of action. The older generation of savants had good reason for thinking this abuse an oppressive burden: the modern savants have an equally good reason for welcoming it, because, leaving their little corner of knowledge out of account, they are part of the "general public" themselves, and its needs are theirs. They only require to take themselves less seriously to be able to open their little kingdom successfully to popular curiosity. This easy-going behaviour is called "the modest condescension of the savant to the people"; whereas in reality he has only "descended" to himself, so far as he is not a savant but a plebeian. Rise to the conception of a people, you learned men; you can never have one noble or high enough. If you thought much of the people, you would have compassion towards them, and shrink from offering your historical aquafortis as a refreshing drink. But you really think very little of them, for you dare not take any reasonable pains for their future; and you act like practical pessimists, men who feel the coming catastrophe and become indifferent and careless of their own and others' existence. "If only the earth last for us: and if it do not last, it is no matter." Thus they come to live an ironical existence.

VIII.

It may seem a paradox, though it is none, that I should attribute a kind of "ironical self-consciousness" to an age that is generally so honestly, and clamorously, vain of its historical training; and should see a suspicion hovering near it that there is really nothing to be proud of, and a fear lest the time for rejoicing at historical knowledge may soon have gone by. Goethe has shown a similar riddle in man's nature, in his remarkable study of Newton: he finds a "troubled feeling of his own error" at the base—or rather on the height—of his being, just as if he was conscious at times of having a deeper insight into things, that vanished the moment after. This gave him a certain ironical view of his own nature. And one finds that the greater and more developed "historical men" are conscious of all the superstition and absurdity in the belief that a people's education need be so extremely historical as it is; the mightiest nations, mightiest in action and influence, have lived otherwise, and their youth has been trained otherwise. The knowledge gives a sceptical turn to their minds. "The absurdity and superstition," these sceptics say, "suit men like ourselves, who come as the latest withered shoots of a gladder and mightier stock, and fulfil Hesiod's prophecy, that men will one day be born gray-headed, and that Zeus will destroy that generation as soon as the sign be visible." Historical culture is really a kind of inherited grayness, and those who have borne its mark from childhood must believe instinctively in the old age of mankind. To old age belongs the old man's business of looking back and casting up his accounts, of seeking consolation in the memories of the past,—in historical culture. But the human race is tough and persistent, and will not admit that the lapse of a thousand years, or a hundred thousand, entitles any one to sum up its progress from the past to the future; that is, it will not be observed as a whole at all by that infinitesimal atom, the individual man. What is there in a couple of thousand years—the period of thirty-four consecutive human lives of sixty years each—to make us speak of youth at the beginning, and "the old age of mankind" at the end of them? Does not this paralysing belief in a fast-fading humanity cover the misunderstanding of a theological idea, inherited from the Middle Ages, that the end of the world is approaching and we are waiting anxiously for the judgment? Does not the increasing demand for historical judgment give us that idea in a new dress? as if our time were the latest possible time, and commanded to hold that universal judgment of the past, which the Christian never expected from a man, but from "the Son of Man." The memento mori, spoken to humanity as well as the individual, was a sting that never ceased to pain, the crown of mediæval knowledge and consciousness.

The opposite message of a later time, memento vivere, is spoken rather timidly, without the full power of the lungs; and there is something almost dishonest about it. For mankind still keeps to its memento mori, and shows it by the universal need for history; science may flap its wings as it will, it has never been able to gain the free air. A deep feeling of hopelessness has remained, and taken the historical colouring that has now darkened and depressed all higher education. A religion that, of all the hours of man's life, thinks the last the most important, that has prophesied the end of earthly life and condemned all creatures to live in the fifth act of a tragedy, may call forth the subtlest and noblest powers of man, but it is an enemy to all new planting, to all bold attempts or free aspirations. It opposes all flight into the unknown, because it has no life or hope there itself. It only lets the new bud press forth on sufferance, to blight it in its own good time: "it might lead life astray and give it a false value." What the Florentines did under the influence of Savonarola's exhortations, when they made the famous holocaust of pictures, manuscripts, masks and mirrors, Christianity would like to do with every culture that allured to further effort and bore that memento vivere on its standard. And if it cannot take the direct way—the way of main force—it gains its end all the same by allying itself with historical culture, though generally without its connivance; and speaking through its mouth, turns away every fresh birth with a shrug of its shoulders, and makes us feel all the more that we are late-comers and Epigoni, that we are, in a word, born with gray hair. The deep and serious contemplation of the unworthiness of all past action, of the world ripe for judgment, has been whittled down to the sceptical consciousness that it is anyhow a good thing to know all that has happened, as it is too late to do anything better. The historical sense makes its servants passive and retrospective. Only in moments of forgetfulness, when that sense is dormant, does the man who is sick of the historical fever ever act; though he only analyses his deed again after it is over (which prevents it from having any further consequences), and finally puts it on the dissecting table for the purposes of history. In this sense we are still living in the Middle Ages, and history is still a disguised theology; just as the reverence with which the unlearned layman looks on the learned class is inherited through the clergy. What men gave formerly to the Church they give now, though in smaller measure, to science. But the fact of giving at all is the work of the Church, not of the modern spirit, which among its other good qualities has something of the miser in it, and is a bad hand at the excellent virtue of liberality.

These words may not be very acceptable, any more than my derivation of the excess of history from the mediæval memento mori and the hopelessness that Christianity bears in its heart towards all future ages of earthly existence. But you should always try to replace my hesitating explanations by a better one. For the origin of historical culture, and of its absolutely radical antagonism to the spirit of a new time and a "modern consciousness," must itself be known by a historical process. History must solve the problem of history, science must turn its sting against itself. This threefold "must" is the imperative of the "new spirit," if it is really to contain something new, powerful, vital and original. Or is it true that we Germans—to leave the Romance nations out of account—must always be mere "followers" in all the higher reaches of culture, because that is all we can be? The words of Wilhelm Wackernagel are well worth pondering: "We Germans are a nation of 'followers,' and with all our higher science and even our faith, are merely the successors of the ancient world. Even those who are opposed to it are continually breathing the immortal spirit of classical culture with that of Christianity: and if any one could separate these two elements from the living air surrounding the soul of man, there would not be much remaining for a spiritual life to exist on." Even if we would rest content with our vocation to follow antiquity, even if we decided to take it in an earnest and strenuous spirit and to show our high prerogative in our earnestness,—we should yet be compelled to ask whether it were our eternal destiny to be pupils of a fading antiquity. We might be allowed at some time to put our aim higher and further above us. And after congratulating ourselves on having brought that secondary spirit of Alexandrian culture in us to such marvellous productiveness—through our "universal history"—we might go on to place before us, as our noblest prize, the still higher task of striving beyond and above this Alexandrian world; and bravely find our prototypes in the ancient Greek world, where all was great, natural and human. But it is just there that we find the reality of a true unhistorical culture—and in spite of that, or perhaps because of it, an unspeakably rich and vital culture. Were we Germans nothing but followers, we could not be anything greater or prouder than the lineal inheritors and followers of such a culture.

This however must be added. The thought of being Epigoni, that is often a torture, can yet create a spring of hope for the future, to the individual as well as the people: so far, that is, as we can regard ourselves as the heirs and followers of the marvellous classical power, and see therein both our honour and our spur. But not as the late and bitter fruit of a powerful stock, giving that stock a further spell of cold life, as antiquaries and grave-diggers. Such late-comers live truly an ironical existence. Annihilation follows their halting walk on tiptoe through life. They shudder before it in the midst of their rejoicing over the past. They are living memories, and their own memories have no meaning; for there are none to inherit them. And thus they are wrapped in the melancholy thought that their life is an injustice, which no future life can set right again.

Suppose that these antiquaries, these late arrivals, were to change their painful ironic modesty for a certain shamelessness. Suppose we heard them saying, aloud, "The race is at its zenith, for it has manifested itself consciously for the first time." We should have a comedy, in which the dark meaning of a certain very celebrated philosophy would unroll itself for the benefit of German culture. I believe there has been no dangerous turning-point in the progress of German culture in this century that has not been made more dangerous by the enormous and still living influence of this Hegelian philosophy. The belief that one is a late-comer in the world is, anyhow, harmful and degrading: but it must appear frightful and devastating when it raises our late-comer to godhead, by a neat turn of the wheel, as the true meaning and object of all past creation, and his conscious misery is set up as the perfection of the world's history. Such a point of view has accustomed the Germans to talk of a "world-process," and justify their own time as its necessary result. And it has put history in the place of the other spiritual powers, art and religion, as the one sovereign; inasmuch as it is the "Idea realising itself," the "Dialectic of the spirit of the nations," and the "tribunal of the world."

History understood in this Hegelian way has been contemptuously called God's sojourn upon earth,—though the God was first created by the history. He, at any rate, became transparent and intelligible inside Hegelian skulls, and has risen through all the dialectically possible steps in his being up to the manifestation of the Self: so that for Hegel the highest and final stage of the world-process came together in his own Berlin existence. He ought to have said that everything after him was merely to be regarded as the musical coda of the great historical rondo,—or rather, as simply superfluous. He has not said it; and thus he has implanted in a generation leavened throughout by him the worship of the "power of history," that practically turns every moment into a sheer gaping at success, into an idolatry of the actual: for which we have now discovered the characteristic phrase "to adapt ourselves to circumstances." But the man who has once learnt to crook the knee and bow the head before the power of history, nods "yes" at last, like a Chinese doll, to every power, whether it be a government or a public opinion or a numerical majority; and his limbs move correctly as the power pulls the string. If each success have come by a "rational necessity," and every event show the victory of logic or the "Idea," then—down on your knees quickly, and let every step in the ladder of success have its reverence! There are no more living mythologies, you say? Religions are at their last gasp? Look at the religion of the power of history, and the priests of the mythology of Ideas, with their scarred knees! Do not all the virtues follow in the train of the new faith? And shall we not call it unselfishness, when the historical man lets himself be turned into an "objective" mirror of all that is? Is it not magnanimity to renounce all power in heaven and earth in order to adore the mere fact of power? Is it not justice, always to hold the balance of forces in your hands and observe which is the stronger and heavier? And what a school of politeness is such a contemplation of the past! To take everything objectively, to be angry at nothing, to love nothing, to understand everything—makes one gentle and pliable. Even if a man brought up in this school will show himself openly offended, one is just as pleased, knowing it is only meant in the artistic sense of ira et studium, though it is really sine ira et studio.

What old-fashioned thoughts I have on such a combination of virtue and mythology! But they must out, however one may laugh at them. I would even say that history always teaches—"it was once," and morality—"it ought not to be, or have been." So history becomes a compendium of actual immorality. But how wrong would one be to regard history as the judge of this actual immorality! Morality is offended by the fact that a Raphael had to die at thirty-six; such a being ought not to die. If you came to the help of history, as the apologists of the actual, you would say: "he had spoken everything that was in him to speak, a longer life would only have enabled him to create a similar beauty, and not a new beauty," and so on. Thus you become an advocatus diaboli by setting up the success, the fact, as your idol: whereas the fact is always dull, at all times more like calf than a god. Your apologies for history are helped by ignorance: for it is only because you do not know what a natura naturans like Raphael is, that you are not on fire when you think it existed once and can never exist again. Some one has lately tried to tell us that Goethe had out-lived himself with his eighty-two years: and yet I would gladly take two of Goethe's "outlived" years in exchange for whole cartloads of fresh modern lifetimes, to have another set of such conversations as those with Eckermann, and be preserved from all the "modern" talk of these esquires of the moment. How few living men have a right to live, as against those mighty dead! That the many live and those few live no longer, is simply a brutal truth, that is, a piece of unalterable folly, a blank wall of "it was once so" against the moral judgment "it ought not to have been." Yes, against the moral judgment! For you may speak of what virtue you will, of justice, courage, magnanimity, of wisdom and human compassion,—you will find the virtuous man will always rise against the blind force of facts, the tyranny of the actual, and submit himself to laws that are not the fickle laws of history. He ever swims against the waves of history, either by fighting his passions, as the nearest brute facts of his existence, or by training himself to honesty amid the glittering nets spun round him by falsehood. Were history nothing more than the "all-embracing system of passion and error," man would have to read it as Goethe wished Werther to be read;—just as if it called to him, "Be a man and follow me not!" But fortunately history also keeps alive for us the memory of the great "fighters against history," that is, against the blind power of the actual; it puts itself in the pillory just by glorifying the true historical nature in men who troubled themselves very little about the "thus it is," in order that they might follow a "thus it must be" with greater joy and greater pride. Not to drag their generation to the grave, but to found a new one—that is the motive that ever drives them onward; and even if they are born late, there is a way of living by which they can forget it—and future generations will know them only as the first-comers.

IX.

Is perhaps our time such a "first-comer"? Its historical sense is so strong, and has such universal and boundless expression, that future times will commend it, if only for this, as a first-comer—if there be any future time, in the sense of future culture. But here comes a grave doubt. Close to the modern man's pride there stands his irony about himself, his consciousness that he must live in a historical, or twilit, atmosphere, the fear that he can retain none of his youthful hopes and powers. Here and there one goes further into cynicism, and justifies the course of history, nay, the whole evolution of the world, as simply leading up to the modern man, according to the cynical canon:—"what you see now had to come, man had to be thus and not otherwise, no one can stand against this necessity." He who cannot rest in a state of irony flies for refuge to the cynicism. The last decade makes him a present of one of its most beautiful inventions, a full and well-rounded phrase for this cynicism: he calls his way of living thoughtlessly and after the fashion of his time, "the full surrender of his personality to the world-process." The personality and the world-process! The world-process and the personality of the earthworm! If only one did not eternally hear the word "world, world, world," that hyperbole of all hyperboles; when we should only speak, in a decent manner, of "man, man, man"! Heirs of the Greeks and Romans, of Christianity? All that seems nothing to the cynics. But "heirs of the world-process"; the final target of the world-process; the meaning and solution of all riddles of the universe, the ripest fruit on the tree of knowledge!—that is what I call a right noble thought: by this token are the firstlings of every time to be known, although they may have arrived last. The historical imagination has never flown so far, even in a dream; for now the history of man is merely the continuation of that of animals and plants: the universal historian finds traces of himself even in the utter depths of the sea, in the living slime. He stands astounded in face of the enormous way that man has run, and his gaze quivers before the mightier wonder, the modern man who can see all this way! He stands proudly on the pyramid of the world-process: and while he lays the final stone of his knowledge, he seems to cry aloud to listening Nature: "We are at the top, we are the top, we are the completion of Nature!"

O thou too proud European of the nineteenth century, art thou not mad? Thy knowledge does not complete Nature, it only kills thine own nature! Measure the height of what thou knowest by the depths of thy power to do. Thou climbest the sunbeams of knowledge up towards heaven—but also down to Chaos. Thy manner of going is fatal to thee; the ground slips from under thy feet into the unknown; thy life has no other stay, but only spider's webs that every new stroke of thy knowledge tears asunder.—But not another serious word about this, for there is a lighter side to it all.

The moralist, the artist, the saint and the statesman may well be troubled, when they see that all foundations are breaking up in mad unconscious ruin, and resolving themselves into the ever flowing stream of becoming; that all creation is being tirelessly spun into webs of history by the modern man, the great spider in the mesh of the world-net. We ourselves may be glad for once in a way that we see it all in the shining magic mirror of a philosophical parodist, in whose brain the time has come to an ironical consciousness of itself, to a point even of wickedness, in Goethe's phrase. Hegel once said, "when the spirit makes a fresh start, we philosophers are at hand." Our time did make a fresh start—into irony, and lo! Edward von Hartmann was at hand, with his famous Philosophy of the Unconscious—or, more plainly, his philosophy of unconscious irony. We have seldom read a more jovial production, a greater philosophical joke than Hartmann's book. Any one whom it does not fully enlighten about "becoming," who is not swept and garnished throughout by it, is ready to become a monument of the past himself. The beginning and end of the world-process, from the first throb of consciousness to its final leap into nothingness, with the task of our generation settled for it;—all drawn from that clever fount of inspiration, the Unconscious, and glittering in Apocalyptic light, imitating an honest seriousness to the life, as if it were a serious philosophy and not a huge joke,—such a system shows its creator to be one of the first philosophical parodists of all time. Let us then sacrifice on his altar, and offer the inventor of a true universal medicine a lock of hair, in Schleiermacher's phrase. For what medicine would be more salutary to combat the excess of historical culture than Hartmann's parody of the world's history?

If we wished to express in the fewest words what Hartmann really has to tell us from his mephitic tripod of unconscious irony, it would be something like this: our time could only remain as it is, if men should become thoroughly sick of this existence. And I fervently believe he is right. The frightful petrifaction of the time, the restless rattle of the ghostly bones, held naïvely up to us by David Strauss as the most beautiful fact of all—is justified by Hartmann not only from the past, ex causis efficientibus, but also from the future, ex causa finali. The rogue let light stream over our time from the last day, and saw that it was very good,—for him, that is, who wishes to feel the indigestibility of life at its full strength, and for whom the last day cannot come quickly enough. True, Hartmann calls the old age of life that mankind is approaching the "old age of man": but that is the blessed state, according to him, where there is only a successful mediocrity; where art is the "evening's amusement of the Berlin financier," and "the time has no more need for geniuses, either because it would be casting pearls before swine, or because the time has advanced beyond the stage where the geniuses are found, to one more important," to that stage of social evolution, in fact, in which every worker "leads a comfortable existence, with hours of work that leave him sufficient leisure to cultivate his intellect." Rogue of rogues, you say well what is the aspiration of present-day mankind: but you know too what a spectre of disgust will arise at the end of this old age of mankind, as the result of the intellectual culture of stolid mediocrity. It is very pitiful to see, but it will be still more pitiful yet. "Antichrist is visibly extending his arms:" yet it must be so, for after all we are on the right road—of disgust at all existence. "Forward then, boldly, with the world-process, as workers in the vineyard of the Lord, for it is the process alone that can lead to redemption!"

The vineyard of the Lord! The process! To redemption! Who does not see and hear in this how historical culture, that only knows the word "becoming," parodies itself on purpose and says the most irresponsible things about itself through its grotesque mask? For what does the rogue mean by this cry to the workers in the vineyard? By what "work" are they to strive boldly forward? Or, to ask another question:—what further has the historically educated fanatic of the world-process to do,—swimming and drowning as he is in the sea of becoming,—that he may at last gather in that vintage of disgust, the precious grape of the vineyard? He has nothing to do but to live on as he has lived, love what he has loved, hate what he has hated, and read the newspapers he has always read. The only sin is for him to live otherwise than he has lived. We are told how he has lived, with monumental clearness, by that famous page with its large typed sentences, on which the whole rabble of our modern cultured folk have thrown themselves in blind ecstasy, because they believe they read their own justification there, haloed with an Apocalyptic light. For the unconscious parodist has demanded of every one of them, "the full surrender of his personality to the world-process, for the sake of his end, the redemption of the world": or still more clearly,—"the assertion of the will to live is proclaimed to be the first step on the right road: for it is only in the full surrender to life and its sorrow, and not in the cowardice of personal renunciation and retreat, that anything can be done for the world-process.... The striving for the denial of the individual will is as foolish as it is useless, more foolish even than suicide.... The thoughtful reader will understand without further explanation how a practical philosophy can be erected on these principles, and that such a philosophy cannot endure any disunion, but only the fullest reconciliation with life."

The thoughtful reader will understand! Then one really could misunderstand Hartmann! And what a splendid joke it is, that he should be misunderstood! Why should the Germans of to-day be particularly subtle? A valiant Englishman looks in vain for "delicacy of perception" and dares to say that "in the German mind there does seem to be something splay, something blunt-edged, unhandy and infelicitous." Could the great German parodist contradict this? According to him, we are approaching "that ideal condition in which the human race makes its history with full consciousness": but we are obviously far from the perhaps more ideal condition, in which mankind can read Hartmann's book with full consciousness. If we once reach it, the word "world-process" will never pass any man's lips again without a smile. For he will remember the time when people listened to the mock gospel of Hartmann, sucked it in, attacked it, reverenced it, extended it and canonised it with all the honesty of that "German mind," with "the uncanny seriousness of an owl," as Goethe has it. But the world must go forward, the ideal condition cannot be won by dreaming, it must be fought and wrestled for, and the way to redemption lies only through joyousness, the way to redemption from that dull, owlish seriousness. The time will come when we shall wisely keep away from all constructions of the world-process, or even of the history of man; a time when we shall no more look at masses but at individuals, who form a sort of bridge over the wan stream of becoming. They may not perhaps continue a process, but they live out of time, as contemporaries: and thanks to history that permits such a company, they live as the Republic of geniuses of which Schopenhauer speaks. One giant calls to the other across the waste spaces of time, and the high spirit-talk goes on, undisturbed by the wanton noisy dwarfs who creep among them. The task of history is to be the mediator between these, and even to give the motive and power to produce the great man. The aim of mankind can lie ultimately only in its highest examples.

Our low comedian has his word on this too, with his wonderful dialectic, which is just as genuine as its admirers are admirable. "The idea of evolution cannot stand with our giving the world-process an endless duration in the past, for thus every conceivable evolution must have taken place, which is not the case (O rogue!); and so we cannot allow the process an endless duration in the future. Both would raise the conception of evolution to a mere ideal (And again rogue!), and would make the world-process like the sieve of the Danaides. The complete victory of the logical over the illogical (O thou complete rogue!) must coincide with the last day, the end in time of the world-process." No, thou clear, scornful spirit, so long as the illogical rules as it does to-day,—so long, for example, as the world-process can be spoken of as thou speakest of it, amid such deep-throated assent,—the last day is yet far off. For it is still too joyful on this earth, many an illusion still blooms here—like the illusion of thy contemporaries about thee. We are not yet ripe to be hurled into thy nothingness: for we believe that we shall have a still more splendid time, when men once begin to understand thee, thou misunderstood, unconscious one! But if, in spite of that, disgust shall come throned in power, as thou hast prophesied to thy readers; if thy portrayal of the present and the future shall prove to be right,—and no one has despised them with such loathing as thou,—I am ready then to cry with the majority in the form prescribed by thee, that next Saturday evening, punctually at twelve o'clock, thy world shall fall to pieces. And our decree shall conclude thus—from to-morrow time shall not exist, and the Times shall no more be published. Perhaps it will be in vain, and our decree of no avail: at any rate we have still time for a fine experiment. Take a balance and put Hartmann's "Unconscious" in one of the scales, and his "World-process" in the other. There are some who believe they weigh equally; for in each scale there is an evil word—and a good joke.

When they are once understood, no one will take Hartmann's words on the world-process as anything but a joke. It is, as a fact, high time to move forward with the whole battalion of satire and malice against the excesses of the "historical sense," the wanton love of the world-process at the expense of life and existence, the blind confusion of all perspective. And it will be to the credit of the philosopher of the Unconscious that he has been the first to see the humour of the world-process, and to succeed in making others see it still more strongly by the extraordinary seriousness of his presentation. The existence of the "world" and "humanity" need not trouble us for some time, except to provide us with a good joke: for the presumption of the small earthworm is the most uproariously comic thing on the face of the earth. Ask thyself to what end thou art here, as an individual; and if no one can tell thee, try then to justify the meaning of thy existence a posteriori, by putting before thyself a high and noble end. Perish on that rock! I know no better aim for life than to be broken on something great and impossible, animæ magnæ prodigus. But if we have the doctrines of the finality of "becoming," of the flux of all ideas, types, and species, of the lack of all radical difference between man and beast (a true but fatal idea as I think),—if we have these thrust on the people in the usual mad way for another generation, no one need be surprised if that people drown on its little miserable shoals of egoism, and petrify in its self-seeking. At first it will fall asunder and cease to be a people. In its place perhaps individualist systems, secret societies for the extermination of non-members, and similar utilitarian creations, will appear on the theatre of the future. Are we to continue to work for these creations and write history from the standpoint of the masses; to look for laws in it, to be deduced from the needs of the masses, the laws of motion of the lowest loam and clay strata of society? The masses seem to be worth notice in three aspects only: first as the copies of great men, printed on bad paper from worn-out plates, next as a contrast to the great men, and lastly as their tools: for the rest, let the devil and statistics fly away with them! How could statistics prove that there are laws in history? Laws? Yes, they may prove how common and abominably uniform the masses are: and should we call the effects of leaden folly, imitation, love and hunger—laws? We may admit it: but we are sure of this too—that so far as there are laws in history, the laws are of no value and the history of no value either. And least valuable of all is that kind of history which takes the great popular movements as the most important events of the past, and regards the great men only as their clearest expression, the visible bubbles on the stream. Thus the masses have to produce the great man, chaos to bring forth order; and finally all the hymns are naturally sung to the teeming chaos. Everything is called "great" that has moved the masses for some long time, and becomes, as they say, a "historical power." But is not this really an intentional confusion of quantity and quality? When the brutish mob have found some idea, a religious idea for example, which satisfies them, when they have defended it through thick and thin for centuries then, and then only, will they discover its inventor to have been a great man. The highest and noblest does not affect the masses at all. The historical consequences of Christianity, its "historical power," toughness and persistence prove nothing, fortunately, as to its founder's greatness, They would have been a witness against him. For between him and the historical success of Christianity lies a dark heavy weight of passion and error, lust of power and honour, and the crushing force of the Roman Empire. From this, Christianity had its earthly taste, and its earthly foundations too, that made its continuance in this world possible. Greatness should not depend on success; Demosthenes is great without it. The purest and noblest adherents of Christianity have always doubted and hindered, rather than helped, its effect in the world, its so-called "historical power"; for they were accustomed to stand outside the "world," and cared little for the "process of the Christian Idea." Hence they have generally remained unknown to history, and their very names are lost. In Christian terms the devil is the prince of the world, and the lord of progress and consequence: he is the power behind all "historical power," and so will it remain, however ill it may sound to-day in ears that are accustomed to canonise such power and consequence. The world has become skilled at giving new names to things and even baptizing the devil. It is truly an hour of great danger. Men seem to be near the discovery that the egoism of individuals, groups or masses has been at all times the lever of the "historical movements": and yet they are in no way disturbed by the discovery, but proclaim that "egoism shall be our god." With this new faith in their hearts, they begin quite intentionally to build future history on egoism: though it must be a clever egoism, one that allows of some limitation, that it may stand firmer; one that studies history for the purpose of recognising the foolish kind of egoism. Their study has taught them that the state has a special mission in all future egoistic systems: it will be the patron of all the clever egoisms, to protect them with all the power of its military and police against the dangerous outbreaks of the other kind. There is the same idea in introducing history—natural as well as human history—among the labouring classes, whose folly makes them dangerous. For men know well that a grain of historical culture is able to break down the rough, blind instincts and desires, or to turn them to the service of a clever egoism. In fact they are beginning to think, with Edward von Hartmann, of "fixing themselves with an eye to the future in their earthly home, and making themselves comfortable there." Hartmann calls this life the "manhood of humanity" with an ironical reference to what is now called "manhood";—as if only our sober models of selfishness were embraced by it; just as he prophesies an age of graybeards following on this stage,—obviously another ironical glance at our ancient time-servers. For he speaks of the ripe discretion with which "they view all the stormy passions of their past life and understand the vanity of the ends they seem to have striven for." No, a manhood of crafty and historically cultured egoism corresponds to an old age that hangs to life with no dignity but a horrible tenacity, where the

"last scene of all
That ends this strange eventful history,
Is second childishness and mere oblivion,
Sans teeth, sans eyes, sans taste, sans everything."

Whether the dangers of our life and culture come from these dreary, toothless old men, or from the so-called "men" of Hartmann, we have the right to defend our youth with tooth and claw against both of them, and never tire of saving the future from these false prophets. But in this battle we shall discover an unpleasant truth—that men intentionally help, and encourage, and use, the worst aberrations of the historical sense from which the present time suffers.

They use it, however, against youth, in order to transform it into that ripe "egoism of manhood" they so long for: they use it to overcome the natural reluctance of the young by its magical splendour, which unmans while it enlightens them. Yes, we know only too well the kind of ascendency history can gain; how it can uproot the strongest instincts of youth, passion, courage, unselfishness and love; can cool its feeling for justice, can crush or repress its desire for a slow ripening by the contrary desire to be soon productive, ready and useful; and cast a sick doubt over all honesty and downrightness of feeling. It can even cozen youth of its fairest privilege, the power of planting a great thought with the fullest confidence, and letting it grow of itself to a still greater thought. An excess of history can do all that, as we have seen, by no longer allowing a man to feel and act unhistorically: for history is continually shifting his horizon and removing the atmosphere surrounding him. From an infinite horizon he withdraws into himself, back into the small egoistic circle, where he must become dry and withered: he may possibly attain to cleverness, but never to wisdom. He lets himself be talked over, is always calculating and parleying with facts. He is never enthusiastic, but blinks his eyes, and understands how to look for his own profit or his party's in the profit or loss of somebody else. He unlearns all his useless modesty, and turns little by little into the "man" or the "graybeard" of Hartmann. And that is what they want him to be: that is the meaning of the present cynical demand for the "full surrender of the personality to the world-process"—for the sake of his end, the redemption of the world, as the rogue E. von Hartmann tells us. Though redemption can scarcely be the conscious aim of these people: the world were better redeemed by being redeemed from these "men" and "graybeards." For then would come the reign of youth.

X.

And in this kingdom of youth I can cry Land! Land! Enough, and more than enough, of the wild voyage over dark strange seas, of eternal search and eternal disappointment! The coast is at last in sight. Whatever it be, we must land there, and the worst haven is better than tossing again in the hopeless waves of an infinite scepticism. Let us hold fast by the land: we shall find the good harbours later and make the voyage easier for those who come after us.

The voyage was dangerous and exciting. How far are we even now from that quiet state of contemplation with which we first saw our ship launched! In tracking out the dangers of history, we have found ourselves especially exposed to them. We carry on us the marks of that sorrow which an excess of history brings in its train to the men of the modern time. And this present treatise, as I will not attempt to deny, shows the modern note of a weak personality in the intemperateness of its criticism, the unripeness of its humanity, in the too frequent transitions from irony to cynicism, from arrogance to scepticism. And yet I trust in the inspiring power that directs my vessel instead of genius; I trust in youth, that has brought me on the right road in forcing from me a protest against the modern historical education, and a demand that the man must learn to live, above all, and only use history in the service of the life that he has learned to live. He must be young to understand this protest; and considering the premature grayness of our present youth, he can scarcely be young enough if he would understand its reason as well. An example will help me. In Germany, not more than a century ago, a natural instinct for what is called "poetry" was awakened in some young men. Are we to think that the generations who had lived before that time had not spoken of the art, however really strange and unnatural it may have been to them? We know the contrary; that they had thought, written, and quarrelled about it with all their might—in "words, words, words." Giving life to such words did not prove the death of the word-makers; in a certain sense they are living still. For if, as Gibbon says, nothing but time—though a long time—is needed for a world to perish, so nothing but time—though still more time—is needed for a false idea to be destroyed in Germany, the "Land of Little-by-little." In any event, there are perhaps a hundred men more now than there were a century ago who know what poetry is: perhaps in another century there will be a hundred more who have learned in the meantime what culture is, and that the Germans have had as yet no culture, however proudly they may talk about it. The general satisfaction of the Germans at their culture will seem as foolish and incredible to such men as the once lauded classicism of Gottsched, or the reputation of Ramler as the German Pindar, seemed to us. They will perhaps think this "culture" to be merely a kind of knowledge about culture, and a false and superficial knowledge at that. False and superficial, because the Germans endured the contradiction between life and knowledge, and did not see what was characteristic in the culture of really educated peoples, that it can only rise and bloom from life. But by the Germans it is worn like a paper flower, or spread over like the icing on a cake; and so must remain a useless lie for ever.

The education of youth in Germany starts from this false and unfruitful idea of culture. Its aim, when faced squarely, is not to form the liberally educated man, but the professor, the man of science, who wants to be able to make use of his science as soon as possible, and stands on one side in order to see life clearly. The result, even from a ruthlessly practical point of view, is the historically and æsthetically trained Philistine, the babbler of old saws and new wisdom on Church, State and Art, the sensorium that receives a thousand impressions, the insatiable belly that yet knows not what true hunger and thirst is. An education with such an aim and result is against nature. But only he who is not quite drowned in it can feel that; only youth can feel it, because it still has the instinct of nature, that is the first to be broken by that education. But he who will break through that education in his turn, must come to the help of youth when called upon; must let the clear light of understanding shine on its unconscious striving, and bring it to a full, vocal consciousness. How is he to attain such a strange end?

Principally by destroying the superstition that this kind of education is necessary. People think nothing but this troublesome reality of ours is possible. Look through the literature of higher education in school and college for the last ten years, and you will be astonished—and pained—to find how much alike all the proposals of reform have been; in spite of all the hesitations and violent controversies surrounding them. You will see how blindly they have all adopted the old idea of the "educated man" (in our sense) being the necessary and reasonable basis of the system. The monotonous canon runs thus: the young man must begin with a knowledge of culture, not even with a knowledge of life, still less with life and the living of it. This knowledge of culture is forced into the young mind in the form of historical knowledge; which means that his head is filled with an enormous mass of ideas, taken second-hand from past times and peoples, not from immediate contact with life. He desires to experience something for himself, and feel a close-knit, living system of experiences growing within himself. But his desire is drowned and dizzied in the sea of shams, as if it were possible to sum up in a few years the highest and notablest experiences of ancient times, and the greatest times too. It is the same mad method that carries our young artists off to picture-galleries, instead of the studio of a master, and above all the one studio of the only master, Nature. As if one could discover by a hasty rush through history the ideas and technique of past times, and their individual outlook on life! For life itself is a kind of handicraft that must be learned thoroughly and industriously, and diligently practised, if we are not to have mere botchers and babblers as the issue of it all!

Plato thought it necessary for the first generation of his new society (in the perfect state) to be brought up with the help of a "mighty lie." The children were to be taught to believe that they had all lain dreaming for a long time under the earth, where they had been moulded and formed by the master-hand of Nature. It was impossible to go against the past, and work against the work of gods! And so it had to be an unbreakable law of nature, that he who is born to be a philosopher has gold in his body, the fighter has only silver, and the workman iron and bronze. As it is not possible to blend these metals, according to Plato, so there could never be any confusion between the classes: the belief in the æterna veritas of this arrangement was the basis of the new education and the new state. So the modern German believes also in the æterna veritas of his education, of his kind of culture: and yet this belief will fail—as the Platonic state would have failed—if the mighty German lie be ever opposed by the truth, that the German has no culture because he cannot build one on the basis of his education. He wishes for the flower without the root or the stalk; and so he wishes in vain. That is the simple truth, a rude and unpleasant truth, but yet a mighty one.

But our first generation must be brought up in this "mighty truth," and must suffer from it too; for it must educate itself through it, even against its own nature, to attain a new nature and manner of life, which shall yet proceed from the old. So it might say to itself, in the old Spanish phrase, "Defienda me Dios de my," God keep me from myself, from the character, that is, which has been put into me. It must taste that truth drop by drop, like a bitter, powerful medicine. And every man in this generation must subdue himself to pass the judgment on his own nature, which he might pass more easily on his whole time:—"We are without instruction, nay, we are too corrupt to live, to see and hear truly and simply, to understand what is near and natural to us. We have not yet laid even the foundations of culture, for we are not ourselves convinced that we have a sincere life in us." We crumble and fall asunder, our whole being is divided, half mechanically, into an inner and outer side; we are sown with ideas as with dragon's teeth, and bring forth a new dragon-brood of them; we suffer from the malady of words, and have no trust in any feeling that is not stamped with its special word. And being such a dead fabric of words and ideas, that yet has an uncanny movement in it, I have still perhaps the right to say cogito ergo sum, though not vivo ergo cogito. I am permitted the empty esse, not the full green vivere. A primary feeling tells me that I am a thinking being but not a living one, that I am no "animal," but at most a "cogital." "Give me life, and I will soon make you a culture out of it"—will be the cry of every man in this new generation, and they will all know each other by this cry. But who will give them this life?

No god and no man will give it—only their own youth. Set this free, and you will set life free as well. For it only lay concealed, in a prison; it is not yet withered or dead—ask your own selves!

But it is sick, this life that is set free, and must be healed. It suffers from many diseases, and not only from the memory of its chains. It suffers from the malady which I have spoken of, the malady of history. Excess of history has attacked the plastic power of life, that no more understands how to use the past as a means of strength and nourishment. It is a fearful disease, and yet, if youth had not a natural gift for clear vision, no one would see that it is a disease, and that a paradise of health has been lost. But the same youth, with that same natural instinct of health, has guessed how the paradise can be regained. It knows the magic herbs and simples for the malady of history, and the excess of it. And what are they called?

It is no marvel that they bear the names of poisons:—the antidotes to history are the "unhistorical" and the "super-historical." With these names we return to the beginning of our inquiry and draw near to its final close.

By the word "unhistorical" I mean the power, the art of forgetting, and of drawing a limited horizon round one's self. I call the power "super-historical" which turns the eyes from the process of becoming to that which gives existence an eternal and stable character, to art and religion. Science—for it is science that makes us speak of "poisons"—sees in these powers contrary powers: for it considers only that view of things to be true and right, and therefore scientific, which regards something as finished and historical, not as continuing and eternal. Thus it lives in a deep antagonism towards the powers that make for eternity—art and religion,—for it hates the forgetfulness that is the death of knowledge, and tries to remove all limitation of horizon and cast men into an infinite boundless sea, whose waves are bright with the clear knowledge—of becoming!

If they could only live therein! Just as towns are shaken by an avalanche and become desolate, and man builds his house there in fear and for a season only; so life is broken in sunder and becomes weak and spiritless, if the avalanche of ideas started by science take from man the foundation of his rest and security, the belief in what is stable and eternal. Must life dominate knowledge, or knowledge life? Which of the two is the higher, and decisive power? There is no room for doubt: life is the higher, and the dominating power, for the knowledge that annihilated life would be itself annihilated too. Knowledge presupposes life, and has the same interest in maintaining it that every creature has in its own preservation. Science needs very careful watching: there is a hygiene of life near the volumes of science, and one of its sentences runs thus:—The unhistorical and the super-historical are the natural antidotes against the overpowering of life by history; they are the cures for the historical disease. We who are sick of the disease may suffer a little from the antidote. But this is no proof that the treatment we have chosen is wrong.

And here I see the mission of the youth that forms the first generation of fighters and dragon-slayers: it will bring a more beautiful and blessed humanity and culture, but will have itself no more than a glimpse of the promised land of happiness and wondrous beauty. This youth will suffer both from the malady and its antidotes: and yet it believes in strength and health and boasts a nature closer to the great

Nature than its forebears, the cultured men and graybeards of the present. But its mission is to shake to their foundations the present conceptions of "health" and "culture," and erect hatred and scorn in the place of this rococo mass of ideas. And the clearest sign of its own strength and health is just the fact that it can use no idea, no party-cry from the present-day mint of words and ideas to symbolise its own existence: but only claims conviction from the power in it that acts and fights, breaks up and destroys; and from an ever heightened feeling of life when the hour strikes. You may deny this youth any culture—but how would youth count that a reproach? You may speak of its rawness and intemperateness—but it is not yet old and wise enough to be acquiescent. It need not pretend to a ready-made culture at all; but enjoys all the rights—and the consolations—of youth, especially the right of brave unthinking honesty and the consolation of an inspiring hope.

I know that such hopeful beings understand all these truisms from within, and can translate them into a doctrine for their own use, through their personal experience. To the others there will appear, in the meantime, nothing but a row of covered dishes, that may perhaps seem empty: until they see one day with astonished eyes that the dishes are full, and that all ideas and impulses and passions are massed together in these truisms that cannot lie covered for long. I leave those doubting ones to time, that brings all things to light; and turn at last to that great company of hope, to tell them the way and the course of their salvation, their rescue from the disease of history, and their own history as well, in a parable; whereby they may again become healthy enough to study history anew, and under the guidance of life make use of the past in that threefold way—monumental, antiquarian, or critical. At first they will be more ignorant than the "educated men" of the present: for they will have unlearnt much and have lost any desire even to discover what those educated men especially wish to know: in fact, their chief mark from the educated point of view will be just their want of science; their indifference and inaccessibility to all the good and famous things. But at the end of the cure, they are men again and have ceased to be mere shadows of humanity. That is something; there is yet hope, and do not ye who hope laugh in your hearts?

How can we reach that end? you will ask. The Delphian god cries his oracle to you at the beginning of your wanderings, "Know thyself." It is a hard saying: for that god "tells nothing and conceals nothing but merely points the way," as Heraclitus said. But whither does he point?

In certain epochs the Greeks were in a similar danger of being overwhelmed by what was past and foreign, and perishing on the rock of "history." They never lived proud and untouched. Their "culture" was for a long time a chaos of foreign forms and ideas,—Semitic, Babylonian, Lydian and Egyptian,—and their religion a battle of all the gods of the East; just as German culture and religion is at present a death-struggle of all foreign nations and bygone times. And yet, Hellenic culture was no mere mechanical unity, thanks to that Delphic oracle. The Greeks gradually learned to organise the chaos, by taking Apollo's advice and thinking back to themselves, to their own true necessities, and letting all the sham necessities go. Thus they again came into possession of themselves, and did not remain long the Epigoni of the whole East, burdened with their inheritance. After that hard fight, they increased and enriched the treasure they had inherited by their obedience to the oracle, and they became the ancestors and models for all the cultured nations of the future.

This is a parable for each one of us: he must organise the chaos in himself by "thinking himself back" to his true needs. He will want all his honesty, all the sturdiness and sincerity in his character to help him to revolt against second-hand thought, second-hand learning, second-hand action. And he will begin then to understand that culture can be something more than a "decoration of life"—a concealment and disfiguring of it, in other words; for all adornment hides what is adorned. And thus the Greek idea, as against the Roman, will be discovered in him, the idea of culture as a new and finer nature, without distinction of inner and outer, without convention or disguise, as a unity of thought and will, life and appearance. He will learn too, from his own experience, that it was by a greater force of moral character that the Greeks were victorious, and that everything which makes for sincerity is a further step towards true culture, however this sincerity may harm the ideals of education that are reverenced at the time, or even have power to shatter a whole system of merely decorative culture.

Schopenhauer as Educator.

I.

When the traveller, who had seen many countries and nations and continents, was asked what common attribute he had found everywhere existing among men, he answered, "They have a tendency to sloth." Many may think that the fuller truth would have been, "They are all timid." They hide themselves behind "manners" and "opinions." At bottom every man knows well enough that he is a unique being, only once on this earth; and by no extraordinary chance will such a marvellously picturesque piece of diversity in unity as he is, ever be put together a second time. He knows this, but hides it like an evil conscience;—and why? From fear of his neighbour, who looks for the latest conventionalities in him, and is wrapped up in them himself. But what is it that forces the man to fear his neighbour, to think and act with his herd, and not seek his own joy? Shyness perhaps, in a few rare cases, but in the majority it is idleness, the "taking things easily," in a word the "tendency to sloth," of which the traveller spoke. He was right; men are more slothful than timid, and their greatest fear is of the burdens that an uncompromising honesty and nakedness of speech and action would lay on them. It is only the artists who hate this lazy wandering in borrowed manners and ill-fitting opinions, and discover the secret of the evil conscience, the truth that each human being is a unique marvel. They show us, how in every little movement of his muscles the man is an individual self, and further—as an analytical deduction from his individuality—a beautiful and interesting object, a new and incredible phenomenon (as is every work of nature), that can never become tedious. If the great thinker despise mankind, it is for their laziness; they seem mere indifferent bits of pottery, not worth any commerce or improvement. The man who will not belong to the general mass, has only to stop "taking himself easily"; to follow his conscience, which cries out to him, "Be thyself! all that thou doest and thinkest and desirest, is not—thyself!"

Every youthful soul hears this cry day and night, and quivers to hear it: for she divines the sum of happiness that has been from eternity destined for her, if she think of her true deliverance; and towards this happiness she can in no wise be helped, so long as she lies in the chains of Opinion and of Fear. And how comfortless and unmeaning may life become without this deliverance! There is no more desolate or Ishmaelitish creature in nature than the man who has broken away from his true genius, and does nothing but peer aimlessly about him. There is no reason to attack such a man at all, for he is a mere husk without a kernel, a painted cloth, tattered and sagging, a scarecrow ghost, that can rouse no fear, and certainly no pity. And though one be right in saying of a sluggard that he is "killing time," yet in respect of an age that rests its salvation on public opinion,—that is, on private laziness,—one must be quite determined that such a time shall be "killed," once and for all: I mean that it shall be blotted from life's true History of Liberty. Later generations will be greatly disgusted, when they come to treat the movements of a period in which no living men ruled, but shadow-men on the screen of public opinion; and to some far posterity our age may well be the darkest chapter of history, the most unknown because the least human. I have walked through the new streets of our cities, and thought how of all the dreadful houses that these gentlemen with their public opinion have built for themselves, not a stone will remain in a hundred years, and that the opinions of these busy masons may well have fallen with them. But how full of hope should they all be who feel that they are no citizens of this age! If they were, they would have to help on the work of "killing their time," and of perishing with it,—when they wish rather to quicken the time to life, and in that life themselves to live.

But even if the future leave us nothing to hope for, the wonderful fact of our existing at this present moment of time gives us the greatest encouragement to live after our own rule and measure; so inexplicable is it, that we should be living just to-day, though there have been an infinity of time wherein we might have arisen; that we own nothing but a span's length of it, this "to-day," and must show in it wherefore and whereunto we have arisen. We have to answer for our existence to ourselves; and will therefore be our own true pilots, and not admit that our being resembles a blind fortuity. One must take a rather impudent and reckless way with the riddle; especially as the key is apt to be lost, however things turn out. Why cling to your bit of earth, or your little business, or listen to what your neighbour says? It is so provincial to bind oneself to views which are no longer binding a couple of hundred miles away. East and West are signs that somebody chalks up in front of us to fool such cowards as we are. "I will make the attempt to gain freedom," says the youthful soul; and will be hindered, just because two nations happen to hate each other and go to war, or because there is a sea between two parts of the earth, or a religion is taught in the vicinity, which did not exist two thousand years ago. "And this is not—thyself," the soul says. "No one can build thee the bridge, over which thou must cross the river of life, save thyself alone. There are paths and bridges and demi-gods without number, that will gladly carry thee over, but only at the price of thine own self: thy self wouldst thou have to give in pawn, and then lose it. There is in the world one road whereon none may go, except thou: ask not whither it lead, but go forward. Who was it that spake that true word— 'A man has never risen higher than when he knoweth not whither his road may yet lead him'?"

But how can we "find ourselves" again, and how can man "know himself"? He is a thing obscure and veiled: if the hare have seven skins, man can cast from him seventy times seven, and yet will not be able to say "Here art thou in very truth; this is outer shell no more." Also this digging into one's self, this straight, violent descent into the pit of one's being, is a troublesome and dangerous business to start. A man may easily take such hurt, that no physician can heal him. And again, what were the use, since everything bears witness to our essence,—our friendships and enmities, our looks and greetings, our memories and forgetfulnesses, our books and our writing! This is the most effective way:—to let the youthful soul look back on life with the question, "What hast thou up to now truly loved, what has drawn thy soul upward, mastered it and blessed it too?" Set up these things that thou hast honoured before thee, and, maybe, they will show thee, in their being and their order, a law which is the fundamental law of thine own self. Compare these objects, consider how one completes and broadens and transcends and explains another, how they form a ladder on which thou hast all the time been climbing to thy self: for thy true being lies not deeply hidden in thee, but an infinite height above thee, or at least above that which thou dost commonly take to be thyself. The true educators and moulders reveal to thee the real groundwork and import of thy being, something that in itself cannot be moulded or educated, but is anyhow difficult of approach, bound and crippled: thy educators can be nothing but thy deliverers. And that is the secret of all culture: it does not give artificial limbs, wax noses, or spectacles for the eyes—a thing that could buy such gifts is but the base coin of education. But it is rather a liberation, a removal of all the weeds and rubbish and vermin that attack the delicate shoots, the streaming forth of light and warmth, the tender dropping of the night rain; it is the following and the adoring of Nature when she is pitifully-minded as a mother;—her completion, when it bends before her fierce and ruthless blasts and turns them to good, and draws a veil over all expression of her tragic unreason—for she is a step-mother too, sometimes.

There are other means of "finding ourselves," of coming to ourselves out of the confusion wherein we all wander as in a dreary cloud; but I know none better than to think on our educators. So I will to-day take as my theme the hard teacher Arthur Schopenhauer, and speak of others later.

II.

In order to describe properly what an event my first look into Schopenhauer's writings was for me, I must dwell for a minute on an idea, that recurred more constantly in my youth, and touched me more nearly, than any other. I wandered then as I pleased in a world of wishes, and thought that destiny would relieve me of the dreadful and wearisome duty of educating myself: some philosopher would come at the right moment to do it for me,—some true philosopher, who could be obeyed without further question, as he would be trusted more than one's self. Then I said within me: "What would be the principles, on which he might teach thee?" And I pondered in my mind what he would say to the two maxims of education that hold the field in our time. The first demands that the teacher should find out at once the strong point in his pupil, and then direct all his skill and will, all the moisture and all the sunshine, to bring the fruit of that single virtue to maturity. The second requires him to raise to a higher power all the qualities that already exist, cherish them and bring them into a harmonious relation. But, we may ask, should one who has a decided talent for working in gold be made for that reason to learn music? And can we admit that Benvenuto Cellini's father was right in continually forcing him back to the "dear little horn"—the "cursed piping," as his son called it? We cannot think so in the case of such a strong and clearly marked talent as his, and it may well be that this maxim of harmonious development applies only to weaker natures, in which there is a whole swarm of desires and inclinations, though they may not amount to very much, singly or together. On the other hand, where do we find such a blending of harmonious voices—nay, the soul of harmony itself—as we see in natures like Cellini's, where everything—knowledge, desire, love and hate—tends towards a single point, the root of all, and a harmonious system, the resultant of the various forces, is built up through the irresistible domination of this vital centre? And so perhaps the two maxims are not contrary at all; the one merely saying that man must have a centre, the other, a circumference as well. The philosophic teacher of my dream would not only discover the central force, but would know how to prevent its being destructive of the other powers: his task, I thought, would be the welding of the whole man into a solar system with life and movement, and the discovery of its paraphysical laws.

In the meantime I could not find my philosopher, however I tried; I saw how badly we moderns compare with the Greeks and Romans, even in the serious study of educational problems. You can go through all Germany, and especially all the universities, with this need in your heart, and will not find what you seek; many humbler wishes than that are still unfulfilled there. For example, if a German seriously wish to make himself an orator, or to enter a "school for authors," he will find neither master nor school: no one yet seems to have thought that speaking and writing are arts which cannot be learnt without the most careful method and untiring application. But, to their shame, nothing shows more clearly the insolent self-satisfaction of our people than the lack of demand for educators; it comes partly from meanness, partly from want of thought. Anything will do as a so-called "family tutor," even among our most eminent and cultured people; and what a menagerie of crazy heads and mouldy devices mostly go to make up the belauded Gymnasium! And consider what we are satisfied with in our finishing schools,—our universities. Look at our professors and their institutions! And compare the difficulty of the task of educating a man to be a man! Above all, the wonderful way in which the German savants fall to their dish of knowledge, shows that they are thinking more of Science than mankind; and they are trained to lead a forlorn hope in her service, in order to encourage ever new generations to the same sacrifice. If their traffic with knowledge be not limited and controlled by any more general principles of education, but allowed to run on indefinitely,—"the more the better,"—it is as harmful to learning as the economic theory of laisser faire to common morality. No one recognises now that the education of the professors is an exceedingly difficult problem, if their humanity is not to be sacrificed or shrivelled up:—this difficulty can be actually seen in countless examples of natures warped and twisted by their reckless and premature devotion to science. There is a still more important testimony to the complete absence of higher education, pointing to a greater and more universal danger. It is clear at once why an orator or writer cannot now be educated,—because there are no teachers; and why a savant must be a distorted and perverted thing,—because he will have been trained by the inhuman abstraction, science. This being so, let a man ask himself: "Where are now the types of moral excellence and fame for all our generation—learned and unlearned, high and low—the visible abstract of constructive ethics for this age? Where has vanished all the reflection on moral questions that has occupied every great developed society at all epochs?" There is no fame for that now, and there are none to reflect: we are really drawing on the inherited moral capital which our predecessors accumulated for us, and which we do not know how to increase, but only to squander. Such things are either not mentioned in our society, or, if at all, with a naïve want of personal experience that makes one disgusted. It comes to this, that our schools and professors simply turn aside from any moral instruction or content themselves with formulæ; virtue is a word and nothing more, on both sides, an old-fashioned word that they laugh at—and it is worse when they do not laugh, for then they are hypocrites.

An explanation of this faint-heartedness and ebbing of all moral strength would be difficult and complex: but whoever is considering the influence of Christianity in its hour of victory on the morality of the mediæval world, must not forget that it reacts also in its defeat, which is apparently its position to-day. By its lofty ideal, Christianity has outbidden the ancient Systems of Ethics and their invariable naturalism, with which men came to feel a dull disgust: and afterwards when they did reach the knowledge of what was better and higher, they found they had no longer the power, for all their desire, to return to its embodiment in the antique virtues. And so the life of the modern man is passed in see-sawing between Christianity and Paganism, between a furtive or hypocritical approach to Christian morality, and an equally shy and spiritless dallying with the antique: and he does not thrive under it. His inherited fear of naturalism, and its more recent attraction for him, his desire to come to rest somewhere, while in the impotence of his intellect he swings backwards and forwards between the "good" and the "better" course—all this argues an instability in the modern mind that condemns it to be without joy or fruit. Never were moral teachers more necessary and never were they more unlikely to be found: physicians are most in danger themselves in times when they are most needed and many men are sick. For where are our modern physicians who are strong and sure-footed enough to hold up another or lead him by the hand? There lies a certain heavy gloom on the best men of our time, an eternal loathing for the battle that is fought in their hearts between honesty and lies, a wavering of trust in themselves, which makes them quite incapable of showing to others the way they must go.

So I was right in speaking of my "wandering in a world of wishes" when I dreamt of finding a true philosopher who could lift me from the slough of insufficiency, and teach me again simply and honestly to be in my thoughts and life, in the deepest sense of the word, "out of season"; simply and honestly—for men have now become such complicated machines that they must be dishonest, if they speak at all, or wish to act on their words.

With such needs and desires within me did I come to know Schopenhauer.

I belong to those readers of Schopenhauer who know perfectly well, after they have turned the first page, that they will read all the others, and listen to every word that he has spoken. My trust in him sprang to life at once, and has been the same for nine years. I understood him as though he had written for me (this is the most intelligible, though a rather foolish and conceited way of expressing it). Hence I never found a paradox in him, though occasionally some small errors: for paradoxes are only assertions that carry no conviction, because the author has made them himself without any conviction, wishing to appear brilliant, or to mislead, or, above all, to pose. Schopenhauer never poses: he writes for himself, and no one likes to be deceived—least of all a philosopher who has set this up as his law: "deceive nobody, not even thyself," neither with the "white lies" of all social intercourse, which writers almost unconsciously imitate, still less with the more conscious deceits of the platform, and the artificial methods of rhetoric. Schopenhauer's speeches are to himself alone; or if you like to imagine an auditor, let it be a son whom the father is instructing. It is a rough, honest, good-humoured talk to one who "hears and loves." Such writers are rare. His strength and sanity surround us at the first sound of his voice: it is like entering the heights of the forest, where we breathe deep and are well again. We feel a bracing air everywhere, a certain candour and naturalness of his own, that belongs to men who are at home with themselves, and masters of a very rich home indeed: he is quite different from the writers who are surprised at themselves if they have said something intelligent, and whose pronouncements for that reason have something nervous and unnatural about them. We are just as little reminded in Schopenhauer of the professor with his stiff joints worse for want of exercise, his narrow chest and scraggy figure, his slinking or strutting gait. And again his rough and rather grim soul leads us not so much to miss as to despise the suppleness and courtly grace of the excellent Frenchmen; and no one will find in him the gilded imitations of pseudo-gallicism that our German writers prize so highly. His style in places reminds me a little of Goethe, but is not otherwise on any German model. For he knows how to be profound with simplicity, striking without rhetoric, and severely logical without pedantry: and of what German could he have learnt that? He also keeps free from the hair-splitting, jerky and (with all respect) rather un-German manner of Lessing: no small merit in him, for Lessing is the most tempting of all models for prose style. The highest praise I can give his manner of presentation is to apply his own phrase to himself:—"A philosopher must be very honest to avail himself of no aid from poetry or rhetoric." That honesty is something, and even a virtue, is one of those private opinions which are forbidden in this age of public opinion; and so I shall not be praising Schopenhauer, but only giving him a distinguishing mark, when I repeat that he is honest, even as a writer; so few of them are, that we are apt to mistrust every one who writes at all. I only know a single author that I can rank with Schopenhauer, or even above him, in the matter of honesty; and that is Montaigne. The joy of living on this earth is increased by the existence of such a man. The effect on myself, at any rate, since my first acquaintance with that strong and masterful spirit, has been, that I can say of him as he of Plutarch—"As soon as I open him, I seem to grow a pair of wings." If I had the task of making myself at home on the earth, I would choose him as my companion.

Schopenhauer has a second characteristic in common with Montaigne, besides honesty; a joy that really makes others joyful. "Aliis lætus, sibi sapiens." There are two very different kinds of joyfulness. The true thinker always communicates joy and life, whether he is showing his serious or comic side, his human insight or his godlike forbearance: without surly looks or trembling hands or watery eyes, but simply and truly, with fearlessness and strength, a little cavalierly perhaps, and sternly, but always as a conqueror: and it is this that brings the deepest and intensest joy, to see the conquering god with all the monsters that he has fought. But the joyfulness one finds here and there in the mediocre writers and limited thinkers makes some of us miserable; I felt this, for example, with the "joyfulness" of David Strauss. We are generally ashamed of such a quality in our contemporaries, because they show the nakedness of our time, and of the men in it, to posterity. Such fils de joie do not see the sufferings and the monsters, that they pretend, as philosophers, to see and fight; and so their joy deceives us, and we hate it; it tempts to the false belief that they have gained some victory. At bottom there is only joy where there is victory: and this applies to true philosophy as much as to any work of art. The contents may be forbidding and serious, as the problem of existence always is; the work will only prove tiresome and oppressive, if the slipshod thinker and the dilettante have spread the mist of their insufficiency over it: while nothing happier or better can come to man's lot than to be near one of those conquering spirits whose profound thought has made them love what is most vital, and whose wisdom has found its goal in beauty. They really speak: they are no stammerers or babblers; they live and move, and have no part in the danse macabre of the rest of humanity. And so in their company one feels a natural man again, and could cry out with Goethe—"What a wondrous and priceless thing is a living creature! How fitted to his surroundings, how true, and real!"

I have been describing nothing but the first, almost physiological, impression made upon me by Schopenhauer, the magical emanation of inner force from one plant of Nature to another, that follows the slightest contact. Analysing it, I find that this influence of Schopenhauer has three elements, his honesty, his joy, and his consistency. He is honest, as speaking and writing for himself alone; joyful, because his thought has conquered the greatest difficulties; consistent, because he cannot help being so. His strength rises like a flame in the calm air, straight up, without a tremor or deviation. He finds his way, without our noticing that he has been seeking it: so surely and cleverly and inevitably does he run his course, as if by some law of gravitation. If any one have felt what it means to find, in our present world of Centaurs and Chimæras, a single-hearted and unaffected child of nature who moves unconstrained on his own road, he will understand my joy and surprise in discovering Schopenhauer: I knew in him the educator and philosopher I had so long desired. Only, however, in his writings: which was a great loss. All the more did I exert myself to see behind the book the living man whose testament it was, and who promised his inheritance to such as could, and would, be more than his readers—his pupils and his sons.

III.

I get profit from a philosopher, just so far as he can be an example to me. There is no doubt that a man can draw whole nations after him by his example; as is shown by Indian history, which is practically the history of Indian philosophy. But this example must exist in his outward life, not merely in his books; it must follow the way of the Grecian philosophers, whose doctrine was in their dress and bearing and general manner of life rather than in their speech or writing. We have nothing yet of this "breathing testimony" in German philosophical life; the spirit has, apparently, long completed its emancipation, while the flesh has hardly begun; yet it is foolish to think that the spirit can be really free and independent when this victory over limitation—which is ultimately a formative limiting of one's self—is not embodied anew in every look and movement. Kant held to his university, submitted to its regulations, and belonged, as his colleagues and students thought, to a definite religious faith: and naturally his example has produced, above all, University professors of philosophy. Schopenhauer makes small account of the learned tribe, keeps himself exclusive, and cultivates an independence from state and society as his ideal, to escape the chains of circumstance here: that is his value to us. Many steps in the enfranchisement of the philosopher are unknown in Germany; they cannot always remain so. Our artists live more bravely and honourably than our philosophers; and Richard Wagner, the best example of all, shows how genius need not fear a fight to the death with the established forms and ordinances, if we wish to bring the higher truth and order, that lives in him, to the light. The "truth," however, of which we hear so much from our professors, seems to be a far more modest being, and no kind of disturbance is to be feared from her; she is an easy-going and pleasant creature, who is continually assuring the powers that be that no one need fear any trouble from her quarter: for man is only "pure reason." And therefore I will say, that philosophy in Germany has more and more to learn not to be "pure reason": and it may well take as its model "Schopenhauer the man."

It is no less than a marvel that he should have come to be this human kind of example: for he was beset, within and without, by the most frightful dangers, that would have crushed and broken a weaker nature. I think there was a strong likelihood of Schopenhauer the man going under, and leaving at best a residue of "pure reason": and only "at best"—it was more probable that neither man nor reason would survive.

A modern Englishman sketches the most usual danger to extraordinary men who live in a society that worships the ordinary, in this manner:—"Such uncommon characters are first cowed, then become sick and melancholy, and then die. A Shelley could never have lived in England: a race of Shelleys would have been impossible." Our Holderins and Kleists were undone by their unconventionality, and were not strong enough for the climate of the so-called German culture; and only iron natures like Beethoven, Goethe, Schopenhauer and Wagner could hold out against it. Even in them the effect of this weary toiling and moiling is seen in many lines and wrinkles; their breathing is harder and their voice is forced. The old diplomatist who had only just seen and spoken to Goethe, said to a friend—"Voilà un homme qui a eu de grands chagrins!" which Goethe translated to mean "That is a man who has taken great pains in his life." And he adds, "If the trace of the sorrow and activity we have gone through cannot be wiped from our features, it is no wonder that all that survives of us and our struggles should bear the same impress." And this is the Goethe to whom our cultured Philistines point as the happiest of Germans, that they may prove their thesis, that it must be possible to be happy among them—with the unexpressed corollary that no one can be pardoned for feeling unhappy and lonely among them. Hence they push their doctrine, in practice, to its merciless conclusion, that there is always a secret guilt in isolation. Poor Schopenhauer had this secret guilt too in his heart, the guilt of cherishing his philosophy more than his fellow-men; and he was so unhappy as to have learnt from Goethe that he must defend his philosophy at all costs from the neglect of his contemporaries, to save its very existence: for there is a kind of Grand Inquisitor's Censure in which the Germans, according to Goethe, are great adepts: it is called—inviolable silence. This much at least was accomplished by it;—the greater part of the first edition of Schopenhauer's masterpiece had to be turned into waste paper. The imminent risk that his great work would be undone, merely by neglect, bred in him a state of unrest—perilous and uncontrollable;—for no single adherent of any note presented himself. It is tragic to watch his search for any evidence of recognition: and his piercing cry of triumph at last, that he would now really be read (legor et legar), touches us with a thrill of pain. All the traits in which we do not see the great philosopher show us the suffering man, anxious for his noblest possessions; he was tortured by the fear of losing his little property, and perhaps of no longer being able to maintain in its purity his truly antique attitude towards philosophy. He often chose falsely in his desire to find real trust and compassion in men, only to return with a heavy heart to his faithful dog again. He was absolutely alone, with no single friend of his own kind to comfort him; and between one and none there lies an infinity—as ever between something and nothing. No one who has true friends knows what real loneliness means, though he may have the whole world in antagonism round him. Ah, I see well ye do not know what isolation is! Whenever there are great societies with governments and religions and public opinions—where there is a tyranny, in short, there will the lonely philosopher be hated: for philosophy offers an asylum to mankind where no tyranny can penetrate, the inner sanctuary, the centre of the heart's labyrinth: and the tyrants are galled at it. Here do the lonely men lie hid: but here too lurks their greatest danger. These men who have saved their inner freedom, must also live and be seen in the outer world: they stand in countless human relations by their birth, position, education and country, their own circumstances and the importunity of others: and so they are presumed to hold an immense number of opinions, simply because these happen to prevail: every look that is not a denial counts as an assent, every motion of the hand that does not destroy is regarded as an aid. These free and lonely men know that they perpetually seem other than they are. While they wish for nothing but truth and honesty, they are in a net of misunderstanding; and that ardent desire cannot prevent a mist of false opinions, of adaptations and wrong conclusions, of partial misapprehension and intentional reticence, from gathering round their actions. And there settles a cloud of melancholy on their brows: for such natures hate the necessity of pretence worse than death: and the continual bitterness gives them a threatening and volcanic character. They take revenge from time to time for their forced concealment and self-restraint: they issue from their dens with lowering looks: their words and deeds are explosive, and may lead to their own destruction. Schopenhauer lived amid dangers of this sort. Such lonely men need love, and friends, to whom they can be as open and sincere as to themselves, and in whose presence the deadening silence and hypocrisy may cease. Take their friends away, and there is left an increasing peril; Heinrich von Kleist was broken by the lack of love, and the most terrible weapon against unusual men is to drive them into themselves; and then their issuing forth again is a volcanic eruption. Yet there are always some demi-gods who can bear life under these fearful conditions and can be their conquerors: and if you would hear their lonely chant, listen to the music of Beethoven.

So the first danger in whose shadow Schopenhauer lived was—isolation. The second is called—doubting of the truth. To this every thinker is liable who sets out from the philosophy of Kant, provided he be strong and sincere in his sorrows and his desires, and not a mere tinkling thought-box or calculating machine. We all know the shameful state of things implied by this last reservation, and I believe it is only a very few men that Kant has so vitally affected as to change the current of their blood. To judge from what one reads, there must have been a revolution in every domain of thought since the work of this unobtrusive professor: I cannot believe it myself. For I see men, though darkly, as themselves needing to be revolutionised, before any "domains of thought" can be so. In fact, we find the first mark of any influence Kant may have had on the popular mind, in a corrosive scepticism and relativity. But it is only in noble and active spirits who could never rest in doubt that the shattering despair of truth itself could take the place of doubt. This was, for example, the effect of the Kantian philosophy on Heinrich von Kleist. "It was only a short time ago," he writes in his poignant way, "that I became acquainted with the Kantian philosophy; and I will tell you my thought, though I cannot fear that it will rack you to your inmost soul, as it did me.—We cannot decide, whether what we call truth is really truth, or whether it only seems so to us. If the latter, the truth that we amass here does not exist after death, and all our struggle to gain a possession that may follow us even to the grave is in vain. If the blade of this thought do not cut your heart, yet laugh not at another who feels himself wounded by it in his Holy of Holies. My one highest aim has vanished, and I have no more." Yes, when will men feel again deeply as Kleist did, and learn to measure a philosophy by what it means to the "Holy of Holies"? And yet we must make this estimate of what Schopenhauer can mean to us, after Kant, as the first pioneer to bring us from the heights of sceptical disillusionment or "critical" renunciation, to the greater height of tragic contemplation, the nocturnal heaven with its endless crown of stars. His greatness is that he can stand opposite the picture of life, and interpret it to us as a whole: while all the clever people cannot escape the error of thinking one comes nearer to the interpretation by a laborious analysis of the colours and material of the picture; with the confession, probably, that the texture of the canvas is very complicated, and the chemical composition of the colours undiscoverable. Schopenhauer knew that one must guess the painter in order to understand the picture. But now the whole learned fraternity is engaged on understanding the colours and canvas, and not the picture: and only he who has kept the universal panorama of life and being firmly before his eyes, will use the individual sciences without harm to himself; for, without this general view as a norm, they are threads that lead nowhere and only confuse still more the maze of our existence. Here we see, as I said, the greatness of Schopenhauer, that he follows up every idea, as Hamlet follows the Ghost, without allowing himself to turn aside for a learned digression, or be drawn away by the scholastic abstractions of a rabid dialectic. The study of the minute philosophers is only interesting for the recognition that they have reached those stages in the great edifice of philosophy where learned disquisitions for and against, where hair-splitting objections and counter-objections are the rule: and for that reason they evade the demand of every great philosophy to speak sub specie æternitatis—"this is the picture of the whole of life: learn thence the meaning of thine own life." And the converse: "read thine own life, and understand thence the hieroglyphs of the universal life." In this way must Schopenhauer's philosophy always be interpreted; as an individualist philosophy, starting from the single man, in his own nature, to gain an insight into his personal miseries, and needs, and limitations, and find out the remedies that will console them: namely, the sacrifice of the ego, and its submission to the nobler ends, especially those of justice and mercy. He teaches us to distinguish between the true and the apparent furtherance of man's happiness: how neither the attainment of riches, nor honour, nor learning, can raise the individual from his deep despair at his unworthiness; and how the quest for these good things can only have meaning through a universal end that transcends and explains them;—the gaining of power to aid our physical nature by them and, as far as may be, correct its folly and awkwardness. For one's self only, in the first instance: and finally, through one's self, for all. It is a task that leads to scepticism: for there is so much to be made better yet, in one and all!

Applying this to Schopenhauer himself, we come to the third and most intimate danger in which he lived, and which lay deep in the marrow of his being. Every one is apt to discover a limitation in himself, in his gifts of intellect as well as his moral will, that fills him with yearning and melancholy; and as he strives after holiness through a consciousness of sin, so, as an intellectual being, he has a deep longing after the "genius" in himself. This is the root of all true culture; and if we say this means the aspiration of man to be "born again" as saint and genius, I know that one need not be a Buddhist to understand the myth. We feel a strong loathing when we find talent without such aspiration, in the circle of the learned, or among the so-called educated; for we see that such men, with all their cleverness, are no aid but a hindrance to the beginnings of culture, and the blossoming of genius, the aim of all culture. There is a rigidity in them, parallel to the cold arrogance of conventional virtue, which also remains at the opposite pole to true holiness. Schopenhauer's nature contained an extraordinarily dangerous dualism. Few thinkers have felt as he did the complete and unmistakable certainty of genius within them; and his genius made him the highest of all promises,—that there could be no deeper furrow than that which he was ploughing in the ground of the modern world. He knew one half of his being to be fulfilled according to its strength, with no other need; and he followed with greatness and dignity his vocation of consolidating his victory. In the other half there was a gnawing aspiration, which we can understand, when we hear that he turned away with a sad look from the picture of Rancé, the founder of the Trappists, with the words: "That is a matter of grace." For genius evermore yearns after holiness as it sees further and more clearly from its watch-tower than other men, deep into the reconciliation of Thought and Being, the kingdom of peace and the denial of the will, and up to that other shore, of which the Indians speak. The wonder is, that Schopenhauer's nature should have been so inconceivably stable and unshakable that it could neither be destroyed nor petrified by this yearning. Every one will understand this after the measure of his own character and greatness: none of us will understand it in the fulness of its meaning.

The more one considers these three dangers, the more extraordinary will appear his vigour in opposing them and his safety after the battle. True, he gained many scars and open wounds: and a cast of mind that may seem somewhat too bitter and pugnacious. But his single ideal transcends the highest humanity in him. Schopenhauer stands as a pattern to men, in spite of all those scars and scratches. We may even say, that what was imperfect and "all too human" in him, brings us nearer to him as a man, for we see a sufferer and a kinsman to suffering, not merely a dweller on the unattainable heights of genius.

These three constitutional dangers that threatened Schopenhauer, threaten us all. Each one of us bears a creative solitude within himself and his consciousness of it forms an exotic aura of strangeness round him. Most men cannot endure it, because they are slothful, as I said, and because their solitude hangs round them a chain of troubles and burdens. No doubt, for the man with this heavy chain, life loses almost everything that one desires from it in youth—joy, safety, honour: his fellow-men pay him his due of—isolation! The wilderness and the cave are about him, wherever he may live. He must look to it that he be not enslaved and oppressed, and become melancholy thereby. And let him surround himself with the pictures of good and brave fighters such as Schopenhauer.

The second danger, too, is not rare. Here and there we find one dowered by nature with a keen vision; his thoughts dance gladly in the witches' Sabbath of dialectic; and if he uncautiously give his talent the rein, it is easy to lose all humanity and live a ghostly life in the realm of "pure reason": or through the constant search for the "pros and cons" of things, he may go astray from the truth and live without courage or confidence, in doubt, denial and discontent, and the slender hope that waits on disillusion: "No dog could live long thus!"

The third danger is a moral or intellectual hardening: man breaks the bond that united him to his ideal: he ceases to be fruitful and reproduce himself in this or that province, and becomes an enemy or a parasite of culture. The solitude of his being has become an indivisible, unrelated atom, an icy stone. And one can perish of this solitude as well as of the fear of it, of one's self as well as one's self-sacrifice, of both aspiration and petrifaction: and to live is ever to be in danger.

Beside these dangers to which Schopenhauer would have been constitutionally liable, in whatever century he had lived, there were also some produced by his own time; and it is essential to distinguish between these two kinds, in order to grasp the typical and formative elements in his nature. The philosopher casts his eye over existence, and wishes to give it a new standard value; for it has been the peculiar task of all great thinkers to be law-givers for the weight and stamp in the mint of reality. And his task will be hindered if the men he sees near him be a weakly and worm-eaten growth. To be correct in his calculation of existence, the unworthiness of the present time must be a very small item in the addition. The study of ancient or foreign history is valuable, if at all, for a correct judgment on the whole destiny of man; which must be drawn not only from an average estimate but from a comparison of the highest destinies that can befall individuals or nations. The present is too much with us; it directs the vision even against the philosopher's will: and it will inevitably be reckoned too high in the final sum. And so he must put a low figure on his own time as against others, and suppress the present in his picture of life, as well as in himself; must put it into the background or paint it over; a difficult, and almost impossible task. The judgment of the ancient Greek philosophers on the value of existence means so much more than our own, because they had the full bloom of life itself before them, and their vision was untroubled by any felt dualism between their wish for freedom and beauty on the grand scale, and their search after truth, with its single question "What is the real worth of life?" Empedocles lived when Greek culture was full to overflowing with the joy of life, and all ages may take profit from his words; especially as no other great philosopher of that great time ventured to contradict them. Empedocles is only the clearest voice among them—they all say the same thing, if a man will but open his ears. A modern thinker is always in the throes of an unfulfilled desire; he is looking for life,—warm, red life,—that he may pass judgment on it: at any rate he will think it necessary to be a living man himself, before he can believe in his power of judging. And this is the title of the modern philosophers to sit among the great aiders of Life (or rather of the will to live), and the reason why they can look from their own out-wearied time and aspire to a truer culture, and a clearer explanation. Their yearning is, however, their danger; the reformer in them struggles with the critical philosopher. And whichever way the victory incline, it also implies a defeat. How was Schopenhauer to escape this danger?

We like to consider the great man as the noble child of his age, who feels its defects more strongly and intimately than the smaller men: and therefore the struggle of the great man against his age is apparently nothing but a mad fight to the death with himself. Only apparently, however: he only fights the elements in his time that hinder his own greatness, in other words his own freedom and sincerity. And so, at bottom, he is only an enemy to that element which is not truly himself, the irreconcilable antagonism of the temporal and eternal in him. The supposed "child of his age" proves to be but a step-child. From boyhood Schopenhauer strove with his time, a false and unworthy mother to him, and as soon as he had banished her, he could bring back his being to its native health and purity. For this very reason we can use his writings as mirrors of his time; it is no fault of the mirror if everything contemporary appear in it stricken by a ravaging disease, pale and thin, with tired looks and hollow eyes,—the step-child's sorrow made visible. The yearning for natural strength, for a healthy and simple humanity, was a yearning for himself: and as soon as he had conquered his time within him, he was face to face with his own genius. The secret of nature's being and his own lay open, the step-mother's plot to conceal his genius from him was foiled. And now he could turn a fearless eye towards the question, "What is the real worth of life?" without having any more to weigh a bloodless and chaotic age of doubt and hypocrisy. He knew that there was something higher and purer to be won on this earth than the life of his time, and a man does bitter wrong to existence who only knows it and criticises it in this hateful form. Genius, itself the highest product of life, is now summoned to justify life, if it can: the noble creative soul must answer the question:—"Dost thou in thy heart say 'Yea!' unto this existence? Is it enough for thee? Wilt thou be its advocate and its redeemer? One true 'Yea!' from thy lips, and the sorely accused life shall go free." How shall he answer? In the words of Empedocles.

IV.

The last hint may well remain obscure for a time: I have something more easy to explain, namely how Schopenhauer can help us to educate ourselves in opposition to our age, since we have the advantage of really knowing our age, through him;—if it be an advantage! It may be no longer possible in a couple of hundred years. I sometimes amuse myself with the idea that men may soon grow tired of books and their authors, and the savant of to-morrow come to leave directions in his will that his body be burned in the midst of his books, including of course his own writings. And in the gradual clearing of the forests, might not our libraries be very reasonably used for straw and brushwood? Most books are born from the smoke and vapour of the brain: and to vapour and smoke may they well return. For having no fire within themselves, they shall be visited with fire. And possibly to a later century our own may count as the "Dark age," because our productions heated the furnace hotter and more continuously than ever before. We are anyhow happy that we can learn to know our time; and if there be any sense in busying ourselves with our time at all, we may as well do it as thoroughly as we can, so that no one may have any doubt about it. The possibility of this we owe to Schopenhauer.

Our happiness would of course be infinitely greater, if our inquiry showed that nothing so hopeful and splendid as our present epoch had ever existed. There are simple people in some corner of the earth to-day—perhaps in Germany—who are disposed to believe in all seriousness that the world was put right two years ago,[1] and that all stern and gloomy views of life are now contradicted by "facts." The foundation of the New German Empire is, to them, the decisive blow that annihilates all the "pessimistic" philosophisers,—no doubt of it. To judge the philosopher's significance in our time, as an educator, we must oppose a widespread view like this, especially common in our universities. We must say, it is a shameful thing that such abominable flattery of the Time-Fetish should be uttered by a herd of so-called reflective and honourable men; it is a proof that we no longer see how far the seriousness of philosophy is removed from that of a newspaper. Such men have lost the last remnant of feeling, not only for philosophy, but also for religion, and have put in its place a spirit not so much of optimism as of journalism, the evil spirit that broods over the day—and the daily paper. Every philosophy that believes the problem of existence to be shelved, or even solved, by a political event, is a sham philosophy. There have been innumerable states founded since the beginning of the world; that is an old story. How should a political innovation manage once and for all to make a contented race of the dwellers on this earth? If any one believe in his heart that this is possible, he should report himself to our authorities: he really deserves to be Professor of Philosophy in a German university, like Harms in Berlin, Jurgen Meyer in Bonn, and Carrière in Munich.

We are feeling the consequences of the doctrine, preached lately from all the housetops, that the state is the highest end of man and there is no higher duty than to serve it: I regard this not a relapse into paganism, but into stupidity. A man who thinks state-service to be his highest duty, very possibly knows no higher one; yet there are both men and duties in a region beyond,—and one of these duties, that seems to me at least of higher value than state-service, is to destroy stupidity in all its forms—and this particular stupidity among them. And I have to do with a class of men whose teleological conceptions extend further than the well-being of a state, I mean with philosophers—and only with them in their relation to the world of culture, which is again almost independent of the "good of the state." Of the many links that make up the twisted chain of humanity, some are of gold and others of pewter.

How does the philosopher of our time regard culture? Quite differently, I assure you, from the professors who are so content with their new state. He seems to see the symptoms of an absolute uprooting of culture in the increasing rush and hurry of life, and the decay of all reflection and simplicity. The waters of religion are ebbing, and leaving swamps or stagnant pools: the nations are drawing away in enmity again, and long to tear each other in pieces. The sciences, blindly driving along, on a laisser faire system, without a common standard, are splitting up, and losing hold of every firm principle. The educated classes are being swept along in the contemptible struggle for wealth. Never was the world more worldly, never poorer in goodness and love. Men of learning are no longer beacons or sanctuaries in the midst of this turmoil of worldliness; they themselves are daily becoming more restless, thoughtless, loveless. Everything bows before the coming barbarism, art and science included. The educated men have degenerated into the greatest foes of education, for they will deny the universal sickness and hinder the physician. They become peevish, these poor nerveless creatures, if one speak of their weakness and combat the shameful spirit of lies in them. They would gladly make one believe that they have outstripped all the centuries, and they walk with a pretence of happiness which has something pathetic about it, because their happiness is so inconceivable. One would not even ask them, as Tannhäuser did Biterolf, "What hast thou, poor wretch, enjoyed!" For, alas! we know far better ourselves, in another way. There is a wintry sky over us, and we dwell on a high mountain, in danger and in need. Short-lived is all our joy, and the sun's rays strike palely on our white mountains. Music is heard; an old man grinds an organ, and the dancers whirl round, and the heart of the wanderer is shaken within him to see it: everything is so disordered, so drab, so hopeless. Even now there is a sound of joy, of clear thoughtless joy! but soon the mist of evening closes round, the note dies away, and the wanderer's footsteps are heard on the gravel; as far as his eye can reach there is nothing but the grim and desolate face of nature.

It may be one-sided, to insist only on the blurred lines and the dull colours in the picture of modern life: yet the other side is no more encouraging, it is only more disturbing. There is certainly strength there, enormous strength; but it is wild, primitive and merciless. One looks on with a chill expectancy, as though into the caldron of a witch's kitchen; every moment there may arise sparks and vapour, to herald some fearful apparition. For a century we have been ready for a world-shaking convulsion; and though we have lately been trying to set the conservative strength of the so-called national state against the great modern tendency to volcanic destructiveness, it will only be, for a long time yet, an aggravation of the universal unrest that hangs over us. We need not be deceived by individuals behaving as if they knew nothing of all this anxiety: their own restlessness shows how well they know it. They think more exclusively of themselves than men ever thought before; they plant and build for their little day, and the chase for happiness is never greater than when the quarry must be caught to-day or to-morrow: the next day perhaps there is no more hunting. We live in the Atomic Age, or rather in the Atomic Chaos. The opposing forces were practically held together in mediæval times by the Church, and in some measure assimilated by the strong pressure which she exerted. When the common tie broke and the pressure relaxed, they rose once more against each other. The Reformation taught that many things were "adiaphora"—departments that needed no guidance from religion: this was the price paid for its own existence. Christianity paid a similar one to guard itself against the far more religious antiquity: and laid the seeds of discord at once. Everything nowadays is directed by the fools and the knaves, the selfishness of the money-makers and the brute forces of militarism. The state in their hands makes a good show of reorganising everything, and of becoming the bond that unites the warring elements; in other words, it wishes for the same idolatry from mankind as they showed to the Church.

And we shall yet feel the consequences. We are even now on the ice-floes in the stream of the Middle Ages: they are thawing fast, and their movement is ominous: the banks are flooded, and giving way. The revolution, the atomistic revolution, is inevitable: but what are those smallest indivisible elements of human society?

There is surely far more danger to mankind in transitional periods like these than in the actual time of revolution and chaos; they are tortured by waiting, and snatch greedily at every moment; and this breeds all kinds of cowardice and selfishness in them: whereas the true feeling of a great and universal need ever inspires men, and makes them better. In the midst of such dangers, who will provide the guardians and champions for Humanity, for the holy and inviolate treasure that has been laid up in the temples, little by little, by countless generations? Who will set up again the Image of Man, when men in their selfishness and terror see nothing but the trail of the serpent or the cur in them, and have fallen from their high estate to that of the brute or the automaton?

There are three Images of Man fashioned by our modern time, which for a long while yet will urge mortal men to transfigure their own lives; they are the men of Rousseau, Goethe, and Schopenhauer. The first has the greatest fire, and is most calculated to impress the people: the second is only for the few, for those contemplative natures "in the grand style" who are misunderstood by the crowd. The third demands the highest activity in those who will follow it: only such men will look on that image without harm, for it breaks the spirit of that merely contemplative man, and the rabble shudder at it. From the first has come forth a strength that led and still leads to fearful revolution: for in all socialistic upheavals it is ever Rousseau's man who is the Typhoeus under the Etna. Oppressed and half crushed to death by the pride of caste and the pitilessness of wealth, spoilt by priests and bad education, a laughing-stock even to himself, man cries in his need on "holy mother Nature," and feels suddenly that she is as far from him as any god of the Epicureans. His prayers do not reach her; so deeply sunk is he in the Chaos of the unnatural. He contemptuously throws aside all the finery that seemed his truest humanity a little while ago—all his arts and sciences, all the refinements of his life,—he beats with his fists against the walls, in whose shadow he has degenerated, and goes forth to seek the light and the sun, the forest and the crag. And crying out, "Nature alone is good, the natural man alone is human," he despises himself and aspires beyond himself: a state wherein the soul is ready for a fearful resolve, but calls the noble and the rare as well from their utter depths.

Goethe's man is no such threatening force; in a certain sense he is a corrective and a sedative to those dangerous agitations of which

Rousseau's man is a prey. Goethe himself in his youth followed the "gospel of kindly Nature" with all the ardour of his soul: his Faust was the highest and boldest picture of Rousseau's man, so far at any rate as his hunger for life, his discontent and yearning, his intercourse with the demons of the heart could be represented. But what comes from these congregated storm-clouds? Not a single lightning flash! And here begins the new Image of man—the man according to Goethe. One might have thought that Faust would have lived a continual life of suffering, as a revolutionary and a deliverer, as the negative force that proceeds from goodness, as the genius of ruin, alike religious and dæmonic, in opposition to his utterly undæmonic companion; though of course he could not be free of this companion, and had at once to use and despise his evil and destructive scepticism—which is the tragic destiny of all revolutionary deliverers. One is wrong, however, to expect anything of the sort: Goethe's man here parts company with Rousseau's; for he hates all violence, all sudden transition—that is, all action: and the universal deliverer becomes merely the universal traveller. All the riches of life and nature, all antiquity—arts, mythologies and sciences—pass before his eager eyes, his deepest desires are aroused and satisfied, Helen herself can hold him no more—and the moment must come for which his mocking companion is waiting. At a fair spot on the earth, his flight comes to an end: his pinions drop, and Mephistopheles is at his side. When the German ceases to be Faust, there is no danger greater than of becoming a Philistine and falling into the hands of the devil—heavenly powers alone can save him. Goethe's man is, as I said, the contemplative man in the grand style, who is only kept from dying of ennui by feeding on all the great and memorable things that have ever existed, and by living from desire to desire. He is not the active man; and when he does take a place among active men, as things are, you may be sure that no good will come of it (think, for example, of the zeal with which Goethe wrote for the stage!); and further, you may be sure that "things as they are" will suffer no change. Goethe's man is a conciliatory and conservative spirit, though in danger of degenerating into a Philistine, just as Rousseau's man may easily become a Catiline. All his virtues would be the better by the addition of a little brute force and elemental passion. Goethe appears to have seen where the weakness and danger of his creation lay, as is clear from Jarno's word to Wilhelm Meister: "You are bitter and ill-tempered—which is quite an excellent thing: if you could once become really angry, it would be still better."

To speak plainly, it is necessary to become really angry in order that things may be better. The picture of Schopenhauer's man can help us here. Schopenhauer's man voluntarily takes upon himself the pain of telling the truth: this pain serves to quench his individual will and make him ready for the complete transformation of his being, which it is the inner meaning of life to realise. This openness in him appears to other men to be an effect of malice, for they think the preservation of their shifts and pretences to be the first duty of humanity, and any one who destroys their playthings to be merely malicious. They are tempted to cry out to such a man, in Faust's words to Mephistopheles:—

"So to the active and eternal
Creative force, in cold disdain
You now oppose the fist infernal"—

and he who would live according to Schopenhauer would seem to be more like a Mephistopheles than a Faust—that is, to our weak modern eyes, which always discover signs of malice in any negation. But there is a kind of denial and destruction that is the effect of that strong aspiration after holiness and deliverance, which Schopenhauer was the first philosopher to teach our profane and worldly generation. Everything that can be denied, deserves to be denied; and real sincerity means the belief in a state of things which cannot be denied, or in which there is no lie. The sincere man feels that his activity has a metaphysical meaning. It can only be explained by the laws of a different and a higher life; it is in the deepest sense an affirmation: even if everything that he does seem utterly opposed to the laws of our present life. It must lead therefore to constant suffering; but he knows, as Meister Eckhard did, that "the quickest beast that will carry you to perfection is suffering." Every one, I should think, who has such an ideal before him, must feel a wider sympathy; and he will have a burning desire to become a "Schopenhauer man";—pure and wonderfully patient, on his intellectual side full of a devouring fire, and far removed from the cold and contemptuous "neutrality" of the so-called scientific man; so high above any warped and morose outlook on life as to offer himself as the first victim of the truth he has won, with a deep consciousness of the sufferings that must spring from his sincerity. His courage will destroy his happiness on earth, he must be an enemy to the men he loves and the institutions in which he grew up, he must spare neither person nor thing, however it may hurt him, he will be misunderstood and thought an ally of forces that he abhors, in his search for righteousness he will seem unrighteous by human standards: but he must comfort himself with the words that his teacher Schopenhauer once used: "A happy life is impossible, the highest thing that man can aspire to is a heroic life; such as a man lives, who is always fighting against unequal odds for the good of others; and wins in the end without any thanks. After the battle is over, he stands like the Prince in the re corvo of Gozzi, with dignity and nobility in his eyes, but turned to stone. His memory remains, and will be reverenced as a hero's; his will, that has been mortified all his life by toiling and struggling, by evil payment and ingratitude, is absorbed into Nirvana." Such a heroic life, with its full "mortification"—corresponds very little to the paltry ideas of the people who talk most about it, and make festivals in memory of great men, in the belief that a great man is great in the sense that they are small, either through exercise of his gifts to please himself or by a blind mechanical obedience to this inner force; so that the man who does not possess the gift or feel the compulsion has the same right to be small as the other to be great. But "gift" and "compulsion" are contemptible words, mere means of escape from an inner voice, a slander on him who has listened to the voice—the great man; he least of all will allow himself to be given or compelled to anything: for he knows as well as any smaller man how easily life can be taken and how soft the bed whereon he might lie if he went the pleasant and conventional way with himself and his fellow-creatures: all the regulations of mankind are turned to the end that the intense feeling of life may be lost in continual distractions. Now why will he so strongly choose the opposite, and try to feel life, which is the same as to suffer from life? Because he sees that men will tempt him to betray himself, and that there is a kind of agreement to draw him from his den. He will prick up his ears and gather himself together, and say, "I will remain mine own." He gradually comes to understand what a fearful decision it is. For he must go down into the depths of being, with a string of curious questions on his lips—"Why am I alive? what lesson have I to learn from life? how have I become what I am, and why do I suffer in this existence?" He is troubled, and sees that no one is troubled in the same way; but rather that the hands of his fellow-men are passionately stretched out towards the fantastic drama of the political theatre, or they themselves are treading the boards under many disguises, youths, men and graybeards, fathers, citizens, priests, merchants and officials,—busy with the comedy they are all playing, and never thinking of their own selves. To the question "To what end dost thou live?" they would all immediately answer, with pride, "To become a good citizen or professor or statesman,"—and yet they are something which can never be changed: and why are they just—this? Ah, and why nothing better? The man who only regards his life as a moment in the evolution of a race or a state or a science, and will belong merely to a history of "becoming," has not understood the lesson of existence, and must learn it over again. This eternal "becoming something" is a lying puppet-show, in which man has forgot himself; it is the force that scatters individuality to the four winds, the eternal childish game that the big baby time is playing in front of us—and with us. The heroism of sincerity lies in ceasing to be the plaything of time. Everything in the process of "becoming" is a hollow sham, contemptible and shallow: man can only find the solution of his riddle in "being" something definite and unchangeable. He begins to test how deep both "becoming" and "being" are rooted in him—and a fearful task is before his soul; to destroy the first, and bring all the falsity of things to the light. He wishes to know everything, not to feed a delicate taste, like Goethe's man, to take delight, from a safe place in the multiplicity of existence: but he himself is the first sacrifice that he brings. The heroic man does not think of his happiness or misery, his virtues or his vices, or of his being the measure of things; he has no further hopes of himself and will accept the utter consequences of his hopelessness. His strength lies in his self-forgetfulness: if he have a thought for himself, it is only to measure the vast distance between himself and his aim, and to view what he has left behind him as so much dross. The old philosophers sought for happiness and truth, with all their strength: and there is an evil principle in nature that not one shall find that which he cannot help seeking. But the man who looks for a lie in everything, and becomes a willing friend to unhappiness, shall have a marvellous disillusioning: there hovers near him something unutterable, of which truth and happiness are but idolatrous images born of the night; the earth loses her dragging weight, the events and powers of earth become as a dream, and a gradual clearness widens round him like a summer evening. It is as though the beholder of these things began to wake, and it had only been the clouds of a passing dream that had been weaving about him. They will at some time disappear: and then will it be day.

V.

But I have promised to speak of Schopenhauer, as far as my experience goes, as an educator, and it is far from being sufficient to paint the ideal humanity which is the "Platonic idea" in Schopenhauer; especially as my representation is an imperfect one. The most difficult task remains;—to say how a new circle of duties may spring from this ideal, and how one can reconcile such a transcendent aim with ordinary action; to prove, in short, that the ideal is educative. One might otherwise think it to be merely the blissful or intoxicating vision of a few rare moments, that leaves us afterwards the prey of a deeper disappointment. It is certain that the ideal begins to affect us in this way when we come suddenly to distinguish light and darkness, bliss and abhorrence; this is an experience that is as old as ideals themselves. But we ought not to stand in the doorway for long; we should soon leave the first stages, and ask the question, seriously and definitely, "Is it possible to bring that incredibly high aim so near us, that it should educate us, or 'lead us out,' as well as lead us upward?"—in order that the great words of Goethe be not fulfilled in our case—"Man is born to a state of limitation: he can understand ends that are simple, present and definite, and is accustomed to make use of means that are near to his hand; but as soon as he comes into the open, he knows neither what he wishes nor what he ought to do, and it is all one whether he be confused by the multitude of objects or set beside himself by their greatness and importance. It is always his misfortune to be led to strive after something which he cannot attain by any ordinary activity of his own." The objection can be made with apparent reason against Schopenhauer's man, that his greatness and dignity can only turn our heads, and put us beyond all community with the active men of the world: the common round of duties, the noiseless tenor of life has disappeared. One man may possibly get accustomed to living in a reluctant dualism, that is, in a contradiction with himself;—becoming unstable, daily weaker and less productive:—while another will renounce all action on principle, and scarcely endure to see others active. The danger is always great when a man is too heavy-laden, and cannot really accomplish any duties. Stronger natures may be broken by it; the weaker, which are the majority, sink into a speculative laziness, and at last, from their laziness, lose even the power of speculation.

With regard to such objections, I will admit that our work has hardly begun, and so far as I know, I only see one thing clearly and definitely—that it is possible for that ideal picture to provide you and me with a chain of duties that may be accomplished; and some of us already feel its pressure. In order, however, to be able to speak in plain language of the formula under which I may gather the new circle of duties, I must begin with the following considerations.

The deeper minds of all ages have had pity for animals, because they suffer from life and have not the power to turn the sting of the suffering against themselves, and understand their being metaphysically. The sight of blind suffering is the spring of the deepest emotion. And in many quarters of the earth men have supposed that the souls of the guilty have entered into beasts, and that the blind suffering which at first sight calls for such pity has a clear meaning and purpose to the divine justice,—of punishment and atonement: and a heavy punishment it is, to be condemned to live in hunger and need, in the shape of a beast, and to reach no consciousness of one's self in this life. I can think of no harder lot than the wild beast's; he is driven to the forest by the fierce pang of hunger, that seldom leaves him at peace; and peace is itself a torment, the surfeit after horrid food, won, maybe, by a deadly fight with other animals. To cling to life, blindly and madly, with no other aim, to be ignorant of the reason, or even the fact, of one's punishment, nay, to thirst after it as if it were a pleasure, with all the perverted desire of a fool—this is what it means to be an animal. If universal nature leads up to man, it is to show us that he is necessary to redeem her from the curse of the beast's life, and that in him existence can find a mirror of itself wherein life appears, no longer blind, but in its real metaphysical significance. But we should consider where the beast ends and the man begins—the man, the one concern of Nature. As long as any one desires life as a pleasure in itself, he has not raised his eyes above the horizon of the beast; he only desires more consciously what the beast seeks by a blind impulse. It is so with us all, for the greater part of our lives. We do not shake off the beast, but are beasts ourselves, suffering we know not what.

But there are moments when we do know; and then the clouds break, and we see how, with the rest of nature, we are straining towards the man, as to something that stands high above us. We look round and behind us, and fear the sudden rush of light; the beasts are transfigured, and ourselves with them. The enormous migrations of mankind in the wildernesses of the world, the cities they found and the wars they wage, their ceaseless gatherings and dispersions and fusions, the doctrines they blindly follow, their mutual frauds and deceits, the cry of distress, the shriek of victory—are all a continuation of the beast in us: as if the education of man has been intentionally set back, and his promise of self-consciousness frustrated; as if, in fact, after yearning for man so long, and at last reaching him by her labour, Nature should now recoil from him and wish to return to a state of unconscious instinct. Ah! she has need of knowledge, and shrinks before the very knowledge she needs: the flame flickers unsteadily and fears its own brightness, and takes hold of a thousand things before the one thing for which knowledge is necessary. There are moments when we all know that our most elaborate arrangements are only designed to give us refuge from our real task in life; we wish to hide our heads somewhere as if our Argus-eyed conscience could not find us out; we are quick to send our hearts on state-service, or money-making, or social duties, or scientific work, in order to possess them no longer ourselves; we are more willing and instinctive slaves of the hard day's work than mere living requires, because it seems to us more necessary not to be in a position to think. The hurry is universal, because every one is fleeing before himself; its concealment is just as universal, as we wish to seem contented and hide our wretchedness from the keener eyes; and so there is a common need for a new carillon of words to hang in the temple of life, and peal for its noisy festival. We all know the curious way in which unpleasant memories suddenly throng on us, and how we do our best by loud talk and violent gestures to put them out of our minds; but the gestures and the talk of our ordinary life make one think we are all in this condition, frightened of any memory or any inward gaze. What is it that is always troubling us? what is the gnat that will not let us sleep? There are spirits all about us, each moment of life has something to say to us, but we will not listen to the spirit-voices. When we are quiet and alone, we fear that something will be whispered in our ears, and so we hate the quiet, and dull our senses in society.

We understand this sometimes, as I say, and stand amazed at the whirl and the rush and the anxiety and all the dream that we call our life; we seem to fear the awakening, and our dreams too become vivid and restless, as the awakening draws near. But we feel as well that we are too weak to endure long those intimate moments, and that we are not the men to whom universal nature looks as her redeemers. It is something to be able to raise our heads but for a moment and see the stream in which we are sunk so deep. We cannot gain even this transitory moment of awakening by our own strength; we must be lifted up—and who are they that will uplift us?

The sincere men who have cast out the beast, the philosophers, artists and saints. Nature—quæ nunquam facit saltum—has made her one leap in creating them; a leap of joy, as she feels herself for the first time at her goal, where she begins to see that she must learn not to have goals above her, and that she has played the game of transition too long. The knowledge transfigures her, and there rests on her face the gentle weariness of evening that men call "beauty." Her words after this transfiguration are as a great light shed over existence: and the highest wish that mortals can reach is to listen continually to her voice with ears that hear. If a man think of all that Schopenhauer, for example, must have heard in his life, he may well say to himself—"The deaf ears, the feeble understanding and shrunken heart, everything that I call mine,—how I despise them! Not to be able to fly but only to flutter one's wings! To look above one's self and have no power to rise! To know the road that leads to the wide vision of the philosopher, and to reel back after a few steps! Were there but one day when the great wish might be fulfilled, how gladly would we pay for it with the rest of life! To rise as high as any thinker yet into the pure icy air of the mountain, where there are no mists and veils, and the inner constitution of things is shown in a stark and piercing clarity! Even by thinking of this the soul becomes infinitely alone; but were its wish fulfilled, did its glance once fall straight as a ray of light on the things below, were shame and anxiety and desire gone for ever—one could find no words for its state then, for the mystic and tranquil emotion with which, like the soul of Schopenhauer, it would look down on the monstrous hieroglyphics of existence and the petrified doctrines of "becoming"; not as the brooding night, but as the red and glowing day that streams over the earth. And what a destiny it is only to know enough of the fixity and happiness of the philosopher to feel the complete unfixity and unhappiness of the false philosopher, 'who without hope lives in desire': to know one's self to be the fruit of a tree that is too much in the shade ever to ripen, and to see a world of sunshine in front, where one may not go!"

There were sorrow enough here, if ever, to make such a man envious and spiteful: but he will turn aside, that he may not destroy his soul by a vain aspiration; and will discover a new circle of duties.

I can now give an answer to the question whether it be possible to approach the great ideal of Schopenhauer's man "by any ordinary activity of our own." In the first place, the new duties are certainly not those of a hermit; they imply rather a vast community, held together not by external forms but by a fundamental idea, namely that of culture; though only so far as it can put a single task before each of us—to bring the philosopher, the artist and the saint, within and without us, to the light, and to strive thereby for the completion of

Nature. For Nature needs the artist, as she needs the philosopher, for a metaphysical end, the explanation of herself, whereby she may have a clear and sharp picture of what she only saw dimly in the troubled period of transition,—and so may reach self-consciousness. Goethe, in an arrogant yet profound phrase, showed how all Nature's attempts only have value in so far as the artist interprets her stammering words, meets her half-way, and speaks aloud what she really means. "I have often said, and will often repeat," he exclaims in one place, "the causa finalis of natural and human activity is dramatic poetry. Otherwise the stuff is of no use at all."

Finally, Nature needs the saint. In him the ego has melted away, and the suffering of his life is, practically, no longer felt as individual, but as the spring of the deepest sympathy and intimacy with all living creatures: he sees the wonderful transformation scene that the comedy of "becoming" never reaches, the attainment, at length, of the high state of man after which all nature is striving, that she may be delivered from herself. Without doubt, we all stand in close relation to him, as well as to the philosopher and the artist: there are moments, sparks from the clear fire of love, in whose light we understand the word "I" no longer; there is something beyond our being that comes, for those moments, to the hither side of it: and this is why we long in our hearts for a bridge from here to there. In our ordinary state we can do nothing towards the production of the new redeemer, and so we hate ourselves in this state with a hatred that is the root of the pessimism which Schopenhauer had to teach again to our age, though it is as old as the aspiration after culture.—Its root, not its flower; the foundation, not the summit; the beginning of the road, not the end: for we have to learn at some time to hate something else, more universal than our own personality with its wretched limitation, its change and its unrest—and this will be when we shall learn to love something else than we can love now. When we are ourselves received into that high order of philosophers, artists and saints, in this life or a reincarnation of it, a new object for our love and hate will also rise before us. As it is, we have our task and our circle of duties, our hates and our loves. For we know that culture requires us to make ready for the coming of the Schopenhauer man;—and this is the "use" we are to make of him;—we must know what obstacles there are and strike them from our path—in fact, wage unceasing war against everything that hindered our fulfilment, and prevented us from becoming Schopenhauer's men ourselves.

VI.

It is sometimes harder to agree to a thing than to understand it; many will feel this when they consider the proposition—"Mankind must toil unceasingly to bring forth individual great men: this and nothing else is its task." One would like to apply to society and its ends a fact that holds universally in the animal and vegetable world; where progress depends only on the higher individual types, which are rarer, yet more persistent, complex and productive. But traditional notions of what the end of society is, absolutely bar the way. We can easily understand how in the natural world, where one species passes at some point into a higher one, the aim of their evolution cannot be held to lie in the high level attained by the mass, or in the latest types developed;—but rather in what seem accidental beings produced here and there by favourable circumstances. It should be just as easy to understand that it is the duty of mankind to provide the circumstances favourable to the birth of the new redeemer, simply because men can have a consciousness of their object. But there is always something to prevent them. They find their ultimate aim in the happiness of all, or the greatest number, or in the expansion of a great commonwealth. A man will very readily decide to sacrifice his life for the state; he will be much slower to respond if an individual, and not a state, ask for the sacrifice. It seems to be out of reason that one man should exist for the sake of another: "Let it be rather for the sake of every other, or, at any rate, of as many as possible!" O upright judge! As if it were more in reason to let the majority decide a question of value and significance! For the problem is—"In what way may your life, the individual life, retain the highest value and the deepest significance? and how may it least be squandered?" Only by your living for the good of the rarest and most valuable types, not for that of the majority,—who are the most worthless types, taken as individuals. This way of thinking should be implanted and fostered in every young man's mind: he should regard himself both as a failure of Nature's handiwork and a testimony to her larger ideas. "She has succeeded badly," he should say; "but I will do honour to her great idea by being a means to its better success."

With these thoughts he will enter the circle of culture, which is the child of every man's self-knowledge and dissatisfaction. He will approach and say aloud: "I see something above me, higher and more human than I: let all help me to reach it, as I will help all who know and suffer as I do, that the man may arise at last who feels his knowledge and love, vision and power, to be complete and boundless, who in his universality is one with nature, the critic and judge of existence." It is difficult to give any one this courageous self-consciousness, because it is impossible to teach love; from love alone the soul gains, not only the clear vision that leads to self-contempt, but also the desire to look to a higher self which is yet hidden, and strive upward to it with all its strength. And so he who rests his hope on a future great man, receives his first "initiation into culture." The sign of this is shame or vexation at one's self, a hatred of one's own narrowness, a sympathy with the genius that ever raises its head again from our misty wastes, a feeling for all that is struggling into life, the conviction that Nature must be helped in her hour of need to press forward to the man, however ill she seem to prosper, whatever success may attend her marvellous forms and projects: so that the men with whom we live are like the débris of some precious sculptures, which cry out—"Come and help us! Put us together, for we long to become complete."

I called this inward condition the "first initiation into culture." I have now to describe the effects of the "second initiation," a task of greater difficulty. It is the passage from the inner life to the criticism of the outer life. The eye must be turned to find in the great world of movement the desire for culture that is known from the immediate experience of the individual; who must use his own strivings and aspirations as the alphabet to interpret those of humanity. He cannot rest here either, but must go higher. Culture demands from him not only that inner experience, not only the criticism of the outer world surrounding him, but action too to crown them all, the fight for culture against the influences and conventions and institutions where he cannot find his own aim,—the production of genius.

Any one who can reach the second step, will see how extremely rare and imperceptible the knowledge of that end is, though all men busy themselves with culture and expend vast labour in her service. He asks himself in amazement—"Is not such knowledge, after all, absolutely necessary? Can Nature be said to attain her end, if men have a false idea of the aim of their own labour?" And any one who thinks a great deal of Nature's unconscious adaptation of means to ends, will probably answer at once: "Yes, men may think and speak what they like about their ultimate end, their blind instinct will tell them the right road." It requires some experience of life to be able to contradict this: but let a man be convinced of the real aim of culture—the production of the true man and nothing else;—let him consider that amid all the pageantry and ostentation of culture at the present time the conditions for his production are nothing but a continual "battle of the beasts": and he will see that there is great need for a conscious will to take the place of that blind instinct. There is another reason also;—to prevent the possibility of turning this obscure impulse to quite different ends, in a direction where our highest aim can no longer be attained. For we must beware of a certain kind of misapplied and parasitical culture; the powers at present most active in its propagation have other casts of thought that prevent their relation to culture from being pure and disinterested.

The first of these is the self-interest of the business men. This needs the help of culture, and helps her in return, though at the price of prescribing her ends and limits. And their favourite sorites is: "We must have as much knowledge and education as possible; this implies as great a need as possible for it, this again as much production, this again as much material wealth and happiness as possible."—This is the seductive formula. Its preachers would define education as the insight that makes man through and through a "child of his age" in his desires and their satisfaction, and gives him command over the best means of making money. Its aim would be to make "current" men, in the same sense as one speaks of the "currency" in money; and in their view, the more "current" men there are, the happier the people. The object of modern educational systems is therefore to make each man as "current" as his nature will allow him, and to give him the opportunity for the greatest amount of success and happiness that can be got from his particular stock of knowledge. He is required to have just so much idea of his own value (through his liberal education) as to know what he can ask of life; and he is assured that a natural and necessary connection between "intelligence and property" not only exists, but is also a moral necessity. All education is detested that makes for loneliness, and has an aim above money-making, and requires a long time: men look askance on such serious education, as mere "refined egoism" or "immoral Epicureanism." The converse of course holds, according to the ordinary morality, that education must be soon over to allow the pursuit of money to be soon begun, and should be just thorough enough to allow of much money being made. The amount of education is determined by commercial interests. In short, "man has a necessary claim to worldly happiness; only for that reason is education necessary."

There is, secondly, the self-interest of the state, which requires the greatest possible breadth and universality of culture, and has the most effective weapons to carry out its wishes. If it be firmly enough established not only to initiate but control education and bear its whole weight, such breadth will merely profit the competition of the state with other states. A "highly civilised state" generally implies, at the present time, the task of setting free the spiritual forces of a generation just so far as they may be of use to the existing institutions,—as a mountain stream is split up by embankments and channels, and its diminished power made to drive mill-wheels, its full strength being more dangerous than useful to the mills. And thus "setting free" comes to mean rather "chaining up." Compare, for example, what the self-interest of the state has done for Christianity. Christianity is one of the purest manifestations of the impulse towards culture and the production of the saint: but being used in countless ways to turn the mills of the state authorities, it gradually became sick at heart, hypocritical and degenerate, and in antagonism with its original aim. Its last phase, the German Reformation, would have been nothing but a sudden flickering of its dying flame, had it not taken new strength and light from the clash and conflagration of states.

In the third place, culture will be favoured by all those people who know their own character to be offensive or tiresome, and wish to draw a veil of so-called "good form" over them. Words, gestures, dress, etiquette, and such external things, are meant to produce a false impression, the inner side to be judged from the outer. I sometimes think that modern men are eternally bored with each other and look to the arts to make them interesting. They let their artists make savoury and inviting dishes of them; they steep themselves in the spices of the East and West, and have a very interesting aroma after it all. They are ready to suit all palates: and every one will be served, whether he want something with a good or bad taste, something sublime or coarse, Greek or Chinese, tragedy or gutter-drama. The most celebrated chefs among the moderns who wish to interest and be interested at any price, are the French; the worst are the Germans. This is really more comforting for the latter, and we have no reason to mind the French despising us for our want of interest, elegance and politeness, and being reminded of the Indian who longs for a ring through his nose, and then proceeds to tattoo himself.

Here I must digress a little. Many things in Germany have evidently been altered since the late war with France, and new requirements for German culture brought over. The war was for many their first venture into the more elegant half of the world: and what an admirable simplicity the conqueror shows in not scorning to learn something of culture from the conquered! The applied arts especially will be reformed to emulate our more refined neighbours, the German house furnished like the French, a "sound taste" applied to the German language by means of an Academy on the French model, to shake off the doubtful influence of Goethe—this is the judgment of our new Berlin Academician, Dubois-Raymond. Our theatres have been gradually moving, in a dignified way, towards the same goal, even the elegant German savant is now discovered—and we must now expect everything that does not conform to this law of elegance, our music, tragedy and philosophy, to be thrust aside as un-German. But there were no need to raise a finger for German culture, did German culture (which the Germans have yet to find) mean nothing but the little amenities that make life more decorative—including the arts of the dancing-master and the upholsterer;—or were they merely interested in academic rules of language and a general atmosphere of politeness. The late war and the self-comparison with the French do not seem to have aroused any further desires, and I suspect that the German has a strong wish for the moment to be free of the old obligations laid on him by his wonderful gifts of seriousness and profundity. He would much rather play the buffoon and the monkey, and learn the arts that make life amusing. But the German spirit cannot be more dishonoured than by being treated as wax for any elegant mould.

And if, unfortunately, a good many Germans will allow themselves to be thus moulded, one must continually say to them, till at last they listen:—"The old German way is no longer yours: it was hard, rough, and full of resistance; but it is still the most valuable material—one which only the greatest modellers can work with, for they alone are worthy to use it. What you have in you now is a soft pulpy stuff: make what you will out of it,—elegant dolls and interesting idols—Richard Wagner's phrase will still hold good, 'The German is awkward and ungainly when he wishes to be polite; he is high above all others, when he begins to take fire.'" All the elegant people have reason to beware of this German fire; it may one day devour them with all their wax dolls and idols.—The prevailing love of "good form" in Germany may have a deeper cause in the breathless seizing at what the moment can give, the haste that plucks the fruit too green, the race and the struggle that cut the furrows in men's brows and stamp the same mark on all their actions. As if there were a poison in them that would not let them breathe, they rush about in disorder, anxious slaves of the "three m's," the moment, the mode and the mob: they see too well their want of dignity and fitness, and need a false elegance to hide their galloping consumption. The fashionable desire of "good form" is bound up with a loathing of man's inner nature: the one is to conceal, the other to be concealed. Education means now the concealment of man's misery and wickedness, his wild-beast quarrels, his eternal greed, his shamelessness in fruition. In pointing out the absence of a German culture, I have often had the reproach flung at me: "This absence is quite natural, for the Germans have been too poor and modest up to now. Once rich and conscious of themselves, our people will have a culture too." Faith may often produce happiness, yet this particular faith makes me unhappy, for I feel that the culture whose future raises such hopes—the culture of riches, politeness, and elegant concealments—is the bitterest foe of that German culture in which I believe. Every one who has to live among Germans suffers from the dreadful grayness and apathy of their lives, their formlessness, torpor and clumsiness, still more their envy, secretiveness and impurity: he is troubled by their innate love of the false and the ignoble, their wretched mimicry and translation of a good foreign thing into a bad German one. But now that the feverish unrest, the quest of gain and success, the intense prizing of the moment, is added to it all, it makes one furious to think that all this sickness can never be cured, but only painted over, by such a "cult of the interesting." And this among a people that has produced a Schopenhauer and a Wagner! and will produce others, unless we are blindly deceiving ourselves; for should not their very existence be a guarantee that such forces are even now potential in the German spirit? Or will they be exceptions, the last inheritors of the qualities that were once called German? I can see nothing to help me here, and return to my main argument again, from which my doubts and anxieties have made me digress. I have not yet enumerated all the forces that help culture without recognising its end, the production of genius. Three have been named; the self-interest of business, of the state, and of those who draw the cloak of "good form" over them. There is fourthly the self-interest of science, and the peculiar nature of her servants—the learned.

Science has the same relation to wisdom as current morality to holiness: she is cold and dry, loveless, and ignorant of any deep feeling of dissatisfaction and yearning. She injures her servants in helping herself, for she impresses her own character on them and dries up their humanity. As long as we actually mean by culture the progress of science, she will pass by the great suffering man and harden her heart, for science only sees the problems of knowledge, and suffering is something alien and unintelligible to her world—though no less a problem for that!

If one accustom himself to put down every experience in a dialectical form of question and answer, and translate it into the language of "pure reason," he will soon wither up and rattle his bones like a skeleton. We all know it: and why is it that the young do not shudder at these skeletons of men, but give themselves blindly to science without motive or measure? It cannot be the so-called "impulse to truth": for how could there be an impulse towards a pure, cold and objectless knowledge? The unprejudiced eye can see the real driving forces only too plainly. The vivisection of the professor has much to recommend it, as he himself is accustomed to finger and analyse all things—even the worthiest! To speak honestly, the savant is a complex of very various impulses and attractive forces—he is a base metal throughout.

Take first a strong and increasing desire for intellectual adventure, the attraction of the new and rare as against the old and tedious. Add to that a certain joy in nosing the trail of dialectic, and beating the cover where the old fox, Thought, lies hid; the desire is not so much for truth as the chase of truth, and the chief pleasure is in surrounding and artistically killing it. Add thirdly a love of contradiction whereby the personality is able to assert itself against all others: the battle's the thing, and the personal victory its aim,—truth only its pretext. The impulse to discover "particular truths" plays a great part in the professor, coming from his submission to definite ruling persons, classes, opinions, churches, governments, for he feels it a profit to himself to bring truth to their side.

The following characteristics of the savant are less common, but still found.—Firstly, downrightness and a feeling for simplicity, very valuable if more than a mere awkwardness and inability to deceive, deception requiring some mother-wit.—(Actually, we may be on our guard against too obvious cleverness and resource, and doubt the man's sincerity.)—Otherwise this downrightness is generally of little value, and rarely of any use to knowledge, as it follows tradition and speaks the truth only in "adiaphora"; it being lazier to speak the truth here than ignore it. Everything new means something to be unlearnt, and your downright man will respect the ancient dogmas and accuse the new evangelist of failing in the sensus recti. There was a similar opposition, with probability and custom on its side, to the theory of Copernicus. The professor's frequent hatred of philosophy is principally a hatred of the long trains of reasoning and artificiality of the proofs. Ultimately the savants of every age have a fixed limit; beyond which ingenuity is not allowed, and everything suspected as a conspirator against honesty.

Secondly, a clear vision of near objects, combined with great shortsightedness for the distant and universal. The professor's range is generally very small, and his eye must be kept close to the object. To pass from a point already considered to another, he has to move his whole optical apparatus. He cuts a picture into small sections, like a man using an opera-glass in the theatre, and sees now a head, now a bit of the dress, but nothing as a whole. The single sections are never combined for him, he only infers their connection, and consequently has no strong general impression. He judges a literary work, for example, by certain paragraphs or sentences or errors, as he can do nothing more; he will be driven to see in an oil painting nothing but a mass of daubs.

Thirdly, a sober conventionality in his likes and dislikes. Thus he especially delights in history because he can put his own motives into the actions of the past. A mole is most comfortable in a mole-hill. He is on his guard against all ingenious and extravagant hypotheses; but digs up industriously all the commonplace motives of the past, because he feels in sympathy with them. He is generally quite incapable of understanding and valuing the rare or the uncommon, the great or the real.

Fourthly, a lack of feeling, which makes him capable of vivisection. He knows nothing of the suffering that brings knowledge, and does not fear to tread where other men shudder. He is cold and may easily appear cruel. He is thought courageous, but he is not,—any more than the mule who does not feel giddiness.

Fifthly, diffidence, or a low estimate of himself. Though he live in a miserable alley of the world, he has no sense of sacrifice or surrender; he appears often to know in his inmost heart that he is not a flying but a crawling creature. And this makes him seem even pathetic.

Sixthly, loyalty to his teachers and leaders. From his heart he wishes to help them, and knows he can do it best with the truth. He has a grateful disposition, for he has only gained admittance through them to the high hall of science; he would never have entered by his own road. Any man to-day who can throw open a new province where his lesser disciples can work to some purpose, is famous at once; so great is the crowd that presses after him. These grateful pupils are certainly a misfortune to their teacher, as they all imitate him; his faults are exaggerated in their small persons, his virtues correspondingly diminished.

Seventhly, he will follow the usual road of all the professors, where a feeling for truth springs from a lack of ideas, and the wheel once started goes on. Such natures become compilers, commentators, makers of indices and herbaria; they rummage about one special department because they have never thought there are others. Their industry has something of the monstrous stupidity of gravitation; and so they can often bring their labours to an end.

Eighthly, a dread of ennui. While the true thinker desires nothing more than leisure, the professor fears it, not knowing how it is to be used. Books are his comfort; he listens to everybody's different thoughts and keeps himself amused all day. He especially chooses books with a personal relation to himself, that make him feel some emotion of like or dislike; books that have to do with himself or his position, his political, æsthetic, or even grammatical doctrines; if he have mastered even one branch of knowledge, the means to flap away the flies of ennui will not fail him.

Ninthly, the motive of the bread-winner, the "cry of the empty stomach," in fact. Truth is used as a direct means of preferment, when she can be attained; or as a way to the good graces of the fountains of honour—and bread. Only, however, in the sense of the "particular truth": there is a gulf between the profitable truths that many serve, and the unprofitable truths to which only those few people devote themselves whose motto is not ingenii largitor venter.

Tenthly, a reverence for their fellow-professors and a fear of their displeasure—a higher and rarer motive than the last, though not uncommon. All the members of the guild are jealously on guard, that the truth which means so much bread and honour and position may really be baptized in the name of its discoverer. The one pays the other reverence for the truth he has found, in order to exact the toll again if he should find one himself. The Untruth, the Error is loudly exploded, that the workers may not be too many; here and there the real truth will be exploded to let a few bold and stiff-necked errors be on show for a time; there is never a lack of "moral idiosyncrasies,"—formerly called rascalities.

Eleventhly, the "savant for vanity," now rather rare. He will get a department for himself somehow, and investigate curiosities, especially if they demand unusual expenditure, travel, research, or communication with all parts of the world. He is quite satisfied with the honour of being regarded as a curiosity himself, and never dreams of earning a living by his erudite studies.

Twelfthly, the "savant for amusement." He loves to look for knots in knowledge and to untie them; not too energetically however, lest he lose the spirit of the game. Thus he does not penetrate the depths, though he often observes something that the microscopic eyes of the bread-and-butter scientist never see.

If I speak, lastly, of the "impulse towards justice" as a further motive of the savant, I may be answered that this noble impulse, being metaphysical in its nature, is too indistinguishable from the rest, and really incomprehensible to mortal mind; and so I leave the thirteenth heading with the pious wish that the impulse may be less rare in the professor than it seems. For a spark in his soul from the fire of justice is sufficient to irradiate and purify it, so that he can rest no more and is driven for ever from the cold or lukewarm condition in which most of his fellows do their daily work.

All these elements, or a part of them, must be regarded as fused and pounded together, to form the Servant of Truth. For the sake of an absolutely inhuman thing—mere purposeless, and therefore motiveless, knowledge—a mass of very human little motives have been chemically combined, and as the result we have the professor,—so transfigured in the light of that pure unearthly object that the mixing and pounding which went to form him are all forgotten! It is very curious. Yet there are moments when they must be remembered,—when we have to think of the professor's significance to culture. Any one with observation can see that he is in his essence and by his origin unproductive, and has a natural hatred of the productive; and thus there is an endless feud between the genius and the savant in idea and practice. The latter wishes to kill Nature by analysing and comprehending it, the former to increase it by a new living Nature. The happy age does not need or know the savant; the sick and sluggish time ranks him as its highest and worthiest.

Who were physician enough to know the health or sickness of our time? It is clear that the professor is valued too highly, with evil consequences for the future genius, for whom he has no compassion, merely a cold, contemptuous criticism, a shrug of the shoulders, as if at something strange and perverted for which he has neither time nor inclination. And so he too knows nothing of the aim of culture.

In fact, all these considerations go to prove that the aim of culture is most unknown precisely where the interest in it seems liveliest. The state may trumpet as it will its services to culture, it merely helps culture in order to help itself, and does not comprehend an aim that stands higher than its own well-being or even existence. The business men in their continual demand for education merely wish for—business. When the pioneers of "good form" pretend to be the real helpers of culture, imagining that all art, for example, is merely to serve their own needs, they are clearly affirming themselves in affirming culture. Of the savant enough has already been said. All four are emulously thinking how they can benefit themselves with the help of culture, but have no thoughts at all when their own interests are not engaged. And so they have done nothing to improve the conditions for the birth of genius in modern times; and the opposition to original men has grown so far that no Socrates could ever live among us, and certainly could never reach the age of seventy.

I remember saying in the third chapter that our whole modern world was not so stable that one could prophesy an eternal life to its conception of culture. It is likely that the next millennium may reach two or three new ideas that might well make the hair of our present generation stand on end. The belief in the metaphysical significance of culture would not be such a horrifying thing, but its effects on educational methods might be so.

It requires a totally new attitude of mind to be able to look away from the present educational institutions to the strangely different ones that will be necessary for the second or third generation. At present the labours of higher education produce merely the savant or the official or the business man or the Philistine or, more commonly, a mixture of all four; and the future institutions will have a harder task;—not in itself harder; as it is really more natural, and so easier; and further, could anything be harder than to make a youth into a savant against nature, as now happens?—But the difficulty lies in unlearning what we know and setting up a new aim; it will be an endless trouble to change the fundamental idea of our present educational system, that has its roots in the Middle Ages and regards the mediæval savant as the ideal type of culture. It is already time to put these objects before us; for some generation must begin the battle, of which a later generation will reap the victory. The solitary man who has understood the new fundamental idea of culture is at the parting of the ways; on the one he will be welcomed by his age, laurels and rewards will be his, powerful parties will uphold him, he will have as many in sympathy behind him as in front, and when the leader speaks the word of deliverance, it will echo through all the ranks. The first duty is to "fight in line," the second to treat as foes all who will not "fall in." On the other way he will find fewer companions; it is steeper and more tortuous. The travellers on the first road laugh at him, as his way is the more troublesome and dangerous; and they try to entice him over. If the two ways cross, he is ill-treated, cast aside or left alone. What significance has any particular form of culture for these several travellers? The enormous throng that press to their end on the first road, understand by it the laws and institutions that enable them to go forward in regular fashion and rule out all the solitary and obstinate people who look towards higher and remoter objects. To the small company on the other road it has quite a different office: they wish to guard themselves, by means of a strong organisation, from being swept away by the throng, to prevent their individual members from fainting on the way or turning in spirit from their great task. These solitary men must finish their work; that is why they should all hold together; and those who have their part in the scheme will take thought to prepare themselves with ever-increasing purity of aim for the birth of the genius, and ensure that the time be ripe for him. Many are destined to help on the labour, even among the second-rate talents, and it is only in submission to such a destiny that they can feel they are living for a duty, and have a meaning and an object in their lives. But at present these talents are being turned from the road their instinct has chosen by the seductive tones of the "fashionable culture," that plays on their selfish side, their vanities and weaknesses; and the time-spirit ever whispers in their ears its flattering counsel:—"Follow me and go not thither! There you are only servants and tools, over-shadowed by higher natures with no scope for your own, drawn by threads, hung with fetters, slaves and automatons. With me you may enjoy your true personality, and be masters, your talents may shine with their own light, and yourselves stand in the front ranks with an immense following round you; and the acclamation of public opinion will rejoice you more than a wandering breath of approval sent down from the cold ethereal heights of genius." Even the best men are snared by such allurements, and the ultimate difference comes not so much from the rarity and power of their talent, as the influence of a certain heroic disposition at the base of them, and an inner feeling of kinship with genius. For there are men who feel it as their own misery when they see the genius in painful toil and struggle, in danger of self-destruction, or neglected by the short-sighted selfishness of the state, the superficiality of the business men, and the cold arrogance of the professors; and I hope there may be some to understand what I mean by my sketch of Schopenhauer's destiny, and to what end Schopenhauer can really educate.

VII.

But setting aside all thoughts of any educational revolution in the distant future;—what provision is required now, that our future philosopher may have the best chance of opening his eyes to a life like Schopenhauer's—hard as it is, yet still livable? What, further, must be discovered that may make his influence on his contemporaries more certain? And what obstacles must be removed before his example can have its full effect and the philosopher train another philosopher? Here we descend to be practical.

Nature always desires the greatest utility, but does not understand how to find the best and handiest means to her end; that is her great sorrow, and the cause of her melancholy. The impulse towards her own redemption shows clearly her wish to give men a significant existence by the generation of the philosopher and the artist: but how unclear and weak is the effect she generally obtains with her artists and philosophers, and how seldom is there any effect at all! She is especially perplexed in her efforts to make the philosopher useful; her methods are casual and tentative, her failures innumerable; most of her philosophers never touch the common good of mankind at all. Her actions seem those of a spendthrift; but the cause lies in no prodigal luxury, but in her inexperience. Were she human, she would probably never cease to be dissatisfied with herself and her bungling. Nature shoots the philosopher at mankind like an arrow; she does not aim, but hopes that the arrow will stick somewhere. She makes countless mistakes that give her pain. She is as extravagant in the sphere of culture as in her planting and sowing. She fulfils her ends in a large and clumsy fashion, using up far too much of her strength. The artist has the same relation to the connoisseurs and lovers of his art as a piece of heavy artillery to a flock of sparrows. It is a fool's part to use a great avalanche to sweep away a little snow, to kill a man in order to strike the fly on his nose. The artist and the philosopher are witnesses against Nature's adaptation of her means, however well they may show the wisdom of her ends. They only reach a few and should reach all—and even these few are not struck with the strength they used when they shot. It is sad to have to value art so differently as cause and effect; how huge in its inception, how faint the echo afterwards! The artist does his work as Nature bids him, for the benefit of other men—no doubt of it; but he knows that none of those men will understand and love his work as he understands and loves it himself. That lonely height of love and understanding is necessary, by Nature's clumsy law, to produce a lower type; the great and noble are used as the means to the small and ignoble. Nature is a bad manager; her expenses are far

greater than her profits: for all her riches she must one day go
bankrupt. She would have acted more reasonably to make the rule of
her household—small expense and hundredfold profit; if there had
been, for example, only a few artists with moderate powers, but an
immense number of hearers to appreciate them, stronger and more
powerful characters than the artists themselves; then the effect of the
art-work, in comparison with the cause, might be a hundred-tongued
echo. One might at least expect cause and effect to be of equal power;
but Nature lags infinitely behind this consummation. An artist, and
especially a philosopher, seems often to have dropped by chance into
his age, as a wandering hermit or straggler cut off from the main body.
Think how utterly great Schopenhauer is, and what a small and absurd
effect he has had! An honest man can feel no greater shame at the
present time than at the thought of the casual treatment Schopenhauer
has received and the evil powers that have up to now killed his effect
among men. First there was the want of readers,—to the eternal shame
of our cultivated age;—then the inadequacy of his first public
adherents, as soon as he had any; further, I think, the crassness of the
modern man towards books, which he will no longer take seriously. As
an outcome of many attempts to adapt Schopenhauer to this enervated
age, the new danger has gradually arisen of regarding him as an odd
kind of pungent herb, of taking him in grains, as a sort of metaphysical
pepper. In this way he has gradually become famous, and I should
think more have heard his name than Hegel's; and, for all that, he is
still a solitary being, who has failed of his effect.—Though the honour
of causing the failure belongs least of all to the barking of his literary
antagonists; first because there are few men with the patience to read
them, and secondly, because any one who does, is sent immediately to
Schopenhauer himself; for who will let a donkey-driver prevent him
from mounting a fine horse, however much he praise his donkey?

Whoever has recognised Nature's unreason in our time, will have to
consider some means to help her; his task will be to bring the free
spirits and the sufferers from this age to know Schopenhauer; and
make them tributaries to the flood that is to overbear all the clumsy
uses to which Nature even now is accustomed to put her philosophers.
Such men will see that the identical obstacles hinder the effect of a

great philosophy and the production of the great philosopher; and so will direct their aims to prepare the regeneration of Schopenhauer, which means that of the philosophical genius. The real opposition to the further spread of his doctrine in the past, and the regeneration of the philosopher in the future, is the perversity of human nature as it is; and all the great men that are to be must spend infinite pains in freeing themselves from it. The world they enter is plastered over with pretence,—including not merely religious dogmas, but such juggling conceptions as "progress," "universal education," "nationalism," "the modern state"; practically all our general terms have an artificial veneer over them that will bring a clearer-sighted posterity to reproach our age bitterly for its warped and stunted growth, however loudly we may boast of our "health." The beauty of the antique vases, says Schopenhauer, lies in the simplicity with which they express their meaning and object; it is so with all the ancient implements; if Nature produced amphoræ, lamps, tables, chairs, helmets, shields, breastplates and the like, they would resemble these. And, as a corollary, whoever considers how we all manage our art, politics, religion and education—to say nothing of our vases!—will find in them a barbaric exaggeration and arbitrariness of expression. Nothing is more unfavourable to the rise of genius than such monstrosities. They are unseen and undiscoverable, the leaden weights on his hand when he will set it to the plough; the weights are only shaken off with violence, and his highest work must to an extent always bear the mark of it.

In considering the conditions that, at best, keep the born philosopher from being oppressed by the perversity of the age, I am surprised to find they are partly those in which Schopenhauer himself grew up. True, there was no lack of opposing influences; the evil time drew perilously near him in the person of a vain and pretentious mother. But the proud republican character of his father rescued him from her and gave him the first quality of a philosopher—a rude and strong virility. His father was neither an official nor a savant; he travelled much abroad with his son,—a great help to one who must know men rather than books, and worship truth before the state. In time he got accustomed to national peculiarities: he made England, France and Italy equally his home, and felt no little sympathy with the

Spanish character. On the whole, he did not think it an honour to be born in Germany, and I am not sure that the new political conditions would have made him change his mind. He held quite openly the opinion that the state's one object was to give protection at home and abroad, and even protection against its "protectors," and to attribute any other object to it was to endanger its true end. And so, to the consternation of all the so-called liberals, he left his property to the survivors of the Prussian soldiers who fell in 1848 in the fight for order. To understand the state and its duties in this single sense may seem more and more henceforth the sign of intellectual superiority; for the man with the furor philosophicus in him will no longer have time for the furor politicus, and will wisely keep from reading the newspapers or serving a party; though he will not hesitate a moment to take his place in the ranks if his country be in real need. All states are badly managed, when other men than politicians busy themselves with politics; and they deserve to be ruined by their political amateurs.

Schopenhauer had another great advantage—that he had never been educated for a professor, but worked for some time (though against his will) as a merchant's clerk, and through all his early years breathed the freer air of a great commercial house. A savant can never become a philosopher: Kant himself could not, but remained in a chrysalis stage to the end, in spite of the innate force of his genius. Any one who thinks I do Kant wrong in saying this does not know what a philosopher is—not only a great thinker, but also a real man; and how could a real man have sprung from a savant? He who lets conceptions, opinions, events, books come between himself and things, and is born for history (in the widest sense), will never see anything at once, and never be himself a thing to be "seen at once"; though both these powers should be in the philosopher, as he must take most of his doctrine from himself and be himself the copy and compendium of the whole world. If a man look at himself through a veil of other people's opinions, no wonder he sees nothing but—those opinions. And it is thus that the professors see and live. But Schopenhauer had the rare happiness of seeing the genius not only in himself, but also outside himself—in Goethe; and this double reflection taught him everything about the aims and culture of the learned. He knew by this experience how the free strong man, to whom all artistic culture was looking, must come to be born; and could he, after this vision, have much desire to busy himself with the so-called "art," in the learned, hypocritical manner of the moderns? He had seen something higher than that—an awful unearthly judgment-scene in which all life, even the highest and completest, was weighed and found too light; he had beheld the saint as the judge of existence. We cannot tell how early Schopenhauer reached this view of life, and came to hold it with such intensity as to make all his writings an attempt to mirror it; we know that the youth had this great vision, and can well believe it of the child. Everything that he gained later from life and books, from all the realms of knowledge, was only a means of colour and expression to him; the Kantian philosophy itself was to him an extraordinary rhetorical instrument for making the utterance of his vision, as he thought, clearer; the Buddhist and Christian mythologies occasionally served the same end. He had one task and a thousand means to execute it; one meaning, and innumerable hieroglyphs to express it.

It was one of the high conditions of his existence that he really could live for such a task—according to his motto vitam impendere vero—and none of life's material needs could shake his resolution; and we know the splendid return he made his father for this. The contemplative man in Germany usually pursues his scientific studies to the detriment of his sincerity, as a "considerate fool," in search of place and honour, circumspect and obsequious, and fawning on his influential superiors. Nothing offended the savants more than Schopenhauer's unlikeness to them.

VIII.

These are a few of the conditions under which the philosophical genius can at least come to light in our time, in spite of all thwarting influences;—a virility of character, an early knowledge of mankind, an absence of learned education and narrow patriotism, of compulsion to earn his livelihood or depend on the state,—freedom in fact, and again freedom; the same marvellous and dangerous element in which the Greek philosophers grew up. The man who will reproach him, as Niebuhr did Plato, with being a bad citizen, may do so, and be himself a good one; so he and Plato will be right together! Another may call this great freedom presumption; he is also right, as he could not himself use the freedom properly if he desired it, and would certainly presume too far with it. This freedom is really a grave burden of guilt; and can only be expiated by great actions. Every ordinary son of earth has the right of looking askance on such endowments; and may Providence keep him from being so endowed—burdened, that is, with such terrible duties! His freedom and his loneliness would be his ruin, and ennui would turn him into a fool, and a mischievous fool at that.

A father may possibly learn something from this that he may use for his son's private education, though one must not expect fathers to have only philosophers for their sons. It is possible that they will always oppose their sons becoming philosophers, and call it mere perversity; Socrates was sacrificed to the fathers' anger, for "corrupting the youth," and Plato even thought a new ideal state necessary to prevent the philosophers' growth from being dependent on the fathers' folly. It looks at present as though Plato had really accomplished something; for the modern state counts the encouragement of philosophy as one of its duties and tries to secure for a number of men at a time the sort of freedom that conditions the philosopher. But, historically, Plato has been very unlucky; as soon as a structure has risen corresponding actually to his proposals, it has always turned, on a closer view, into a goblin-child, a monstrous changeling; compare the ecclesiastical state of the Middle Ages with the government of the "God-born king" of which Plato dreamed! The modern state is furthest removed from the idea of the Philosopher-king (Thank Heaven for that! the Christian will say); but we must think whether it takes that very "encouragement of philosophy" in a Platonic sense, I mean as seriously and honestly as if its highest object were to produce more Platos. If the philosopher seem, as usual, an accident of his time, does the state make it its conscious business to turn the accidental into the necessary and help Nature here also?

Experience teaches us a better way—or a worse: it says that nothing so stands in the way of the birth and growth of Nature's philosopher as the bad philosophers made "by order." A poor obstacle, isn't it? and the same that Schopenhauer pointed out in his famous essay on

University philosophy. I return to this point, as men must be forced to take it seriously, to be driven to activity by it; and I think all writing is useless that does not contain such a stimulus to activity. And anyhow it is a good thing to apply Schopenhauer's eternal theories once more to our own contemporaries, as some kindly soul might think that everything has changed for the better in Germany since his fierce diatribes. Unfortunately his work is incomplete on this side as well, unimportant as the side may be.

The "freedom" that the state, as I said, bestows on certain men for the sake of philosophy is, properly speaking, no freedom at all, but an office that maintains its holder. The "encouragement of philosophy" means that there are to-day a number of men whom the state enables to make their living out of philosophy; whereas the old sages of Greece were not paid by the state, but at best were presented, as Zeno was, with a golden crown and a monument in the Ceramicus. I cannot say generally whether truth is served by showing the way to live by her, since everything depends on the character of the individual who shows the way. I can imagine a degree of pride in a man saying to his fellow-men, "take care of me, as I have something better to do—namely to take care of you." We should not be angry at such a heightened mode of expression in Plato and Schopenhauer; and so they might properly have been University philosophers,—as Plato, for example, was a court philosopher for a while without lowering the dignity of philosophy. But in Kant we have the usual submissive professor, without any nobility in his relations with the state; and thus he could not justify the University philosophy when it was once assailed. If there be natures like Schopenhauer's and Plato's, which can justify it, I fear they will never have the chance, as the state would never venture to give such men these positions, for the simple reason that every state fears them, and will only favour philosophers it does not fear. The state obviously has a special fear of philosophy, and will try to attract more philosophers, to create the impression that it has philosophy on its side,—because it has those men on its side who have the title without the power. But if there should come one who really proposes to cut everything to the quick, the state included, with the knife of truth, the state, that affirms its own existence above all, is justified in banishing him as an enemy, just as it bans a religion that exalts itself to be its judge. The man who consents to be a state philosopher, must also consent to be regarded as renouncing the search for truth in all its secret retreats. At any rate, so long as he enjoys his position, he must recognise something higher than truth—the state. And not only the state, but everything required by it for existence—a definite form of religion, a social system, a standing army; a noli me tangere is written above all these things. Can a University philosopher ever keep clearly before him the whole round of these duties and limitations? I do not know. The man who has done so and remains a state-official, is a false friend to truth; if he has not,—I think he is no friend to truth either.

But general considerations like these are always the weakest in their influence on mankind. Most people will find it enough to shrug their shoulders and say, "As if anything great and pure has ever been able to maintain itself on this earth without some concession to human vulgarity! Would you rather the state persecuted philosophers than paid them for official services?" Without answering this last question, I will merely say that these "concessions" of philosophy to the state go rather far at present. In the first place, the state chooses its own philosophical servants, as many as its institutions require; it therefore pretends to be able to distinguish the good and the bad philosophers, and even assumes there must be a sufficient supply of good ones to fill all the chairs. The state is the authority not only for their goodness but their numbers. Secondly, it confines those it has chosen to a definite place and a definite activity among particular men; they must instruct every undergraduate who wants instruction, daily, at stated hours. The question is whether a philosopher can bind himself, with a good conscience, to have something to teach every day, to any one who wishes to listen. Must he not appear to know more than he does, and speak, before an unknown audience, of things that he could mention without risk only to his most intimate friends? And above all, does he not surrender the precious freedom of following his genius when and wherever it call him, by the mere fact of being bound to think at stated times on a fixed subject? And before young men, too! Is not such thinking in its nature emasculate? And suppose he felt some day that he had no ideas just then—and yet must be in his place and appear to be thinking! What then?

"But," one will say, "he is not a thinker but mainly a depository of thought, a man of great learning in all previous philosophies. Of these he can always say something that his scholars do not know." This is actually the third, and the most dangerous, concession made by philosophy to the state, when it is compelled to appear in the form of erudition, as the knowledge (more specifically) of the history of philosophy. The genius looks purely and lovingly on existence, like a poet, and cannot dive too deep into it;—and nothing is more abhorrent to him than to burrow among the innumerable strange and wrong-headed opinions. The learned history of the past was never a true philosopher's business, in India or Greece; and a professor of philosophy who busies himself with such matters must be, at best, content to hear it said of him, "He is an able scholar, antiquary, philologist, historian,"—but never, "He is a philosopher." I said, "at best": for a scholar feels that most of the learned works written by University philosophers are badly done, without any real scientific power, and generally are dreadfully tedious. Who will blow aside, for example, the Lethean vapour with which the history of Greek philosophy has been enveloped by the dull though not very scientific works of Ritter, Brandis and Zeller? I, at any rate, would rather read Diogenes Laertius than Zeller, because at least the spirit of the old philosophers lives in Diogenes, but neither that nor any other spirit in Zeller. And, after all, what does the history of philosophy matter to our young men? Are they to be discouraged by the welter of opinions from having any of their own; or taught to join the chorus that approves the vastness of our progress? Are they to learn to hate or perhaps despise philosophy? One might expect the last, knowing the torture the students endure for their philosophical examinations, in having to get into their unfortunate heads the maddest efforts of the human mind as well as the greatest and profoundest. The only method of criticising a philosophy that is possible and proves anything at all—namely to see whether one can live by it—has never been taught at the universities; only the criticism of words, and again words, is taught there. Imagine a young head, without much experience of life, being stuffed with fifty systems (in the form of words) and fifty criticisms of them, all mixed up together,—what an overgrown wilderness he will come to be, what contempt he will feel for a philosophical education! It is, of course, not an education in philosophy at all, but in the art of passing a philosophical examination: the usual result being the pious ejaculation of the wearied examinee, "Thank God I am no philosopher, but a Christian and a good citizen!"

What if this cry were the ultimate object of the state, and the "education" or leading to philosophy were merely a leading from philosophy? We may well ask.—But if so, there is one thing to fear—that the youth may some day find out to what end philosophy is thus mis-handled. "Is the highest thing of all, the production of the philosophical genius, nothing but a pretext, and the main object perhaps to hinder his production? And is Reason turned to Unreason?"—Then woe to the whole machinery of political and professorial trickery!

Will it soon become notorious? I do not know; but anyhow university philosophy has fallen into a general state of doubting and despair. The cause lies partly in the feebleness of those who hold the chairs at present: and if Schopenhauer had to write his treatise on university philosophy to-day, he would find the club no longer necessary, but could conquer with a bulrush. They are the heirs and successors of those slip-shod thinkers whose crazy heads Schopenhauer struck at: their childish natures and dwarfish frames remind one of the Indian proverb: "men are born according to their deeds, deaf, dumb, misshapen." Those fathers deserved such sons, "according to their deeds," as the proverb says. Hence the students will, no doubt, soon get on without the philosophy taught at their university, just as those who are not university men manage to do without it already. This can be tested from one's own experience: in my student-days, for example, I found the university philosophers very ordinary men indeed, who had collected together a few conclusions from the other sciences, and in their leisure hours read the newspapers and went to concerts; they were treated by their academic colleagues with politely veiled contempt. They had the reputation of knowing very little, but of never being at a loss for obscure expressions to conceal their ignorance. They had a preference for those obscure regions where a man could not walk long with clear vision. One said of the natural sciences,—"Not one of them can fully explain to me the origin of matter; then what do I care about them all?"—Another said of history, "It tells nothing new to the man with ideas": in fact, they always found reasons for its being more philosophical to know nothing than to learn anything. If they let themselves be drawn to learn, a secret instinct made them fly from the actual sciences and found a dim kingdom amid their gaps and uncertainties. They "led the way" in the sciences in the sense that the quarry "leads the way" for the hunters who are behind him. Recently they have amused themselves with asserting they are merely the watchers on the frontier of the sciences. The Kantian doctrine is of use to them here, and they industriously build up an empty scepticism on it, of which in a short time nobody will take any more notice. Here and there one will rise to a little metaphysic of his own, with the general accompaniment of headaches and giddiness and bleeding at the nose. After the usual ill-success of their voyages into the clouds and the mist, some hard-headed young student of the real sciences will pluck them down by the skirts, and their faces will assume the expression now habitual to them, of offended dignity at being found out. They have lost their happy confidence, and not one of them will venture a step further for the sake of his philosophy. Some used to believe they could find out new religions or reinstate old ones by their systems. They have given up such pretensions now, and have become mostly mild, muddled folk, with no Lucretian boldness, but merely some spiteful complaints of the "dead weight that lies on the intellects of mankind"! No one can even learn logic from them now, and their obvious knowledge of their own powers has made them discontinue the dialectical disputations common in the old days. There is much more care and modesty, logic and inventiveness, in a word, more philosophical method in the work of the special sciences than in the so-called "philosophy," and every one will agree with the temperate words of Bagehot[2] on the present system builders: "Unproved abstract principles without number have been eagerly caught up by sanguine men, and then carefully spun out into books and theories, which were to explain the whole world. But the world goes clear against these abstractions, and it must do so, as they require it to go in antagonistic directions. The mass of a system attracts the young and impresses the unwary; but cultivated people are very dubious about it. They are ready to receive hints and suggestions, and the smallest real truth is ever welcome. But a large book of deductive philosophy is much to be suspected. Who is not almost sure beforehand that the premises will contain a strange mixture of truth and error, and therefore that it will not be worth while to spend life in reasoning over their consequences?" The philosophers, especially in Germany, used to sink into such a state of abstraction that they were in continual danger of running their heads against a beam; but there is a whole herd of Laputan flappers about them to give them in time a gentle stroke on their eyes or anywhere else. Sometimes the blows are too hard; and then these scorners of earth forget themselves and strike back, but the victim always escapes them. "Fool, you do not see the beam," says the flapper; and often the philosopher does see the beam, and calms down. These flappers are the natural sciences and history; little by little they have so overawed the German dream-craft which has long taken the place of philosophy, that the dreamer would be only too glad to give up the attempt to run alone: but when they unexpectedly fall into the others' arms, or try to put leading-strings on them that they may be led themselves, those others flap as terribly as they can, as if they would say, "This is all that is wanting,—that a philosophaster like this should lay his impure hands on us, the natural sciences and history! Away with him!" Then they start back, knowing not where to turn or to ask the way. They wanted to have a little physical knowledge at their back, possibly in the form of empirical psychology (like the Herbartians), or perhaps a little history; and then they could at least make a public show of behaving scientifically, although in their hearts they may wish all philosophy and all science at the devil.

But granted that this herd of bad philosophers is ridiculous—and who will deny it?—how far are they also harmful? They are harmful just because they make philosophy ridiculous. As long as this imitation-thinking continues to be recognised by the state, the lasting effect of a true philosophy will be destroyed, or at any rate circumscribed; nothing does this so well as the curse of ridicule that the representatives of the great cause have drawn on them, for it attacks that cause itself. And so I think it will encourage culture to deprive philosophy of its political and academic standing, and relieve state and university of the task, impossible for them, of deciding between true and false philosophy. Let the philosophers run wild, forbid them any thoughts of office or civic position, hold them out no more bribes,—nay, rather persecute them and treat them ill,—you will see a wonderful result. They will flee in terror and seek a roof where they can, these poor phantasms; one will become a parson, another a schoolmaster, another will creep into an editorship, another write school-books for young ladies' colleges, the wisest of them will plough the fields, the vainest go to court. Everything will be left suddenly empty, the birds flown: for it is easy to get rid of bad philosophers,—one only has to cease paying them. And that is a better plan than the open patronage of any philosophy, whatever it be, for state reasons.

The state has never any concern with truth, but only with the truth useful to it, or rather, with anything that is useful to it, be it truth, half-truth, or error. A coalition between state and philosophy has only meaning when the latter can promise to be unconditionally useful to the state, to put its well-being higher than truth. It would certainly be a noble thing for the state to have truth as a paid servant; but it knows well enough that it is the essence of truth to be paid nothing and serve nothing. So the state's servant turns out to be merely "false truth," a masked actor who cannot perform the office required from the real truth—the affirmation of the state's worth and sanctity. When a mediæval prince wished to be crowned by the Pope, but could not get him to consent, he appointed an antipope to do the business for him. This may serve up to a certain point; but not when the modern state appoints an "anti-philosophy" to legitimise it; for it has true philosophy against it just as much as before, or even more so. I believe in all seriousness that it is to the state's advantage to have nothing further to do with philosophy, to demand nothing from it, and let it go its own way as much as possible. Without this indifferent attitude, philosophy may become dangerous and oppressive, and will have to be persecuted.—The only interest the state can have in the university lies in the training of obedient and useful citizens; and it should hesitate to put this obedience and usefulness in doubt by demanding an examination in philosophy from the young men. To make a bogey of philosophy may be an excellent way to frighten the idle and incompetent from its study; but this advantage is not enough to counterbalance the danger that this kind of compulsion may arouse from the side of the more reckless and turbulent spirits. They learn to know about forbidden books, begin to criticise their teachers, and finally come to understand the object of university philosophy and its examinations; not to speak of the doubts that may be fostered in the minds of young theologians, as a consequence of which they are beginning to be extinct in Germany, like the ibexes in the Tyrol.

I know the objections that the state could bring against all this, as long as the lovely Hegel-corn was yellowing in all the fields; but now that hail has destroyed the crop and all men's hopes of it, now that nothing has been fulfilled and all the barns are empty,—there are no more objections to be made, but rather rejections of philosophy itself. The state has now the power of rejection; in Hegel's time it only wished to have it—and that makes a great difference. The state needs no more the sanction of philosophy, and philosophy has thus become superfluous to it. It will find advantage in ceasing to maintain its professors, or (as I think will soon happen) in merely pretending to maintain them; but it is of still greater importance that the university should see the benefit of this as well. At least I believe the real sciences must see that their interest lies in freeing themselves from all contact with sham science. And further, the reputation of the universities hangs too much in the balance for them not to welcome a severance from methods that are thought little of even in academic circles. The outer world has good reason for its widespread contempt of universities; they are reproached with being cowardly, the small fearing the great, and the great fearing public opinion; it is said that they do not lead the higher thought of the age but hobble slowly behind it, and cleave no longer to the fundamental ideas of the recognised sciences. Grammar, for example, is studied more diligently than ever without any one seeing the necessity of a rigorous training in speech and writing. The gates of Indian antiquity are being opened, and the scholars have no more idea of the most imperishable works of the Indians—their philosophies—than a beast has of playing the harp; though Schopenhauer thinks that the acquaintance with Indian philosophy is one of the greatest advantages possessed by our century. Classical antiquity is the favourite playground nowadays, and its effect is no longer classical and formative; as is shown by the students, who are certainly no models for imitation. Where is now the spirit of Friedrich August Wolf to be found, of whom Franz Passow could say that he seemed a loyal and humanistic spirit with force enough to set half the world aflame? Instead of that a journalistic spirit is arising in the university, often under the name of philosophy; the smooth delivery—the very cosmetics of speech—with Faust and Nathan the Wise for ever on the lips, the accent and the outlook of our worst literary magazines and, more recently, much chatter about our holy German music, and the demand for lectures on Schiller and Goethe,—all this is a sign that the university spirit is beginning to be confused with the Spirit of the Age. Thus the establishment of a higher tribunal, outside the universities, to protect and criticise them with regard to culture, would seem a most valuable thing, and as soon as philosophy can sever itself from the universities and be purified from every unworthy motive or hypocrisy, it will be able to become such a tribunal. It will do its work without state help in money or honours, free from the spirit of the age as well as from any fear of it; being in fact the judge, as Schopenhauer was, of the so-called culture surrounding it. And in this way the philosopher can also be useful to the university, by refusing to be a part of it, but criticising it from afar. Distance will lend dignity.

But, after all, what does the life of a state or the progress of universities matter in comparison with the life of philosophy on earth! For, to say quite frankly what I mean, it is infinitely more important that a philosopher should arise on the earth than that a state or a university should continue. The dignity of philosophy may rise in proportion as the submission to public opinion and the danger to liberty increase; it was at its highest during the convulsions marking the fall of the Roman Republic, and in the time of the Empire, when the names of both philosophy and history became ingrata principibus nomina. Brutus shows its dignity better than Plato; his was a time when ethics cease to have commonplaces. Philosophy is not much regarded now, and we may well ask why no great soldier or statesman has taken it up; and the answer is that a thin phantom has met him under the name of philosophy, the cautious wisdom of the learned professor; and philosophy has soon come to seem ridiculous to him. It ought to have seemed terrible; and men who are called to authority should know the heroic power that has its source there. An American may tell them what a centre of mighty forces a great thinker can prove on this earth. "Beware when the great God lets loose a thinker on this planet," says Emerson.[3] "Then all things are at risk. It is as when a conflagration has broken out in a great city, and no man knows what is safe, or where it will end. There is not a piece of science, but its flank may be turned to-morrow; there is not any literary reputation, not the so-called eternal names of fame, that may not be revised and condemned.... The things which are dear to men at this hour are so on account of the ideas which have emerged on their mental horizon, and which cause the present order of things as a tree bears its apples. A new degree of culture would instantly revolutionise the entire system of human pursuits." If such thinkers are dangerous, it is clear why our university thinkers are not dangerous; for their thoughts bloom as peacefully in the shade of tradition "as ever tree bore its apples." They do not frighten; they carry away no gates of Gaza; and to all their little contemplations one can make the answer of Diogenes when a certain philosopher was praised: "What great result has he to show, who has so long practised philosophy and yet has hurt nobody?" Yes, the university philosophy should have on its monument, "It has hurt nobody." But this is rather the praise one gives to an old woman than to a goddess of truth; and it is not surprising that those who know the goddess only as an old woman are the less men for that, and are naturally neglected by the real men of power.

If this be the case in our time, the dignity of philosophy is trodden in the mire; and she seems herself to have become ridiculous or insignificant. All her true friends are bound to bear witness against this transformation, at least to show that it is merely her false servants in philosopher's clothing who are so. Or better, they must prove by their own deed that the love of truth has itself awe and power.

Schopenhauer proved this and will continue to prove it, more and more.

FOOTNOTES

[1]This was written in 1873.—Tr.

[2]Physics and Politics, chap. v. Nietzsche has altered the order of the sentences without any apparent benefit to his own argument, and to the disadvantage of Bagehot's. I have restored the original order.—Tr.

[3]Essay on "Circles."

www.ingramcontent.com/pod-product-compliance
Lightning Source LLC
Chambersburg PA
CBHW031304170626
46807CB00001B/302